PENGUIN BOOKS

SINGING THE MASTER

Roger D. Abrahams is Professor of Folklore and Folklife at the University of Pennsylvania in Philadelphia. He holds a B.A. from Swarthmore College, an M.A. from Columbia University, and a Ph.D. from the University of Pennsylvania. He is a past president of the American Folklore Society, a former chairman of the English Department at the University of Texas, and a Phi Beta Kappa Visiting Scholar.

Professor Abrahams has done fieldwork in a range of African-American communities, from a ghetto neighborhood in Philadelphia to the Caribbean. He has also studied and written about Anglo-American folk songs and children's lore. Among his most recent books are *African Folktales* and *Afro-American Folktales*.

SINGING

THE

MASTER

The Emergence of African American Culture

in the Plantation South

ROGER D. ABRAHAMS

PENGUIN BOOKS

PENGUIN BOOKS
Published by the Penguin Group
Penguin Books USA Inc., 375 Hudson Street, New York,
New York 10014, U.S.A.
Penguin Books Ltd, 27 Wrights Lane, London W8 5TZ, England
Penguin Books Australia Ltd, Ringwood, Victoria, Australia
Penguin Books Canada Ltd, 10 Alcorn Avenue,
Toronto, Ontario, Canada M4V 3B2
Penguin Books (N.Z.) Ltd, 182–190 Wairau Road,
Auckland 10, New Zealand

Penguin Books Ltd, Registered Offices:
Harmondsworth, Middlesex, England

First published in the United States of America by
Pantheon Books, a division of Random House, Inc., 1992
Reprinted by arrangement with Pantheon Books
Published in Penguin Books 1993

1 3 5 7 9 10 8 6 4 2

THE LIBRARY OF CONGRESS HAS CATALOGUED THE HARDCOVER AS FOLLOWS:
Abrahams, Roger D.
Singing the master: the emergence of African American culture in
the plantation South/Roger D. Abrahams.
p. cm.
Includes bibliographical references and index.
ISBN 0-394-55591-0 (hc.)
ISBN 0 14 01.7919 4 (pbk.)
1. Slaves—Southern States—Social life and customs. 2. Plantation life—
Southern States—History—19th century. 3. Southern States—Social life
and customs—1775–1865. I. Title.
E443.A26 1992
975´.00496—dc20   91–30163

Printed in the United States of America
Designed by Fearn Cutler

To Américo Paredes
Master Liminar and Illuminator

Shuck corn, shell corn,
Carry corn to mill.
Grind de meal, gimme de husk;
Bake de bread, gimme de crus';
Fry de meat, gimme de skin;
And dat's de way to bring 'em in.

Boys, come along and shuck that corn,
Boys, come along to the rattle of the horn;
We shuck and sing till the coming of the morn,
Then we'll have a holiday.

Come to shuck dat corn tonight,
Come to shuck with all you might;
Come for to shuck all in sight,
Come to shuck dat corn tonight.

CONTENTS

ACKNOWLEDGMENTS

This project arose from the work carried out by myself, John Szwed, and others from the project that resulted in our *Afro-American Folk Culture: An Annotated Bibliography* (Philadelphia: ISHI, 1977). We had come upon notices of slave holidays in various places, but, at that point, I was not aware of the significance of the corn-shucking ceremony in the American South.

A number of people have provided sources and references: Chuck Perdue, Glenn Hinson, John Szwed, Doug DeNatale, Hugo Freund, Carol Wood, Frank Korom, Fred Thomsen, Peter Tokofsky, Elizabeth Mackenzie, Cynthia Bidart, Faye McMahon, and Emily Socolov. Jerrilyn McGregory, Tyrone Yarborough, and Cassandra Stancil did some especially valuable research and thinking on the subject of black festivities. David Cressy, Suny Davis, and Bob St. George have filled me in on the extensive literature about festivals in American life, and to them my thanks. The Alabama Historical Commission kindly sent on the pages of the Brewer Manuscript. Herbert Halpert and Kenny Goldstein went through their personal libraries and emerged with a number of new sources. Larry Small led me to the Hardeman book, and Perk Hardeman himself kindly gave me new materials, which filled in my knowledge of corn culture. He also gave me my first and most prized shucking peg. My continuing thanks.

It will become clear how much of the argument is based on the insights into slave culture and community made by Eugene Genovese, Sidney Mintz, John Blassingame, Sterling Stuckey, and Richard Price. Gene Genovese shared his manuscript *Roll, Jordan, Roll* while he was writing it, and the discussions that emerged have stayed with me all these years, finally animating this present work. While I was teaching at the University of Texas at Austin, my colleagues Mody Boatright, Américo Paredes, and Dick Bauman first made me aware of the need to situate folkloristic arguments within a historical context and to regard performances in terms of the confrontation of diverse cultures, not only within but also between cultures. Additionally, ongoing discussions with Sid Mintz and Rich Price have provided me with models of how historical materials might be brought to bear on anthropological arguments.

Charles Joyner provided the opportunity to present some of this material to a group of historians interested in traditional practices, at a conference at the University of South Carolina, Coastal Carolina Campus, in Myrtle Beach. My thanks to him, his wife, Jeanie, and their daughter, Hanna, for hosting a fine conclave. The participants of that conference, especially Rhys Isaac and Shane White, were very helpful in confronting questions raised by the very existence of these data.

My debts to Houston Baker and to Skip Gates will be evident to readers of their work; their collegiality and forthrightness emboldened me to continue to pursue this project.

Not only was John Szwed involved in the project at the outset, but he has listened to the arguments as they developed, always commenting helpfully. Other colleagues, especially at Penn, heard me out repeatedly as the argument developed: Henry Glassie, early on; later, John Roberts, Kenny Goldstein, Margaret Mills, and Bob St. George. All of them gave me useful feedback and, in the case of Kenny and Bob, references to follow up, which had a good payoff. Elsewhere, Rich Price gave the book a very helpful reading in early draft form, as did Ruth Finnegan and Shane White.

Later, Barbara Kirshenblatt-Gimblett, Bob Cantwell, John Vlach, and Bill Ferris gave me the benefit of enthusiastic and informed responses. Phyllis Rackin read a later draft, assisting greatly with an understanding of the range of potential audiences for this argument. Drew Faust, Sam Kinser, and Gene Genovese—bless them—read the book as it was being finished and cautioned me on historiographical uncertainties. Janet Anderson, always my best reader, went beyond herself with this one, encouraging me at every stage of the work. And Dan Frank set out with a will and a way to put it into readable shape. The impact of his thoughtful but thorough reading is reflected in every page of the book. He rescued me from many infelicities and soft arguments. If there are any left they are not his fault.

Dealing with accounts which are suffused with racist language and perspectives may create a problem for those readers offended by the stereotypical portrayal of blacks of an earlier era. The grotesque portraits and patronizing descriptions drawn upon here and the visual illustrations included in these early accounts—to say nothing of the strange orthographical renderings of black speech—all of these are offensive because they call to mind the racist social attitudes of those times. But the analytic procedures developed recently by social historians and folklorists allow access to the materials of everyday life and encourage us to get beyond this initial repulsion to the materials.

As Robert Darnton notes in his overview of these developments, "after generations of struggle to discover 'what actually happened' " during specific historical times, "historians have learned to cope with documentary problems. And if they want to understand what a happening actually meant" to those who participated or looked on, historians "can take advantage of the very elements" that, in the past, have distorted our reading of these journalistic reports. The aims of historical writing have been altered in an attempt to arrive at greater understandings not of what happened when but of how people acted and reacted in the quotidian world. As a result, today "we can read a text . . . not to nail down all the whos, whats, wheres, and whens of an event but rather to see what the event meant to the people who participated in it."[1]

Says historian Greg Dening, isolating just this problem in a different part of the world, where whites and non-whites are confronting each other across cultural boundaries, where each side narrates its own understandings of the exchange:

Storytellers, mythmakers, gossipers, sculpt events with choice words and fine dramatics and pass them on by word of mouth so that their histories are embellished by each occasion of their telling, and in the end get caught by being written down. Participants in the event choose a genre—a diary, a letter, a poem, a newspaper to clothe their interpretations of what has happened. . . . These relics of experience—always interpretations of the experience, never the experience itself—are all that there is of the past. Historians never confront the Past, only the inscriptions that the Past has left. History is always interpretation of interpretation, always a reading of a given text.[2]

Reportage of various sorts, then, may be used jointly to get at meanings in common. Interpretation gets a little more slippery, however, when the meaning of the event is not shared by all involved. Such is the case with the corn shucking. Rather than to attempt to discern the social dimension of the meaning of the event, the number of types of documents that have been discovered allows one to argue that the event had a range of overlapping meanings, all revolving around the open display of work and play.

In the American South before the Civil War a harvest celebration developed surrounding the shucking of the corn. Indian corn never achieved the economic or symbolic importance of cotton, rice, sugar, indigo, or tobacco but was the crop at the center of the harvest feast celebrated primarily on the largest plantations. This event brought together a tremendous number of participants, most of them slaves, who were encouraged by "Old Master" and his family as well as by each other to perform in a style derived from their common African ancestors. This book chronicles this customary practice, and some of its outgrowths.

It may seem surprising that any new ideas regarding the social and cultural life of the plantation in the American South might be put forward. Yet there remains a lack of understanding of how African American cultural forms emerged in the midst of a society that systematically repressed the slaves. The cultural production of slaves needs to be reconsidered if we are to begin to describe effectively the dynamic, expressive interrelations of the two cultures living side by side, which has never been adequately described. This book represents an essay in that direction.

Using richly detailed firsthand accounts, I will describe one event—the harvest corn shucking—as a representative scene in which some of the dynamic features of the interaction between blacks and whites are elaborated. Far from seeking to eliminate the evidences of the "savage" past of the slaves, the planters, I will argue, came to regard their charges as exploitable for their capabilities as both workers and players. The planters constructed situations in which blacks played in front of whites for their mutual enjoyment. The slaves represented an exotic presence to their masters.

By the late eighteenth century, a majority of the slaves were native born and had developed uniquely American traditions of interacting, celebrating, and worshiping. While these folkways developed in the New World, they were, in the main, organized around the moral and aesthetic principles found throughout much of the sub-Saharan world from which they came.

These multiple-voice, complex metrical practices could be carried out, African-style, while the slaves went at a common task: in moving in gang formation to and from the fields; while planting, hoeing, weeding, reaping; or in preparing the cash crop for consumption, at the curing or boiling houses, or at the gin houses in which the cotton was cleaned. Reports of these traditional practices include songs that commented on their lives, even as they amplified the rhythms of the work.

Yet more widely noticed were the evenings' entertainments. Tasks were set for the slaves in the yard behind the Big House, and there the playing broke out as well, the singing and the ring-play dancing that were later to be elaborated into the "plantation scenes" of the American stage. The corn-shucking ceremony was an elaboration of this evening entertainment, a more intense spelling out of the abilities of the slaves to turn their tasks into stylized enterprises. In the organized activities of the corn feasts one can recognize the distinctive ways in which black leadership emerged.

So long as the slaves were singing and dancing, the planters were not threatened by their congregating. Many plantations introduced regular Saturday-night dances into their weekly routine even to the point of providing slaves with the instruments by which slave and master alike might be entertained. The slaves found that by developing musical abilities, individual slaves might gain mobility and be brought into the Big House to provide the music for balls.

Singing and dancing were regarded as signs of happiness, in spite of the fact that many whites could understand that the songs were often about the agonies of separation and alienation. This display served the planters' purposes in many ways. For the working seemed to go better when it was accompanied by singing, and the play that broke out provided the planters with home entertainments.

The slaves performed what was certainly seen as exotic displays by the planters, just as the balls and tournaments of the planters seemed exotic to the slaves—a point one tends to forget. The plantation accounts describe whites watching blacks at play, but we see too the whites costuming themselves and playing roles that were obviously strange and exciting to the slaves, who surely considered them power displays. The planter families repeatedly note that wherever they went, they felt as if they were on show as far as the slaves were concerned, a matter of some jocularity when the displays were done for their own amusement, as at tournaments, but hardly so when they were concerned with more private doings.

In 1819 the Methodist minister John Fanning Watson, observing the style of slave worship, noted:

In the blacks' quarter, the coloured people get together and sing for hours together, short scraps of disjointed affirmations, pledges, or prayers, lengthened out with long repetition *choruses*. These are all sung in merry chorus-manner of the southern harvest field or husking frolic method, of the slave blacks. . . .[3]

For Watson and his readers, participation through anti-phonal song was recognizably African. Watson related the singing to a system of foot-tapping and hand-patting on the leg with the "chorus-manner" registering, thereby, a gathering of stylistic traits that has been consistently noted of Afro-American performances, sacred and secular, work and play, for the last two centuries.

Watson was not a Southerner, certainly did not write exclusively for Southern readers, and indeed was describing a liturgical "error" committed by blacks at a camp meeting in Philadelphia. The essence of the style was not only the call-and-response singing but the pervasive sense of elation emerging from the experience of the slaves at the service.

This account emerged decades before the full-scale development of the minstrel show tradition. The slave song and dance had not yet become an element of American popular culture, in the sense of finding such plantation style and activities within a form of wide-scale popular entertainment. Nevertheless, by the second decade of the century, a musical style had entered into the vernacular imagination as characteristic of slave invention and performance.

Watson identifies the singing in the black quarters while working with the harvest of corn. From late in the eighteenth century until well into the twentieth, the husking, or shucking, was reported as an emblematic scene of the republican virtues widely observable in American agrarian life. The corn harvest developed in a different manner in the North, the South, and the West, depending on the proximity of farms, the availability of workers for the shucking, and how gregarious the neighbors were. For most of America, it was a community effort. On the Southern plantation it was performed by "the hands"—the slaves responsible for carrying out the basic work of producing the cash crop in the fields, the yard, the factory. And they developed the shucking occasion in a substantially different direction, differences that are sufficiently well-reported that they can be used as a channel into the stream of Afro-American culture as it was being created in the plantation yard.

These reports form the body of information at the center of this book. While the bulk of the actual accounts were made after the Civil War and were often affected by a rhetoric of nostalgia, others were written before the war, often by people from outside the South who had come to observe. Additionally, those who had been slaves and who had worked and played on these occasions detailed the practice in many of the same terms. Still others were recorded by abolitionists, hardly enamored of the system out of which the practice developed. To be sure, they were all responding to the widespread idea that the South, and especially the plantation South, was a place of pastoral serenity. But if this is so, the slaves themselves, when they spoke and wrote about the event, subscribed to this pastoral vision, almost as if they were saying that on this one occasion ideology operated successfully. I do not argue that the accounts reflect the way in which masters and slaves responded to each other in any other situation. But such a constellation of voices encourages me to discuss plantation life in terms that take us somewhat beyond the shucking itself. By looking closely at this event and by asking how the proceedings were interpreted by both the planters and the slaves, a further insight is offered into the complex creation of this New World cultural invention, the plantation world.

If I seize upon the corn-shucking accounts as the basis of my argument, it is not simply to discuss how one traditional event developed in the South (though as a folklorist, that was certainly why I first took note of these materials). Rather, I see the event as being characteristic of a dynamic process taking place on the plantation in which the slaves neither divested themselves of their African cultural heritage nor acculturated to the behaviors and performance patterns of their masters. To the contrary, the hands were encouraged to act and perform differently. The practices emerged as forms of active resistance, not in the sense that they attacked the system but rather in the ways in which they maintained alternative perspectives toward time, work, and status. In the process, a new cultural formation emerged, just as the whites on the plantation developed a life-style that was unique, both in itself and in the ways in which it took into account the presence of the culturally distinctive slave population.

An Afro-American culture was developed by the slaves, then, in counterpoint to a planter ideology that, on its face, seemed to regard them as part of the family. For the last twenty-five years historians have asked the question: What went on in the slave quarters that resulted in the development of an alternative culture scheme in the face of the surveillance of planters who were by turns hostile and paternalistic? Here I will attempt to relocate that question somewhat, for the evidence I have been able to gather concerning the interaction of whites and blacks indicates that a good deal of culture building was taking place in the yard between the Big House and the slave quarters, in contested areas betwixt and between the two worlds.

Much of the evidence of this cultural interaction is derived from a literature that is far from objective in its rendering of either black or white cultural patterns. To the contrary, the documents of the plantation experience are all marked by the rhetorical strategies of observers who were commenting on the viability and the humanity of this strange institution. It is not my task to discard racist stereotypical accounts but rather to explore the convenient fictions on which they rest, and to see how deeply these fictions affected the ways in which slave life was approached and how actual practices were affected by these attitudes.

Such an essentially racist and often nostalgic literature included a good deal of information about black/white relations. They carry the message that the slaves had maintained their own ways and that these were sufficiently attractive and productive that the plantation was able to accommodate and even encourage these differences.

Not only did some planters become aware that their slaves had a different set of cultural practices, but they encouraged a display of these differences in the slave dances and holidays. Such entertainments provided them with the sense that the plantation was inhabited by their family writ-large and gave them a break from the grindingly dull routine of a frontier life-style dedicated to producing surplus crops for the world market. However, the slaves came to recognize in the obligatory play and performance an opportunity for cultural invention and social commentary.

The planters did not understand fully what the hands were saying and doing as they carried out these work displays and entertainments. Rather, my overwhelming impression of life on the plantation is that the representatives of two cultures lived cheek to jowl for a matter of centuries, entertaining each other, subtly imitating each other in selective ways, but never fully comprehending the extent and meaning of these differences.

Clearly, this event, the corn shucking, meant something quite different to the black participants and the white observers. To white onlookers, the event was an entertainment verging on the spectacular; to the slaves, it was an opportunity to celebrate together. The difference cannot be overstressed. To whites, this was a spectator event; to slaves, it was a time of mutual participation in working, eating, and dancing.

No study of the culture of African American peoples can be carried out without bearing in mind that it is commenting on the largest social question faced by all Americans, black or white, yellow or red: How have "people of color" (and especially blacks) developed a significantly different culture while similar culturally different "ethnic" populations have become acculturated and assimilated to the so-called American mainstream? Another and more positive formulation of the question would ask how African Americans have preserved their significantly different ways of speaking, interacting, performing, and celebrating despite acculturative pressures?

From this perspective, slave cultural developments on the

plantation reveal how subjugated peoples are brought into a position of cultural as well as political submission. I hope to show that any such convergence of cultures, even under the most repressive regimes, may be usefully complicated through a consideration of the dynamics of stereotyping as it arises between the two or more groups coming together. The theme of resistance will be found in the lore of other subjugated or subordinated peoples, techniques that emerge from within the disempowered group which build upon the stereotype image imposed upon them by those in control. This complex cultural exchange emerges from the very kinds of events, festivals, and ceremonies that seem to be models of and models for a system of labor exploitation.

On first reading, these documents seem to record the continuing fealty paid the master by the slaves on his and nearby plantations. They also seem to present slaves as willingly accepting the role of singing and dancing "naturals" in this moment of public display and feasting. But the record also bespeaks a good deal of imitational behavior not so easily accounted for as simple acquiescence to a subordinate status.

I do not mean to overvalue these reports. They are anecdotal in the extreme. They do not argue a case that the corn shucking was universally practiced throughout the plantation South. Indeed, the reports are sufficiently isolated that I have not felt it useful to look closely at the authors and their professed purpose. In a sufficient number of them, the account emerges in the midst of memoirs of pleasant days. In others, they are made as commentary on the humanity or lack of it in black/white interactions on the plantation. Still others were elicited as records of what actual life in the yard and the quarters was like long after the system was no longer in place. But all of them carried one strong message: that these were significant experiences for everyone involved—the shuckers and the spectators on the portico. Those in attendance were forced to recognize the vitality of the occasion and the ways in which it provided an opportunity for the slaves alone to achieve some sense of shared feelings, values, and experiences, even while they entertained those looking on.

SINGING

THE

MASTER

CHAPTER ONE

"Ain't You Gwine to the Shucking of the Corn?"

In the two generations of plantation life immediately preceding the Civil War, the corn-shucking harvest ceremony became an important seasonal event throughout the Tidewater and low-country areas of the Chesapeake, as well as some areas of the Piedmont. Elsewhere, it was widely found in both lowland and upland settlements in the Carolinas and Georgia as well as Kentucky, Tennessee, Alabama, Mississippi, and East Texas. It developed throughout the area in which cotton was cultivated but was not limited only to cotton plantations.

It was regarded as a slaves' holiday, one which called for the field workers to enter freely into a work party as a prelude to a feast and a dance.[1] As one former slave, Sara Colquitt, explained to her WPA interviewer, "Marsa would have de corn hauled up to de crib, and piled as a house. Den he would invite de hands 'round to come and hope shuck it. . . . Us had two leaders or generals and choose up two sides. Den we'd see which side could win first and holler and sing."[2]

In the corn shucking, the slaves found that if they were willing to assume the role of happy workers, the planters would provide them with a feast and dance that would be remembered by both blacks and whites almost a century later. While far from universally found throughout the South, the corn feast was widely practiced in those areas which supported large cotton and tobacco plantations.

According to the reports, hundreds of workers were involved. Henry A. Woods, raised on a plantation, put it at "a hundred or more,"[3] the traveler Charles Lanman noted "perhaps two hundred,"[4] and the ex-slave Francis Fedric remembered "men to the number of three or four hundred. . . ."[5] The quantity of corn shucked was also immense, often described as being heaped as high as a house. And the amount of food prepared was sufficient to the occasion. Large tubs and whole animals are often mentioned. The feast and frolic called for a great deal of planning by everyone, slaves and masters alike, both in the gathering of the corn and in the organization of the work party followed by a feast and dance.

In the early fall, the corn was cut on the stalk and gathered into shocks, awaiting the end of the harvest. In the South, the corn would be brought in after the other crops were harvested, and a shucking would occur sometime between early November and mid-December. Fedric, who escaped from slavery, remembered: "In the autumn, about the 1st of November, the slaves commence gathering the Indian-corn, pulling it off the stalk and throwing it into heaps." At some point in the next few days, these piles were conveyed to the plantation yard.[6]

The corn was "carted home, and thrown into heaps sixty or seventy yards long, seven or eight feet wide," Fedric noted.[7] He recalled one corn pile a hundred and eighty yards long! Others exclaimed about such great piles, including the famous ex-slave Booker T. Washington, who recalled that there were "thousands of bushels, sometimes, . . . piled up in the shape of a mound, often to the height of fifty or sixty feet."[8] Jethro Rumple, a planter, similarly described the corn piled in a "huge long heap, straight or crescent-shaped" containing "thirty, fifty, or a hundred loads of corn. . . ."[9] Even after allowing for the fact that these were reminiscences and therefore potentially subject to exaggeration, the event clearly was extraordinarily outsized in relation to everyday life.

The event was commonly held at night, so pine knots were also gathered in abundance to light the occasion, and to provide warmth as well, should the night be chilly. Charles Lanman exclaimed about the quantities and qualities of this "light wood . . . employed for the several purposes of tempering the night air, affording necessary light, and rendering the approaching scene as cheerful as possible."[10] Mary Livermore, a Yankee teacher teaching on a Virginia plantation before the war, remembered the drama inherent in the "pitch pine knots . . . gathered in large quantities to illuminate the festive occasion."[11] Some ex-slaves recalled the lightwood illumination with similar feelings. "Dem old pine knots would burn for a long time and throw a fine bright light," one of them pointed out, reminding herself of the ". . . grand sight out dar at night wid dat old harvest moon a-shinin, fire a-burnin, and dem old torches lit up."[12]

As the corn heap grew in the yard near the pens, anticipation grew that a shucking might be held soon. On the plantation at which Livermore was teaching, she reported, the planter agreed to have a shucking at the urging of the children of the family.[13] But other accounts indicate that it was certain slaves who called for the occasion. Dr. John Wyeth, who came from a planter family, remembered that "[T]he negroes on one plantation were privileged to invite those of other places near by to come. . . ."[14]

Whoever initiated the idea, the master was responsible for sending out the "news" of the oncoming event in some form. Many remembered that the invitation itself came from the master. Booker T. Washington, for instance, noted, "Invitations would be sent around by the master himself to the neighbouring planters, inviting their slaves on a certain night to attend. . . . one or two hundred men, women, and children would come together."[15]

The invitation was a come-one, come-all sort, "free to any who wished to come, so that if the familiar sound of a number of negroes singing corn songs at one place was heard, any negro man or boy felt he had a right to go, and they generally went. . . ." Thus remarked George Brewer, raised on a plantation. (That female field slaves were included in the invitation is clear from the images we have of the occasion, but the shuckers were predominantly men.) Brewer further recalled: "Several negroes that were experts in 'corn songs' were asked to come and tell others to come."[16] Again, the ex-slaves concurred with these details: "De owners of slaves use to giv' cornshuckin' parties, an' invite slaves from yuther plantations."[17] "A week or more from the time, the news began to spread around when it was going to be; and as soon as it was dark, then neighbors began to drop in."[18]

On the appointed night, voices were heard singing from afar, first from one direction and then another, heralding the arrival of groups of slaves from the various plantations, all of them carrying pine-knot lanterns to light their way.

> You gwine, ain't you gwine,
> Ain't you gwine to the shuckin' of the corn?
> Oh yes I gwine to stay to morning
> When Gable blows his horn,
> Am gwine to stay till the coming of the dawn.[19]

The festive atmosphere of this convergence of slave gangs was remembered in remarkably similar terms by blacks and whites from different states. William Wells Brown, in one of the classic accounts of plantation life, told from the perspective of an escaped slave, wrote: ". . . the negroes dropped in from the neighboring plantations, singing as they came. . . . Often when approaching the place, the singers would speculate on what they were going to have for supper."

> All dem puty gals will be dar,
>   Shuck dat corn before you eat.
> Dey will fix it fer us rare,
>   Shuck dat corn before you eat.
> I know dat supper will be big,
>   Shuck dat corn before you eat.
> I think I smell a fine roast pig,
>   Shuck dat corn before you eat.
> A supper is provided so dey said,
>   Shuck dat corn before you eat.
> I hope dey'll have some nice wheat bread,
>   Shuck dat corn before you eat.
> [etc.]

Brown continued: ". . . slaves from plantations five or six miles away, would assemble. . . ." The effect was stunning to him even in remembrance: "To hear three or four of these gangs coming from different directions, their leaders giving out the words, and the whole company joining in the chorus," was enough to make the listener forget the pale imitations represented in even the best of the blackface minstrel shows of the time.[20]

In his memoirs, *Reminiscences of an Old Georgia Lawyer*, Garnett Andrews, a member of a planter family, describes in similar terms the approach of the various groups singing on the road: ". . . a solitary refrain might be heard a mile or two away, then another would join . . . , until they arrived, singing, at the corn-pile . . . making the night air resonant with melody. . . ."[21]

Mary Livermore also remembered, "Long before we saw their dusky figures, we heard their melodious songs . . . through the woods as they marched toward the . . . plantation." The groups converged "in four companies from as many different directions, by cart paths, and through the forest . . . ," coming together at the crossroads where they "saluted and marched together." The effect of the torches carried aloft, the singing and the shouting as the gangs encountered each other, dazzled her: ". . . the whole place brilliant with blazing pine knots, their enthusiasm knew no bounds."[22]

The groups of slaves were met in the yard by the master of the plantation who, along with his own slaves, had been waiting for their arrival. Other whites from the neighborhood often attended as well, invited by the master to enjoy the entertainment, seated on the portico above the spectacle. The slaves assembled in the yard, and the master came down and gave welcome to all. Some of the accounts include actual speeches. John Cabell Chenault reported of one occasion: "Mr. Norris . . . [in] the front of the portico rapped for silence [and said], 'Men, you have done me the kindness to come here tonight.' " Following a discussion of the work to be done, and the feasting and dance which were to come, Chenault reports his host to have said to the slaves, "I thank each of you now for this volunteer service. . . ."[23]

Before the arrival, the heap of corn was divided. Sometimes this was done simply by making two mounds, or dividing the one in half. One observer, James Lamar, remembered that one shucker was put at about the center of the pile, as he was "known to be a fast shucker," and proceeded to shuck through it, at that point, thus cutting it in two.[24] But more commonly the mass of ears was divided by a long fence rail or pole laid down the center. An early Kentucky observer, Dr. Daniel Drake, described this elaborate process:

They paced the rick and estimated its contractions and expansions with the eye, till they were able to fix on the spot on which the end of the dividing rail should be. The choice depended on the tossing of a chip, one side of which had been spit upon; the first choice of men was decided in the same manner, and in a few minutes the rick was charged upon by the rival forces.[25]

Another member of a planter family, James Avirett, remembered the use of a tape measure to ensure "an honest, fair division of that immense corn pile, as nearly equal in bulk and barrels as . . . well-trained eyes and hands can make it."[26]

Pacing the rick and laying the rail was important, for once the sides were chosen, there was further negotiating to do. Says Drake, "The captains planted themselves on each side of the rail" and then entered into what he called "the great contest," to see if further advantage might be had for one side or the other, "for it was lawful to cause the rail to slide or fall toward your own end, [thus] shortening it and lengthening the other. . . ."²⁷

The descriptions of how the pole was laid differ from one account to another. Joel Chandler Harris, from north Georgia, remembered that the pole was laid across the ground, and the corn laid on top,²⁸ while David Barrow, who came from the southwestern part of the state, noted that a fence rail was laid "across the top of the corn-pile, so that the vertical plane, passing through the rail, will divide the pile. . . ."²⁹

After the division, two teams were chosen which would then contend for a prize. These teams were commonly chosen by the "captains," or "generals." Being chosen as captain was, according to one ex-slave, the Rev. I. M. Lowery, "no little honor." He recalled that the captains were elected and once the honor was bestowed, each paraded about, with his "hat or his cap . . . decorated with the office, and everybody—white and black—did him honor."³⁰

As to how the captains achieved their position, the accounts do not agree. Indeed, the accounts indicate that numerous local traditions existed for the purpose. David Barrow remembered that "two 'gin'r'ls' are chosen from among the most famous cornshuckers. . . ,"³¹ while Lewis Paine, a Northerner residing some years in the South, noted that "[e]ach party selects two of the shrewdest and best singers among the slaves, to mount the pile and sing. . . ."³²

The accounts do agree that the captains chose the teams, and that each captain would have one, two, or three friends whom they knew to be good shuckers on their side. At the time of choosing sides, the master would often make another speech, reminding the sides of the rules against fighting, moving the rail, or throwing ears at each other excessively, and promising drink while the shucking was going on, and a feast—and often a dance—afterward. The planter wanted to ensure that the occasion provided a good time, but because it usually involved drinking, he needed to maintain some semblance of order.

Now the contest began in earnest. The captains sat, knelt, or stood at the top of their side of the pile and exhorted their followers to shuck as fast as they could, shouting out the first lines of songs to which their followers could respond vocally and through the timing of their movements, throwing the shucks in one direction and the shelled ears in another. The effect was dramatic, for the songs rang out and could be heard miles away.

> *Come to shuck that corn to-night,*
> *Come to shuck with all your might.*
> *Come to shuck all in sight,*
> *Come to shuck that corn to-night.*[33]

The men would stand or sit around the edges of the pile, in a ring. The shuckers picked up an ear with their left hand with the silk top facing upward, and tore downward with their right, often with the aid of a hardwood pin strapped onto and emerging from the palm of the right hand. Their left hand then fastened on the back half of the shuck and tore it off to the shank, or butt. The ear was then broken off, the shuck thrown behind the shucker, and the ear thrown back into the pile or directly into a pen. A good shucker could do the whole sequence in a matter of seconds.[34]

The shucks and ears flew through the air. One side would taunt the other, with jokes or in song:

Massa's niggers am slick and fat,
   Oh! Oh! Oh!
Shine just like a new beaver hat,
   Oh! Oh! Oh!
Turn out here and shuck dis corn,
   Oh! Oh! Oh!
Biggest pile o' corn seen since I was born,
   Oh! Oh! Oh!
Jones's niggers am lean an' po'
   Oh! Oh! Oh!
Don't know whether dey got 'nough to eat or no,
   Oh! Oh! Oh!
Turn out here and shuck dis corn,
   Oh! Oh! Oh!
Biggest pile o' corn seen since I was born,
   Oh! Oh! Oh![35]

When the contest got heated, some of the younger whites watching would come and play in the residue. James Lamar remembered this moment in the event: "[F]or a while the shucked corn would rain down upon the pile, and . . . accumulated behind the men, a state of things not to be resisted by any small boy." They proceeded to turn "summersets," bury each other underneath the shucks, run races through them, and push each other down, "rejoicing in the harmless falls, and shouting and screaming with delighted glee. . . ."[36]

Avirett noticed that whites of courtship age would make wagers on the outcome, "here a pair of kid gloves, there a handsome driving whip or a silver dog whistle."[37] This seems to have been the extent of the involvement of those watching from the portico.

As the shucking proceeded, occasionally a shout was heard when one of the shuckers found a red ear, a signal of good fortune and more. As one ex-slave, Marinda Brown, recalled, "Ever'body that found a red ear had t'be kissed. I didn't like that much though!"[38] Another, Lina Hunter, remembered that ". . . evvy Nigger dat found a red ear got a extra swig of liquor."[39] As the rhyme had it:

> *Pull de husk, break de ear*
> *Whoa, Ise got de red ear here.*[40]

The shucking itself, and especially the spirit of contest, encouraged the captains to display their song-leading abilities. The descriptions of the singing in the reports are wonderfully vivid, for it seemed both joyous and exotic to the whites who listened. James Lamar provided a characteristically nostalgic paean to the leader and his songs:

They have a leader or foreman who is responsible for the "composition." This he sings one or two lines at a time, in some cases as loud as he can bawl, in others in a subdued crooning sort of way. . . . [T]he very spirit of the song . . . , seems to enter into the shuckers and regulate their movements. . . . [T]he bringing out of the choral refrain . . . is noise in measured time and infallibility of movement. It is pleasing to the ear, and wonderful in its effect upon the feelings. . . .[41]

The captains' singing and cajoling emphasized the simultaneous work and play—a point underscored by the sung responses. Again, the relation between the pace of the work and that of the songs was repeatedly noted. James Lamar remembered "a very effective one, considered as a stimulus to rapid shucking, which began with the chorus: . . . *Pull de co'n* . . . :

> *Pull down,*
> *Pull de co'n.*
> *Every body,*
> *Pull de co'n.*
> *Pull fas' an,*
> *Pull de co'n.*
> *Wake up, Sambo,*
> *Pull de co'n.*
> *Roosters crowin',*
> *Pull de co'n.*
> *Day's a-breakin*
> *Pull de co'n."*[42]

Many of the songs had refrains that encouraged the shuckers:

> *Up Roanoke and down the river,*
> *Oho, we are 'most done.*
>
> *Up Roanoke and down the river.*
> *Oho, we are 'most done.*
>
> *Two canoes, and nary paddle.*
> *Oho, we are 'most done.*
>
> *Two canoes, and nary paddle.*
> *Oho, we are 'most done.*[43]

On occasion the singing would subside, and joking and storytelling might take its place. As Paine described it: "They sing awhile, then tell stories, and joke and laugh awhile. At last they get to making all the different noises the human voice is capable of, all at the same time—each one of each party doing its best to win the victory."[44] But as the pile gets lower, excitement mounts, the singing and shouting make it appear "that Bedlam had broken loose, . . ."[45] Again there are tricks to try to trip up the other side. David Barrow noted, for instance, that "should his side seem to be gaining, one of their opponents will knock the leader off the cornpile, and thus cause a momentary panic."[46] Sometimes fights broke out near the close of the contest.[47] As the pile got smaller, the fever of the crowd would grow. The shuckers would pick up the pace, often with a song that underscored the pitch of the contest:

> *Lookin' fur de las' year [ear],*
> *Bang-a-ma-lango!*
> *Lookin' fur de las' year,*
> *Bang-a-ma-lango!*
> *Roun' up de co'n boys,*
> *Bang-a-ma-lango!*
> *Roun' up de co'n boys,*
> *Bang-a-ma-lango!*[48]

But, as Paine described it, as the outcome became clear, the "victorious party" erupted, "peal[ing] forth their shouts and jests in a deafening volley, . . . as though kingdom come was already in their possession."[49] It is not clear how the victors were rewarded, though one ex-slave, Ida Henry, remarked that "de prize would usually be a suit of clothes or something to wear and which would be given at some later time."[50]

At the sounds of victory, on a number of plantations, a "chairing" was carried out. The winners searched out the host (or "Young Marster" or the overseer) and tossed him onto their shoulders and carried him around the great house,

often beating on pans and buckets, while singing a song special to the "walkaround" that made fun of the man aloft. For example:

> Oh, Mr. Reid iz er mighty fine man,—
> Er mighty fine man indeed;
> He plants all de taters,
> He plows all de corn,
> He weighs all de cotton,
> An' blows de dinner-horn;
> Mr. Reid iz er mighty fine man.[51]

As one North Carolinian remembered it, "Old Marster" didn't have the stamina to stay up throughout the event: "About midnight, when the husking was over . . . the master of the house, . . . was gotten out of bed, his hair combed, his shoes blacked, his clothes brushed, and taken for a ride around the house in a chair, all to the tune of gay songs used for these occasions."[52]

When the shucking was over and the winners were declared, the master called for the food to be served. Meat and drink were served in abundance, marking the different character of the occasion, for these were valued, scarce commodities for the slaves (though standard fare for the planter, his family, and his guests). As Letitia Burwell remembered: "[A]fter all the corn was shucked, they had a feast of roasted pigs, mutton, beef, pies and cakes."[53] One of the commonplaces of the white corn-shucking literature is the epic list of the foods and drinks available: "Fresh meats, chicken-pie, ham, cold turkey, fried chicken, hot coffee, and several kinds of plate pies . . ." made up one such catalog;[54] another listed "loaf, biscuits, ham, pork, chicken pie, pumpkin custard, sweet cakes, apple pie, grape pie, coffee, sweet milk, buttermilk, preserves, in short a rich feast of everything yielded by the farm."[55]

Again, matters of scale tended to overwhelm these descriptions, as regards not only the number of foods, but the amounts that had to be prepared. As planter James Love pointed out, "the big chicken pot pie with its wealth of dumpling had to be cooked out of doors in the 'wash kettle,' " for there were no pots big enough in the ordinary kitchen.[56]

The reports suggest that slave women did the cooking while the men were shucking. Livermore, however, says that "the cooking began early in the morning," when "all the resources of the 'niggah kitchen,' where the meals of the field hand were prepared, were duly monopolized."[57] Avirett claims that the food, while prepared by "several of the servants," drew the active participation of 'ole Mistuss.' "[58] But the planter-diarist John Dorris goes further in a speech in which he indicates that the planter's wife did the cooking with some help from "her neighbors."[59] And in one report on the food preparation and service, the ex-slave Fedric says, "it being usual to kill an ox, on such an occasion . . . Mr., Mrs., and the Misses Taylor, waited on the slaves at supper." (This may have meant that they stood to the side and watched throughout; the exact meaning is unclear.)[60]

The division of duties was almost certainly derived from everyday life, and the women who did most of the cooking were connected with the Big House whether or not the planter's family was involved in the service. The other women, the field slaves, almost certainly entered into the shucking. Illustrations from books and magazines reporting the event show women in the corn pile along with the men. As a number of reporters indicated, it was a matter of whether their hands were hard enough to carry out the task of shucking, for profound calluses, or "horns," on the hands were necessary to enable them to bear the constant friction of the leaves. By the end of the event even the best shuckers would have a good many cuts on their hands from the edges of the leaves.

As the eating started, one of the captains or another good talker among the slaves took on the role of the master of ceremonies to toast the health of the host and hostess, and to hold forth on other subjects: "Jokes of questionable elegance and delicacy are uttered to a considerable extent," Charles Lanman remembered of this part of the occasion, "and many compliments paid to the *lib'ral and magnan' mous massa ob dis plantation.*"[61]

After the feast, the tables were cleared, the fiddler was sent for, and dancing began. Nettie Powell reminisced many years afterward about her own experiences at shuckings, that when "the task was over," and the "sumptuous supper" was served, there was a dance in which old and young joined. The music was supplied by old-time fiddlers with much beating of straws.[62] The visitor from the North, William Cullen Bryant, was struck by the dancing: "various dances, capering, prancing and drumming with 'heel and toe upon the floor' . . . came after the feast.[63]

This might go on for hours, sometimes even till cockcrow. While most of the accounts simply describe the carousers as disbanding, a few call attention to a more formal closing. Ex-slave William Wells Brown recalled that "[o]n leaving the corn-shucking farm, each gang of men, headed by their leader, would sing during the entire journey home."[64] In a similar vein, Mary Ross Banks, a white woman raised on a plantation, reminisced: "[M]any of the visitors snatch up the brands, and waving them high over their heads, start home as happy and lighthearted, apparently as unfatigued as when they came into the yard four hours ago . . . singing on their way home. . . ."[65]

> *Fare you well, fare you well.*
> *Weell ho. Weell ho.*
> *Fare you well, young ladies all.*
> *Weell ho. Weell ho.*
> *Fare you well, I'm going away.*
> *Weell ho. Weell ho.*
> *I'm going away to Canada.*
> *Weell ho. Weell ho.*[66]

The corn shuckings persisted in the memories of a great many people, long after the system under which they flourished was dead. Indeed, one diarist writing during the Civil

War, on November 3, 1863, heard the sounds of a corn shucking going on through the chill night air and wrote, "I felt that probably for the last time I heard the songs of the negroes at one of their only convivial gatherings, songs and sounds which I have been familiar with from my infancy. Old things are passing away."[67]

Nicey Kinney, an ex-slave in Georgia, remembered such scenes, too. Her master did not live for very long after the war, but as long as he was alive he kept up the old ways. "One night he let his farm hands have a big corn-shucking," with the supper and the liquor traditional to the event. And "[a]s was the custom in them days, some of them niggers got Old Master up on their shoulders and toted him up to the big house . . . ," cavorting, singing, "gay as they was." When they let him down onto the portico in front of his door, "he told Old Mistress that he din't want no supper 'cept a little coffee and bread, and he strangled on the first bite . . . he was nigh . . . gone into the glory of the next world, . . . a good man."[68]

David Barrow, reporting in the 1880s, indicated that in fact the slaves had valued the shuckings sufficiently that they maintained the tradition under the condition of freedom. He pointed out that they were still taking place among the black freemen farmers in his area of southwest Georgia, for "[w]ith the larger liberty they enjoy there has come increased social intercourse. . . ." In addition, he goes on, "the great number of small farmers who have sprung up in the South since the war necessitates mutual aid in larger undertakings. . . ."[69] The corn shuckings were remembered as long as there were blacks and whites who had experienced them, and were written about for the next seventy-five years by ex-slaves, ex–plantation dwellers, even by many who exulted in the death of the system under which the slaves' holiday had arisen.

The corn shucking, then, was a fully developed traditional event calling for a great deal of planning and eliciting the excitement of the entire plantation community. Nevertheless, it was a slaves' holiday as both planters and ex-slaves maintained. The corn shucking was a time in which the slaves were called upon not only to carry out extensive work but to enjoy themselves while doing it, and to entertain those whites who came to watch the proceedings. Till now, this event has received scant attention from historians. Doubtless this is because it represents such an apparent capitulation to the image of the happy slave purveyed by the planter-apologists for slavery. But much more than simply a playing out of that stereotypical self-image was going on.

CHAPTER TWO

Orders Within Order:
Cavalier and Slave Culture on the
Plantation

"About seven o'clock in the summer season, the colored people would . . . assemble in the yard belonging to the planter's residence," Emily Burke reminisced about her service as a Yankee schoolteacher in Georgia in the 1840s. She remembered that in the yard, the slaves would kindle their lightwood and carry out their assigned work in grinding corn, while "all the rest join in a dance" around the fire. "In this manner was spent the great part of summer evenings" where the family assembled "on the piazza to witness their pastimes . . ." and, on occasion, the white children descended to the yard and joined in the dancing of a waltz or quadrille.[1]

Sarah Fitzpatrick, an ex-slave from Alabama, remembered a similar pattern involving slaves from a number of quarters: "Young 'Niggers' f'om sev'ral plan'tations used to get together at one 'er der white fo'ks houses an' have a big time," she mused. "White lact to git 'round an' watch 'em, make 'em ring up an' play games an' things lack dat."[2]

The corn shucking provided one of the most potent of

the "scenes and sketches of life on the plantation" which became conventional in the travelers' accounts and, later, in the novels, minstrel shows, and other staged representations of Southern life. These scenes provided a dramatization of the ways slaves and masters had worked out of accommodating to each other's recreative needs. Indeed, the corn shucking seemed to announce that everyone on the plantation was engaged in a vigorous common enterprise, in which nature—the passage of the season and the growth of the crops—was placed at the service of the owners and tillers of the land.

To be sure, the shucking was a display event for both groups. For the planters, it built on the everyday scenes of work and play in which the slaves were the featured performers. For the slaves, it was an opportunity to depart from everyday labor while developing and maintaining their own

traditional practices in the face of enslavement. Hands and masters played roles in a set piece which turned the system of power relationships of the plantation into a comedy and a pastoral romance. In the process the social structure was revealed, tested, reaffirmed.

In *The Mind of the South* W. J. Cash described the theatrical features of life on the plantation as "a sort of stage piece out of the eighteenth century . . . its social pattern was manorial, its civilization that of the Cavalier, its ruling class an aristocracy coextensive with the planter group." The planter families themselves built upon this putative past, proclaiming descent from "gentlefolk [from] . . . the ruling classes of Europe." Cash concludes that "the gentlemanly idea, driven from England by Cromwell, had taken refuge in the South and fashioned for itself a world . . . singularly polished and mellow and poised, wholly dominated by ideals of honor and chivalry and *noblesse*."[3]

But Cash also noticed the cultural complications arising from such a self-conscious attempt to project an image and a history. Numerous features of plantation life were responses to altered geographical and social conditions as they moved west, set up new plantations, and introduced new cash crops. Planters established households that included slave hands from altogether different cultural systems living with them in areas which were unique to slave and master alike. In a long and breathless sentence reminiscent of his contemporary William Faulkner, Cash meditates:

. . . in this society in which the infant son of the planter was commonly suckled by a black mammy, in which gray old black men were his most loved storytellers, in which black stalwarts were among the chiefest heroes and mentors of his boyhood, and in which his usual, often practically his only, companions until he was past the age of puberty were black boys (and girls) of the plantation—in this society in which by far the greater number of white boys of whatever degree were more or less shaped by such companionship, and which nearly the whole body of whites, young and old, had constantly before their eyes the example, had constantly before their ears the accent, of the Negro, the relationship between the two groups was, by the second generation, nothing less than organic.

He concludes: "Negro entered into white man as profoundly as white man entered into Negro—subtly influencing every gesture, every word, every emotion and idea, every attitude."[4]

While the plantation did establish certain patterns of interaction by which commerce between the races was practiced, no deep sense of cultural reciprocity developed. The white children played in the quarters; the black hands ceremonially welcomed the return of master and mistress from

journeys, and greeted their guests as they arrived. From this a set of customs emerged which became central to "the etiquette of race relations," as Bertram Doyle referred to it.[5]

In the main, the institution that came to be called "the plantation" throughout the English-speaking world was an invention of Europeans. Seizing territories either from the indigenous populations or newly opened up through the process of voyage and discovery, this system of production was essentially an early commercial enterprise, conducted to produce crops for trade in international markets. However, the social and cultural system that emerged from the social organization centering on the production of surplus crops brought back into play the terms of the manorial relationships. The older social system had turned, too, on organizing agricultural production, using the passage of the seasons as times for celebrations that reaffirmed the social structure. That this was a new social system is beyond doubt, as Eugene Genovese and Elizabeth Fox-Genovese have shown.[6] That it masked its innovations in an older set of vocabularies and through display occasions which self-consciously appropriated past traditions also cannot be doubted.

The planters certainly were exercising their power through the act of tolerance in the corn shucking. In bringing the field hands into the yard, addressing them individually and collectively, and providing them with an abundant repast, the master was able to actively play the part of the kind and demanding patriarch. He animated the occasion by extending the plantation household beyond his own family, by being able to call the names of the slaves on other plantations as well. And by actually thanking the slaves for coming, he brought his own conception of himself as a magnanimous leader into the center of the proceedings.

As in harvest ceremonies in England, local social structure

in the plantation South was translated into spectacle while the economic enterprise carried out in common by all members of the working community was celebrated. The spectacle was all the more dramatic because it featured members of the lowest social order in the plantation social order— the field hands.

Planters were drawn to such displays in the first place because the festivities dramatized the success of their own enterprise even while it made palpable their "dream of self-sufficiency," as Gerald Mullin phrased it.[7] Each planter sought to establish a little world unto itself, one which was self-contained and controlled, and in which he and his family not only profited, but did so with honor and were accorded respect and given deference. And, ideally, the planters were able to assemble a cadre of slave laborers who carried out the tasks on which the agricultural enterprise depended, as well as to arrange training of artisans who could maintain and improve the operation.

In this contained world a particular social structure existed among the slaves, in which status was determined by the proximity of a slave's role to the planter or the Big House.

The corn shucking occurred in the yard because it was close to the corn pen, the outbuilding where the shucked corn would be stored. By situating the event in the environs of the Big House, the planter also proclaimed that he regarded the activity as a family event. The extensiveness of the co-ordinated effort and the dimensions of the largess involved in feeding the crew were evidence of the planter's ability to maintain his prominence within the home plantation and in the larger community of blacks and whites. The planter could develop a reputation as both a good manager of his resources and an effective paterfamilias due the deference of one in such a position.

The great planter was called upon to play a number of roles: benevolent provider and protector, genial and gregarious neighbor and host, and commercial and diplomatic

leader. He gave impetus and direction to this capitalist enterprise which was cloaked in precapitalist agricultural terms. To his slaves as to his family, he was called upon to build his house well and to run it efficiently.

The corn shucking developed during a historical period in which major shifts occurred in the populations of both planters and slaves. The success of cotton as a cash crop, beginning in the 1790s, made it possible for many yeomen farmers to expand their holdings and to add slaves to their work force.[8] Not only had the ratio of blacks to whites altered on many of the older and more populous plantations in the Tidewater regions and the Piedmont following the American Revolution, but the slave population altered from predominantly African-born to one almost exclusively native-born.[9] The corn shucking, it seems clear, could not have been carried on in this manner and scale before the 1790s.

More important, the slave population on the larger plantations increasingly was made up of those born and raised there. The planters were less fearful of slave uprisings or desertions among hands born in the New World and raised on the plantation. These slaves lived longer, were more fully integrated into the larger family design of the planters, and often produced hands who could learn the crafts needed to make the plantation more fully self-sufficient.

As new ideas for planting, cultivating, harvesting, and rotating crops were introduced throughout the United States, a different relationship arose between workers and owners or employers, and a different intensity and scale of work began to be expected. While this regime was not as widely called for in the South, notions of rationalized work scheduling became increasingly apparent in plantation records.[10]

Yet the older way of conceiving of the workplace on the plantation in family terms was maintained, even as the work itself was viewed in terms of task organization.[11] In conceiving of the work in terms of separable tasks and a process of production, the planters drifted increasingly into a conception of work as a contract between themselves and the slaves, in which they took on the burden of providing food, clothing, shelter, and other forms of protection. Implicitly, the slaves negotiated to carry out the work in their own fashion. The corn shucking was, from this perspective, a dramatization of the gang-organization of work that was brought by these hoe-agriculturalists from Africa.

The corn shucking was a reminder, then, for everyone on the plantation, of the continuing reliance on slaves as a labor force for bringing in the cash crop on which the economic success of the operation depended. Calling on the workers from neighboring plantations permitted the development of a feeling of self-sufficiency for an entire neighborhood. By extending the enterprise beyond the individual farm, the planters established a pattern by which it came to be understood that during the harvest period on plantations that opted to have such a feast, travel on the roads between the plantations would be more open to social visiting among the slaves. Undoubtedly, there were many unneighborly masters who were not prepared to enter into the kind of social and cultural negotiation with the slaves called for in holding any kind of bee or frolic.

The slaves lived by a different calendar than the masters. As the planter James Battle Avirett explained: "The three great feasts on the plantation are 'Crismus, hog killin', and corn shuckin' '—the first an immovable one but the last two are movable feasts in the African almanac."[12] These three holidays, all surrounding the close of the agricultural year, and all carrying messages of the plenitude of the enterprise, measured the days in which the slaves came to feel entitled to a break in the plantation regime.[13]

For the slaves, the time from the close of work on Saturday until late Sunday was their most extended period of rest and relaxation. Saturday night was the time for slave dances and frolics. On Sunday they were able to tend their own garden plots, and more and more in the nineteenth century, to engage in worship.

For the planters, Sunday was the day of high ceremony, a time to go to church and to gather with others of their station. As the Northern tutor Phillip Fithian noted of his Virginia employers, it was "a general custom . . . with Gentlemen to invite one another home to dine, after church; and to consult about, determine their common business, either before or after service, discussing important matters such as the price of tobacco and grain and the merits of their fighting cocks and horses."[14] And Sunday was also provisioning day, in which master and slave came together to allocate and receive rations, an activity which was attended by a certain degree of ceremony.

Monthly court days intensified this official sense of gathering for high display and discussion in the planters' calendar. The various ranks assembled in the county seat, for these were market and trading days. As the historian Rhys Isaac has recently noticed, "On court days economic exchange was openly merged with social exchange (both plentifully sealed by the taking of liquor) and also expressed in conventional forms of aggression—in bantering, swearing and fighting."[15] To this was added the high ceremony of some of the established church holidays, when, as T. H. Breen says, "rituals took place around courthouses and Anglican churches . . . occasions [in which] the number of the local gentry asserted their claim to cultural dominance, and before an audience of their country neighbors."[16]

The slave holidays were dictated, in the main, by points of repose in the agricultural year, immediately following times of intense labor. In addition to the respite from work, the holidays called for major feasts and dances. While the corn shucking was ubiquitous but by no means omnipresent in the South, a number of similar kinds of frolics were held in midsummer, at first frost, and after the major crop was brought in, and then at Christmas. Indeed, Christmas was the only holiday season shared by slaves and masters. Christmas became the time in which the slaves animated the Big House with their presence.[17] Often dressed in their Sunday finery, they freely entered the house expecting to be given their "Christmas Gift." A good deal of boisterous activities, joking, and laughing was reported. Clearly this was a time of license in which their gifts were produced on demand.

If the slaves lived by a calendar somewhat at variance from that of the planters, there was one area of culture in which each group took part in the life of the other: at points of life-passage, especially funerals and weddings. Reports of shared expressions of sentiment, in tears and in laughter, are extraordinarily widespread throughout writings on plantation life. This was especially the case among the adult women, but far from exclusive to them. Even in the midst of the Civil War, Lucy Breckinridge recorded a number of details of the wedding between the slaves Jim and Matilda on her home plantation. She made cakes for the party, as was the clear custom, as well as a headdress for the bride. She and a friend not only attended the wedding ("The Episcopal service was read by 'Uncle Ned' . . . ") but responded positively when they were "begged" to witness the dancing afterward. "They had banjoes and fiddles and danced quite prettily," she recorded in her diary.[18]

Births and deaths also prompted well-managed social dramas, especially with slaves who had the honor and trust of the family in the great house. The most important enactment of the etiquette of race relations took place at the deathbed. As Bertram Doyle pointed out, whites and blacks were expected to take a place of honor at each others' passing as a means of dramatizing their mutual respect and affection. Furthermore, the funerals themselves, of whites and blacks alike, were treated with a great deal of respect by everyone.[19]

Slaves and masters spent little time in mutual celebration, however. Rather, the play of each group provided an entertainment for the other. Just as whites observed blacks in the

evenings' entertainments and the corn shucking, so a number of eyewitness accounts reveal the slaves looking in on dances and other entertainments in the great house. As the ex-slave James Boyd reported, after recalling the corn shuckings and the Christmas dances of the slaves, at which the master and his family were present, "W'en de white folks had dere big balls we niggers would cook an' wait on de white folks and watch 'em dance, but we had lots of fun on de side."[20]

By the middle of the eighteenth century, the great landed families had begun to prosper in that part of the Tidewater which remained arable, much of the Piedmont, and on the other side of the Appalachians wherever the land would support the raising of cotton or sugar. Throughout this region, large-scale planters deliberately set themselves off from their yeoman neighbors as they built their great houses. Their enterprises were constructed in the image of isolated country villages. These compounds served as headquarters for families which aspired to operate in a dynastic fashion. The houses provided settings for elaborate displays of refinement, elegance, hospitality. In greeting guests and taking their leave, in presenting food and drink and presiding over meals, planters, their wives, and children were constantly called upon to be formally graceful and hospitable.

At the center of the crafted landscape, the mansion served as an embodiment of the integrity and the power of the family residing within, even when the building itself was not always very grand. From the enlarged public rooms the planter families played out their roles to the rest of the world, which on a daily basis meant their slaves. The enduring image of the plantation from observers' reports has the hands as well as the house servants constantly seeking direction from someone in the planter's family. Between such times, they were standing in the doorways or looking in from outside. Repeatedly, the great families felt the omnipresent gaze of their "charges," not only during the public occasions but also whenever privacy would seem called for.

The yard, as a work area, seems to have been a region predominantly populated by certain of the hands, while remaining under the constant surveillance of the planters and their deputies. As Philip Fithian found at Nomini Hall, there were major parts of the yard which the slaves regarded as their exclusive domain.[21] From this perspective, the yard was contested terrain, firmly established as the site for significant work to be carried out under the gaze of those in authority, but under normal circumstances subject to the control of the slaves themselves. That this reflected the planters' own view was indicated by their customary reference to "the yard" not only to mean the space outside the Big House in which work was carried out, but to mean the work force of artisans and animal tenders as well.[22]

The idea of the great house was derived from the English country house in plan, materials, and formality of life-style. In the Chesapeake area, especially, the houses were built on a plan "exactly like middle-sized manors in the south and west of England during the seventeenth and early eighteenth centuries," says David Hackett Fischer, surveying the subject. He describes the "general characteristics . . . typical of the genre: broad fronts of 70 to 100 feet; symmetrical plans; a first floor with a modest number of large rooms; generous proportions and high ceilings; a large central hall open at both ends; and a low 'ground floor' with bed chambers." The house was built sufficiently back from the road or the river to highlight its most dramatic qualities of size, stateliness, and formal integrity.[23]

The formality of the family arrangements might be evident not only within the common rooms that would accommodate a great number of people in dining, dancing, or some other form of social intercourse, but in the arrangement of gardens, terraces, and bowling greens. These were radically differentiated from the yard, both in terms of the activities which took place there and in the appurtenances, for the yards were stripped bare of anything but paraphernalia attached to the technical operation of the plantation. From the slaves' perspective, each different area on the plantation demanded maintenance and provided employment for a larger number of hands who found themselves with greater access to the house and its social benefits.

Emily Burke provides a full inventory of the plantation landscape, beginning at the boundaries and proceeding inward: "[T]here was a paling enclosing all the buildings belonging to the family." She describes the "principal house," in which "the father of the family and all the females lodged," and the house close by, "occupied by the steward . . . where all the white boys belong[ing] to the family had their sleeping apartments." Farther away from the Big House there was a two-room schoolhouse, one room of which was given over to the teacher's quarters. Beyond this, "the cook, the washer-woman, and the milk-maid had each their several houses, the children's nurses always sleeping upon the floor of their mistress' apartment." She gives a catalog of the task-related structures that populated the yard: "the kitchen, the store-house, corn-house, stable, hen-coop, the hound's kennel, the shed for the corn mill"—each a separate building "within the same enclosure." At the edge of the compound, "at a considerable distance from the master's residence, yet not beyond his watchful and jealous eye," stood the "huts of the field servants . . . arranged with a good deal of order . . . ," each with a small plot for gardening.[24]

Thus the symbolic landscape which is centered on the

great house announces formality rather than intimacy, yet constantly places the planters and the slaves within each other's gaze. While many of the slaves were privy to the details of planter family life, one has the impression that a good deal of observation and reporting was being carried out at all times from the house into the quarters.[25] This, of course, was paralleled by the observation of slave work and play by members of the planter family not directly concerned with supervising the slaves' output.

Dell Upton, describing the dynamic of life in this landscape, underscores the fact that while the slaves and masters lived in a common space, they developed alternative ways of encountering the buildings, yards, and fields. The plan-

tation world, from the planter's perspective, was an ordered collection of buildings embodying a "landscape [which] was both articulated and processional." Each building took a place in the social and political economy of means in the plantation community, becoming part of "a network of spaces—rooms in the house, the house itself, the outbuildings, the church with its interior pews and surrounding walled churchyard, the courthouse and its walled yard— that were linked by roads and that functioned as the settings for public interactions that had their own particular character but that worked together to embody the community as a whole."[26]

Anyone entering the planters' world passed a series of what Upton calls "physical barriers that are also social barriers" in the form of terraces, forebuildings, and doors. As the folklorist and social historian Robert St. George detailed this landscape:

The world of the great white planters consisted of contrived collections of buildings and spaces ordered by sequences of social barriers: rows of trees, terraces, dependencies, the kitchen. Finally, the house itself confronted the white visitor with more barriers: portico, doorway, grand stair hall, chambers for waiting, chambers for formal talking, chambers for formal dining.

This crafted social space was developed as "a carefully orchestrated exercize in the definition of status; every barrier passed was a mark of preference." It was the whole effect that created great houses, each of which, as St. George puts it, "was a vortex of local power sustained through its centrality in commerce, education, rituals of hospitality and politics." Finally, the social drama invoked by the house was repeated in the other formal structures within this world:

the courthouse, the church, and other places of public congregation.[27]

The view of the plantation landscape was different if one began in the quarters. For the hands, too, social status was intimately determined every day—by their proximity to the great house, by their degree of access to the planter and his family, by the costume they were called upon to wear, and so on. The slave quarters stood in an articulated, if often hidden, relationship to the great house, and the sight lines naturally went from the slave houses, through the yard and its buildings, into the Big House. The slaves became accolytes in the ceremonial system of the masters. Hands would come into the great house world from the quarters through the yard, into the kitchen and into the dining room through less than grand entrances.[28] Within the quarters, they were known by the character of their labor.[29] The hands most favored in this scheme were those who had established their importance by their place in the yard: the tanners, blacksmiths, carders and weavers of cloth, the needleworkers de-

vising the clothing for the slaves, and the gardeners and the keepers of various animals.[30]

Like so many other features of plantation life, the architectural ideal and the crafting of the landscape derived from the practices of the aristocracy and the country gentry in England. Except in the extraordinary circumstances of those planters elected to public office, or those who also operated as factors, clerics, or in some other role which took them away from home, the planter and his family saw themselves as being cut off from town life. Their isolation was not unlike that registered by so many frontier families—and felt especially strongly by the women. In developing their self-concept as Cavaliers, they maintained some of the elaborate public role playing of the Stuarts without having the depth of clientage that would have enabled them to exercise their gentility and benevolence as often as they would have wished. "The great house was essential to the sustaining of the master's part in social drama," Rhys Isaac perceives. "It stood in a dialectic relationship to him, for it took its meaning from his social existence and, in turn, it contributed powerfully to the shaping of his patterns of behavior."[31]

Some of the great planters sought to create ever more theatrical opportunities by which their public postures of power might better be appreciated. These were events, such as balls and tournaments, in which exaggerated honor seeking and risk taking were the primary themes.[32] The inherent theatricality of festive times in Cavalier England was further developed under the plantation regime.

This theatricality was nowhere more fully embodied than in the image of the planter standing on his portico to welcome his guests, black or white, or riding on his favorite horse to survey his land and supervise his charges. The good master not only had a large number of hands and entertained lavishly, but also looked the part, always well-dressed, even when mounted and riding through his fields.

The possibilities for theatricality in everyday life were endless under this system. As Frederick Douglass noted in his autobiography, even the day on which food and clothing were distributed would be turned into festive drama of a sort. "On allowance day," he said, "those who visited the great house farm were particularly excited . . . they would make the dense old woods, for miles around, ring with their wild notes."[33] At least one great nineteenth-century planter, James Henry Hammond of South Carolina, saw another opportunity in the provisioning day. He required the slaves who came to him for their allowance to wear clean clothes, and to approach with dignity, to which he would respond with deference. As his biographer, Drew Gilpin Faust, pointed out, "Although the overseer could perfectly well have executed such a task, the ceremonial importance of the moment demanded the master's direct participation." Requiring "fresh apparel" made this occasion something more special, "set off . . . from other less sacred events of daily life. . . ." This was, she persuades us, "plantation management as theater, with Hammond starring as paternalist and the blacks all assembled as captive, if not appreciative audience."[34]

Social position was determined by one's position vis à vis the master. This structuring may in fact have been more elaborated by the slaves themselves. Rank among the slaves was determined by the kinds of tasks they were assigned; not only by the intensity of the work but by the relative access to the master, mistress, or others living in the great house. According to one ex-slave, Rosa Stark:

Dere was just two classes to de white folks—buckra slave owners and poor white folks dat didn't own no slaves. Dere was more classes 'mongst de slaves. De fust class was de house servants. Dese was de butler, de maids, de nurses, chambermaids, and de cooks. De nex' class was de carriage drivers and de gardeners, de carpenters, de barber, and de stable men. Then come de nex' class: de wheelwright, wagonners, blacksmiths, and slave fore-men. De nex' class I 'members was de cow men and de niggers dat have care of de dogs. All dese have good houses and never have to work hard or git a beatin'. Then come de cradlers of de wheat, de threshers, and de millers of de corn and de wheat, and de feeders of de cotton gin . . . De lowest class was de common field niggers.[35]

This observer clearly lived on a plantation with a high degree of division of labor, for only on the largest plantations could so many houseworkers and craftsmen and animal tenders be distinguished. As Gerald Mullin has noted, the "good patriarch" was called upon to "maintain two posi-tions, one in the neighborhood, by sumptuous living and feats of hospitality, and the other among his slaves on the plantation, by a benevolent, indulgent, and understanding view of their performance."[36] The good master, from the slaves' perspective, was one who rode about regularly check-ing up on their work, knew each of his charges by name, and recognized the details of each slave's character and ability.

The life-style of the planters and their wives emphasized formality rather than familiarity in personal relationships. While the huge balls and tournaments fed the nostalgic image of the plantation, actual records tell of the loneliness of the life for the planters and their families. Carl Bridenbaugh, surveying the life of the Chesapeake planters, says that "the renowned open hospitality practiced by the gentry sprang initially from the social needs of their isolated existence and only secondarily from the conscious imitation and customs and courtesy of the gentlefolk" in the Old World.[37] After noting that the land was good to the planters, as Susan Bradford Eppes writes, "Lonely at times themselves, they opened their homes to others, who also knew the pangs of homesickness and longing." The more the merrier became the common attitude, leading to the custom in which "crowds collected and were made welcome . . . [and] the lavish hospitality of the South was acquired."[38] The occasions for merrymaking were infrequent, and the balls or tournaments that were held were on the same scale as corn shuckings. As I have pointed out, parties and balls were planned to display wealth as well as hospitality.[39]

Contributing to the note of melancholy in the lives of the planters' families was the necessity for those engaged in this family commercial enterprise to constantly move on to the frontier, to establish new plantations which might support and extend the family prestige. Expanding the family and its domains became the primary means by which a Cavalier might distinguish himself. As Rhys Isaac puts it, "A man could not be a gentleman in the fullest sense in this society unless he was the independent head of his own household, having slaves certainly, and a wife and children, ideally to reflect, in their degrees, the greatness of the master."[40]

Formal gestures were ever-present even within family interactions, and set the terms by which men of honor might dramatize their attitudes, values, and place within society. This system depended upon the identification of the plenitude of the land with the master of the house, and harvest largess became a major occasion for enacting that identity. This was true as much in terms of the lessons of class derived by those who lived in the great house as in the giving of license to the slaves to celebrate. Honor and status were associated with men who could lay claims to the greatest number of productive members in their household, including the size of their slave family. And, by being able to call upon the neighboring slaves, the planter holding a corn shucking would create a grand occasion calling for the displays of deference that we see in these reports.

By the American Revolution, a majority of the slaves were native-born, and sufficient time had passed for there to have developed, as historian Allan Kulikoff put it, "black communities that encompassed both their own and neighboring plantations."[41] Many scholars have been able to reconstruct the ways in which slaves' worship developed and with it, after the Revolution, black churches.[42] At the heart of this literature regarding slave religion was the worship practice of the *ring shout*. In this practice, the slaves formed themselves into a ring which moved counterclockwise in a kind

of holy leaping dance, punctuated by yells, cries, shrieking, and evidence of the descent of the spirit on individuals in the congregation.

Though the ring shout impressed Christian observers as being heathenish and idolatrous, this form of worship did call their attention to the continuous existence of a distinctive Afro-American style of expression. These very same traits were also present in the afterdinner entertainments—the forming into a ring, the singing and moving together—and would become the essence of the display in the corn shucking and other slave holidays.

Says Kulikoff: "Large plantations, especially those villages of a hundred or more slaves owned by the wealthiest gentlemen, became community centers for neighborhood slaves." Perhaps the draw of these community centers was as much for purposes of play as for anything else, since such recreations were within the Cavalier system of condescension and largess for many planters. In many areas at least one plantation had a benevolent enough regime that slave dances and other entertainments were held regularly. Kulikoff also notices that "slaves worked together in the . . . fields and cultivated their gardens, cooked, and talked with each other in the yards surrounding their cabins each evening." While those who lived on smaller farms would have less of a community at home, their isolation was diminished through participation in activities with slaves on other plantations, "through dances and by marrying and establishing families on other plantations."[43]

Interactions between plantations were organized not only in the hush-arbor religious meetings, but more openly around dances, quiltings, hog killings, and other such festive events. (Hush-arbor, also called brush-arbor, meetings were congregations outdoors, at some remove from any habita-

tions.) And as cotton took over from tobacco as the primary cash crop in some areas, harvest season came to last from early November through New Year's Day, when the feasting and revelry were extended to the slaves.

The existence of these times of festive community-building within and between resident slave populations did not testify to the liberality of the planters. Rather, it represented a compromise on their part with regard to the pace by which the slaves' time and energy were put to use. While the planters owned the slaves' production, Kulikoff notes, "they depended upon slave labor for their wealth and learned to tolerate slave direction of the pace of labor."[44] They also came to accept the idea that the slaves were entitled to time for the production of much of their own food, the maintenance of their family life, and the festive events that brought slaves together outside the boundaries of the individual plantation.

The intense isolation of many plantations cannot be overstressed. By living in such close proximity to the slaves and so far from other whites, as noted, the planter families came to rely on slave singing and dancing displays regularly for their entertainments.

From the masters' perspective, the corn shucking may simply have involved temporarily enlarging their household by inviting hands from other plantations to help in the shucking and to experience the openhandedness of the home plantation. From the slaves' point of view, something else was taking place as well. The shucking was an event in which the house servants found themselves serving field hands, not only from their own plantation but from elsewhere. While this might seem to be an onerous task, they saw it less in that light than as an opportunity to demonstrate the prodigality of their master.[45] Shucking dramatized the relations between slaves as well as between slave and master. If the negotiations for power and deference on the part of the slaves are less visible to us than those of the planters, it is not because they did not take place.

As a phenomenon which arose after the founding of the new republic, it is tempting to see in the development of the corn shucking a response to a change in worldview taking place at that time. For it was during this period that, as an outgrowth of the republican enthusiasm of the new nation, work and community cooperation came to be valued as a way of dramatizing the virtues of self-government and the strength of the social contract. Work itself, when celebrated in the house-raising, the log-pulling, or any other kind of bee, marked phases in the passage of life to the extent that these activities were times for courtship, or occasions on which family holdings were materially altered through the construction of a house, a barn, a quilt, or the bringing in of a crop.

The historian Daniel Blake Smith has argued that sentimentalism of this special character was introduced into the ideal of the self-sufficient planter household. Earlier in the eighteenth century, the family was a self-sufficient organization not only economically but psychologically, a "peaceable kingdom" marked by "self-restraint, stifled emotion and rare intimacy." Smith characterizes the earlier planter families as emotionally cool: "From the formal, calculated grandiloquence of courtship to the calm resignation in times of death, *la vie intime* among the planter class suggested a rather cold, astringent atmosphere."[46]

But ". . . by the early 1800's," Smith continues, "planter families," along with families elsewhere in the new republic, "had turned their emotional energies inward to focus on an intimate, sentimental family unit that stood apart from the larger society as a private enclave for mutual support and sociability."[47] From this perspective, the corn shucking might be regarded as another feature of the warming of the emotional environment, a way in which the planters might grant their beloved house servants the prestige of entertaining the rest of the slaves.

This alteration of sentiments is described as a shift from a patriarchal to a paternalistic worldview by Rhys Isaac and Philip Morgan, among others. Morgan, who admits that the distinction "can be a fine one," nevertheless says that "patriarchalism was [the] more austere code." Paternalistic slaveholders came to expect their hands' gratitude and even affectionate regard in response to their more intimate initiatives. Out of this putative freely given mutual regard emerged the "fiction of the contented and happy slave." In this way, "austere, rigid patriarchalism" was seen to slowly mutate to a more "warm, mellow paternalism" and slavery came to be regarded as "a benign and protective institution."[48] Certainly life in the quarters as well as in the Big House was depicted in these warm hues.

Whites raised on plantations reported that many features of the corn shuckings seem to reflect this sentimentalizing as it was extended to everyone in the planter's family. Certainly from the planter's perspective, the corn shucking was a model of and for black-white interactions with regard to the manner in which the social and economic enterprise was carried out. However, public interactions between slaves and their masters and mistresses remained extraordinarily formal and replete with evidences of a profound, continuous deference and condescension in relations between slaves and masters.

But the shucking also seems to have arisen from the more public dimension of this growing sentimentalization—from the large-scale events by which the planter family's prodigality was displayed. Again, the plantation literature is suffused with descriptions of the most flamboyant of these scenes—the elaborately arranged horse races, the balls and other parties, and especially the neo-medieval tournaments. These last events, involving as they did elaborate costuming and role playing on the theme of courtly love (as understood through its representation in the novels of Sir Walter Scott) and the taking on of heroic names, enacted the theme that preoccupied them: facing the loss of honor and gentility. Genovese, in his overview of the impact of such self-conscious medievalisms in Southern life points out that "the slaveholders who dominated society are supposed to have been in love with the Middle Ages and with feudalism, and to have equated the manors with their own plantations," but that "the Old South was hardly a refurbished medieval society, and few southerners ever pretended that it was." However, the chivalry of the Middle Ages represented a set of lifeways that Southerners admired because they departed so markedly from the alternatives presented to them, especially by the North, in their own times. "Their attempt to identify the divinely inspired, the permanent, the admirable in the medieval experience proved both intellectually powerful and politically significant."[49] While the tournament and other neo-medieval rituals provided the framework for spectacular displays of honor and glory, the Southern attraction to the manorial past also had a more mundane basis: the depiction of arrangements between landholders and slaveowners in terms of family obligations.

However, with the new sentimentalism the householders grew ever more aware of a conflict betwen the privacy implicit in connubial relations and the need to maintain the paraphernalia of display in order to maintain the system of deference and condescension. The very plan of the house and the centrality of its public spaces began to be experienced as inimical to this growing need for privacy, especially between the master and mistress of the plantation. It was in this environment that the great diarists of the plantation families, such as Mary Boykin Chesnut and Gertrude Thomas, expressed great ambivalence in the face of the felt presence of their dependents, especially the servants and the hands.

Says Genovese of the reciprocal arrangement:

The house servants required the protection and support of their white folks, much as the field hands did, and in addition, they needed to maintain their special advantages. The whites required that the house servants, like the field hands, work to provide for them, but in addition they required their love and emotional support far beyond anything the servants needed in return. In the reciprocal dependency of slavery, especially in the Big House, the slaves needed masters and mistresses they could depend on; they did not need masters and mistresses to love them. But the whites needed their servants' love and trust. The slaves had the upper hand, and many of them learned how to use it.[50]

As the planters came to view the system as "a benign and protective institution," says Philip Morgan, "slaves would . . . soon be enveloped in 'domestic affection'; and before long, it would be the master for whom pity would be invoked as 'the greatest slave of all.' "[51]

But as Mary Boykin Chesnut expounded in one of the classic scenes of plantation diary literature, it was the planters' wives who felt the ironies of the situation most fully. For they had to maintain face and demeanor while sharing a dreadful secret: that their husbands presumed that one feature by which their power might be displayed was through sexual access to the slave women:

A magnate who runs a hideous black harem with its consequences under the same roof with his lovely white wife, and his beautiful and accomplished daughters? He holds his head as high and poses as the model of all human virtues to these poor women whom God and the laws have given him. From the height of his awful majesty, he scolds and thunders at them, as if he never did wrong in his life. . . . You see, Mrs. Stowe did not hit the sorest spot. She makes Legree a bachelor.[52]

Among the men running the larger plantations, keeping up their public face remained an important feature of their self-image. The slaves, for their part, played an ever greater supporting role in a drama in which honor and grand display went hand in hand. Just as maintaining oneself as a country squire in England called for the presence of agricultural workers with whom the "governor" might practice magnanimity and receive deference, so the slaves were depended upon to display themselves in set scenes. The corn-shucking reports also reveal that the slaves came to regard their part in these staged scenes as their due in a system of such severe deference. The planters, too, again and again mention that certain celebrations should be regarded as occasions to which the slaves were entitled; but one presumes that these were the planters who played the benevolent and paternal version of their role. At bottom, the system of condescension remained little changed.

CHAPTER THREE

BALLAD-SINGER

An American Version of Pastoral

Not only in the South, but throughout the United States, the harvesting of the Indian corn became a time of celebration. The corn shucking was certainly patterned after the English harvest home. In its community organization, its focus on cooperative intensive labor, the English celebration provided the model for that range of American frontier activities known as "bees" and "frolics."

The husking bee of New England and the old Northwest departed from the harvest home inasmuch as it projected an egalitarian system rather than the hierarchical order of the English countryside event. On the other hand, in the South, the influence of English Cavalier traditions and English attitudes toward class relations are more evident. Balls, processions, tournaments, and other grand ceremonials were taken directly from English elite entertainments, as were many of the activities "within the family," like Christmas, harvest home, and Easter.

Some of the most important symbolic features of the corn shucking were inherent in any harvest ceremony. All harvest ceremonies celebrate the earth's abundance and the techniques of producing food. Agricultural ceremonies reenact the triumph of human order in breaking the ground, sowing the seed, and reaping the benefits of that labor. And insofar as the reaping must involve the concerted effort of the entire community, the shared intensity of the ceremonial moment signifies the community's success in organizing its forces in bringing in the crops.[1]

Song and dance and feasting were features found among Indians, too, and were observed by the earliest European settlers. Moreover, those slaves who had come from the agricultural areas of Africa would have held on to harvest ceremonies of their own. Harvesting often involves paying special attention to the crop which has been brought in through some kind of special elaboration—as here, by heap-

ing it into gigantic proportions; or by making a wreath or some other kind of symbolic form out of the crop.

Certain features unique to the English harvest home were incorporated into the plantation practices. The occasion of the harvest provided the climax for the agricultural operation of the year. In England the crop ripened quickly and had to be brought into the farmyard and effectively gleaned during a very brief period, before the onset of rains which would cause rot to the grain. The English harvest ceremony served as a way of giving thanks for the tremendous effort given by all in the community in harvesting the crop after it had ripened but before the autumn rains began.

Many of the actual practices found in the corn shucking were adapted from seasonal practices of the English countryside: the use of the grain crop as the central symbol for the celebration; the procession and feast, with the speechmaking, singing, and joking; some topsy-turvy behavior and the general overall social-leveling motive which provided the mood of the occasion. This moment at the end of the agricultural year gave palpable presence to the message of natural abundance. The massive display of the crop stacked "high as a house," and the tremendous amount of food prepared and consumed, all bespoke the idea of plenitude.

The English harvest home was infused with a sense of joy in completing the gathering and the reaping. It began with the triumphant bearing of the "last leaf" of the crop (often braided into a corn dolly) by the harvest queen or king. Or the grain wagon was ornamented, made into "the hock cart" and celebrated by all as the "last load." This wagon was commonly decked out with flowers and oak or ash boughs. So, too, the beasts that were carrying in the grain were garlanded. And on this last load would sit the featured members of the harvesting crew—the harvest lord, a harvest queen (often a male cross-dressed as a hag or a beauty), and the rest of the crew responsible for bringing together the grain and the cart in its elaborated form. The most playful members of the crew stood on the load and shouted and blew horns. Each locality seemed to develop different ways of dramatizing the arrival; sometimes the young girls of the area would throw water over the heads of the boys riding on the cart who were busy singing the local harvest song.

In the evening, the mell, kern, or supper was held for all the participants, though notables in the countryside—the blacksmith, wheelwright, constable, parson—were invited as well. The master of the field under harvest ceremonially elevated his workers when he sat down with them and drank their health. The feast was marked with speeches and performances of songs by everyone of all stations. Sometimes they were appropriate to the season; sometimes they were simply favorites of the neighborhood.

Harvest home, then, celebrated the "homing" of the harvested grain called the "corn" in England, the "kirn" in Scotland. It took place throughout rural Britain, and all who helped in the harvest participated in the festivities: not only male and female farmhands of all ages, but blacksmiths and wheelwrights, and local officials such as the village constable and parson.[2]

In England, as the eighteenth-century antiquarian Henry Bourne put it, "The Servant and his Master are alike, and every Thing is done with equal Freedom. They sit at the same Table, converse freely together, and spend the remaining Part of the Night in dancing, singing, etc. without any

Difference or Distinction."[3] In New England, such social leveling was taken for granted, for class marking was frowned upon in all matters. In the South nothing suggests that the slaves and masters ate at the same table—though they often seemed to have drunk from the same bottle.

In some parts of England, there was an authority figure within the ranks of the workers who prefigured the shucking captain—the "harvest lord." Appointed by the farmer celebrating the crop, he was given a bit more pay for his troubles. Thomas Tusser describes the role in his *Five Hundred Points of Good Husbandry*,[4] published in the middle of the sixteenth century: "Grant harvest lord, more, by a penny or twoo,/ to call his fellow better to doo." Like the shucking captains later, he was chosen for his ability to lead the workers, though singing ability was not a criterion.[5] On both sides of the Atlantic, ceremonial speeches were made by both masters and workers, the latter commonly led in England by the harvest lord, in the American South by the shucking captain. Despite these parallels, the shucking captains were not simply descendants of the English figure, for they organized the work and led it in African-patterned ways.

Another feature of English countryside pastimes found in the shucking was the *chairing* of the master. However, the lifting and parading of the corn shucking come from the "heaving" practices associated with the planting rather than the harvesting ceremonial occasion.[6]

The husking bee in the Northern settlements found its niche in the Yankee agricultural calendar somewhat more quickly than its counterpart in the English outposts to the south. From the earliest reports it is clear that the potential for excess in such celebrations was a matter of concern as early as 1617, when Cotton Mather complained; "*Riots . . .*

have too often accustomed our *Huskings*," bringing about a sense of "fearful Ingratitude and Provocation unto the Glorious God." He concludes: "May the *Joy of Harvest* no longer be prostituted into vicious purposes."[7] Obviously, a distinction was being made between righteous joy and untramelled revelry.

The London pamphleteer Ned Ward, while far from being a Puritan, launched a similar attack on New England huskers in one of his Grub Street lampoons about New World life. "Husking of *Indian-Corn*," he rails, "is as good sport for the Amerous *Wag-tailes* in *New England,* as *Maying* amongst us for our forward Youths and Wenches." He goes on to survey local reports of the "*Bastards* got in that Season," a situation which leads some of the "looser *Saints* to call it *Rutting Time.*"[8]

At least a century and a half after the founding of the New England colonies, we have a wry report from the heart of Puritan country, written by Dr. Nathaniel Ames of Dedham, Massachusetts, on October 14, 1767: "Made an husking entertainment. Possibly this leafe may last a Century and fall into the hand of some inquisitive Person. . . ." He proceeded to describe the event as it was practiced at that time, noting that the evening's work was one to which "all the neighboring Swains are invited. . . ." When the corn shelling is finished, "they like the Hottentots give three Cheers or huzza's" but find that they are not able to carry in the results of the work "without a Rhum bottle."[9]

During this same period, the marching song of the Revolution, "Yankee Doodle," spread through Massachusetts as a husking song. Indeed, as J. A. Leo Lemay has reconstructed it, the song actually describes some husking practices, together with other topsy-turvy festival motives:

> *Husking time is coming on*
> *They all begin to laugh sir—*
> *Father is a coming home*
> *To kill the fatted calf sir.*

And later:

> *Now husking time is over*
> *They have a duced frolic*
> *There'l be some as drunk as sots*
> *The rest will have the colic.*[10]

A number of English and European visitors observed huskings in the Northern settlements. Perhaps the most famous of their accounts is that of the Marquise de La Tour du Pin, who, during her exile in upstate New York, was the hostess of such a "frolic." "First the floor of the barn is swept with as much care as for a ball," she begins. "Then, when darkness comes, candles are lit and the people assemble, about thirty of them, black and white. . . ." They proceed to carry out the husking operation while someone sings or tells a story. In the "middle of the night" refreshments are served, a potion of boiling milk, "previously turned with cider" to which molasses and cloves, cinnamon, nutmeg, and other spices have been added. A bowl of this is served to each person, and eaten with toast. The frolic was finished by five o'clock in the morning.[11]

Even in the Northern settlements, then, the husking was strongly identified with slaves. The marquise noted, "Our negroes were often asked to similar frolics. . . ."[12] William Johnston, in his survey of *Slavery in Rhode Island,* reports: "The old corn-huskings of Narragansett were greatly enjoyed by the negroes." As in the South, invitations were sent out to slave masters in the neighborhood, ". . . and in return the invited guests sent their slaves to aid the host. . . ." After the husking took place, there was a "repast" and then "the recreations of dancing commenced" for blacks and whites separately. As in the South, slaves provided the entertainment for the white guests, for, as planters, they had "natural musicians among their slaves." The account ends thus: "bountiful preparations were made, and like amusements were enjoyed by them in the large kitchens and outhouses, the places of their residences."[13]

Johnston related the event to English harvest practices, remarking that "[t]he amusements of the slaves" in Rhode Island "were like those of the English servants." So did another visitor to the North in 1691, Admiral Bartholomew James of the Royal Navy. He noted a similarity between "the ceremony of husking corn" and "the . . . 'harvest home' in England, with the additional amusement of kissing the girls whenever the [huskers] met with a red corncob. . . ."[14]

At some places in the North, the red ear was ceremonially elaborated. Indeed, one of the best-known American poems of the late eighteenth century, "The Hasty Pudding" by Joel Barlow, contains a description of a husking bee including the mock-heroic discovery of the red ear:

> *The laws of husking every wight can tell,*
> *And sure no laws he ever keeps so well;*
> *For each red ear, a general kiss he gains;*
> *With each smut ear he smuts the luckless swains;*
> *But when to some fair maid the prise is cast,*
> *Red as her lip, and taper as her waist,*
> *She walks the round, and calls one favored beau,*
> *Who leaps the luscious tribute to bestow.*[15]

This discovery and the giving of the prize were developed, in some areas of the North, into a ceremony: "[H]e or she who first finds a red ear of corn is made king or queen of the revels that follow . . . ," notes one commentator. That is, at the end of all the husking, "a procession is formed, headed by the farmer and his wife," and they parade "in triumph followed by all their hands, leading the victorious maid carrying her patent of royalty—the red ear—in her hand." They go from "the "huskin' barn to another large granary which has been effectively decorated with green boughs and corn ears." There a throne stands in the midst of a rough-plank floor covered with sawdust. Here the queen is crowned and enthroned, and sits in court.[16]

This little scene underscores the feature of the husking

bee that was notably absent from the Southern shucking—interaction between the sexes. Indeed, most of the reports of the husking underscore that the event provided an opportunity for eligible members of the opposite sex to meet after the corn was husked.

Insofar as the Southern planters traced their ancestry to the seventeenth-century Cavaliers, they could draw upon the approach to old holiday pastimes formulated by James I. From James's perspective, theater and country pastimes were deeply related. As he put forth in his influential letter to his son Henry, *Basilikon Doron,*

... to allure them to a common amitie among themselues, certaine days in the yeere would be appointed, for delighting the people with publicke spectacles of all honest games, and exercise of armes: as also for conueening of neighbors, for entertaining friendship and heartliness, by honest feast and merriness: For I cannot see what greater superstition can be in making playes and lawful games in Maie, and good cheere at Christmas, then in eat fish in Lent. . . ."[17]

This patronizing perspective was later developed into James's more famous work, "A Declaration of Sports," issued on May 24, 1618, and reissued by Charles I in 1632.[18] Festivities were encouraged in which the court pageantry was translated into country terms, drawing upon the participation of residents of the countryside.

The Southern planters seized upon the various agricultural festivals, such as the corn shucking, as a way of authorizing the delegation of power attending the ownership of the land and the slaves. In this, they operated essentially in the same relationship with the seasonal passage as did the great landholders in England.[19]

In England, the politics of country life had developed out of the need of James I to assert hegemony over the nation in his pursuit of the powers of a divine kingship. He was assisted by Archbishop Laud, who made the entire realm sacred by bringing it under the ordering principles of the church calendar. The ideas concerning land and natural abundance were elaborated by Laud into what Leah Marcus usefully has called the doctrine of *survivalism:* "a type of agrarian consciousness that fuses cyclical, communal economic activities, like sowing and harvesting, with the maintenance of old collective customs and collective village order."[20] In both the Old World and the New, after the development of international markets for agricultured cash crops, the celebration of the passing of the seasons was maintained "from ancient practice" and adapted by country gentry as a means of rationalizing their power base, which lay in the ownership of land.

Benjamin Franklin, Thomas Jefferson, and many other commentators on the political economy of the new nation articulated the ideal of a yeoman citizenry in which a mean would be found between savagery and decadence, based on the virtues of the rational agriculturalist. Their hopes were echoed by others in Europe who saw the United States as a noble political experiment. British commentator Richard Price enthusiastically responded to the egalitarian promise of the Revolution. He saw in this new style of independent action the possibility of achieving a happy "middle state" of existence, that "between the *savage* and the *refined,* or between the wild and the luxurious state." Where the state produced "an independent and hardy yeomanry," Price maintained, the result was a citizenry "trained in arms . . . clothed in homespun—of simple manners—strangers to luxury—drawing plenty from the ground—and that plenty, gathered easily by the hand of industry."[21] And nowhere was industry so fully illustrated, and with such an egalitarian note, than in the the frontier bee and frolic.[22]

This vision of the independent farmer of the middle way, commonly associated historically with Thomas Jefferson, was not wholly shared by that man's neighbors in Virginia and elsewhere in the South. The Southern planters clung to many of the more aristocratic features which had characterized the Cavalier perspective in England. As opposed to the democratic drama of the frontier bee, work parties on the plantation involved a bringing together of workers who were not landholders but slaves. Indeed, at the center of the pastoral drama of the plantation were combat displays, with the workers used as contestants. For instance, in many plantations, cotton picking was turned into a contest with prizes offered for winners.[23] Thus, the shucking contests themselves were symptomatic of the planters' passion for such competitions. Descriptions of the gouging and wrestling matches between the designated slave "bullies" of the area are legion in plantation literature, especially in the Mississippi River basin.

It would be mistaken to presume that all the country amusements common to English agricultural life endured the transatlantic journey to the South. In all colonies, a number of English countryside traditions were lost: the morris dancing, annual wakes and ridings, and the craft holidays. As American historian Richard Bushman has noted, this loss occurred not so much from a distrust of such festivities by the more sober settlers, but because these traditions were often tied to specific locales in England.[24]

In their Old World setting, local traditions were strongly associated with the bounds of a parish. One of the most common of these practices was "the beating of the bounds," a ceremony and celebration in which members of the community, once a year, would walk from boundary stone to boundary stone, circumscribing the parish. In such a situation, on certain days such as Christmas, mummers or carollers or morris dancers could go from door to door, often masked and costumed, and no one needed to worry about the presence of strangers—indeed, the players often dressed as vagabonds or "gypsies" as a way of playing upon this fact. Whenever something unusual happened, the bells of the local church would be rung, and the congregation would organize a bonfire for that night. Thus these practices used a vocabulary of celebration that could be seen or heard throughout the bounded community.

In contrast, on the frontier, and especially in the South, the population was so dispersed that this parish mode of organization simply did not hold for the countryside. Moreover, the planters established their domiciles in the midst of their land, to allow them oversight of their slaves.[25] Further, as David Cressy has demonstrated, the British calendar celebrations marked by bells and bonfires were commonly connected with annual commemorations of significant historical happenings, the most enduring being Guy Fawkes Day.[26] In most cases these events were of little interest to Americans, especially after Independence.

Unlike the local traditions commemorating historical events in Great Britain, the practices relating to agriculture were maintained to some extent, at least in the Chesapeake area. For instance, the Swiss visitor Francis Louis Michel noted of the Virginians that "the custom of the country, when the harvest is to be gathered in, is to prepare a dinner, to which the neighbors are invited." He recognized that the occasion was more celebratory than useful, for the thirty or forty people attending only had to work two hours to earn their neighbor's largess. He concludes: "This is one of the principal festivals or times of rejoicing."[27]

By the end of the eighteenth century, the times for the slave holidays were more or less established. By then, the plantations were sufficiently successful, the number of the slaves was sufficiently large, and the slaves had acculturated to the plantation environment as a community of workers. Moreover, the husking of the corn had become something of a social event in the North and on the frontiers as well. Such harvest ceremonies provided opportunities for expression of the local sense of community wherever they were found.

But the corn-husking ceremony also provided a forceful reminder to the whole nation that the adoption of this crop and its technology had been a by-product of the encounter with Indians under early settlement conditions. Centered on the earliest subsistence crop throughout the United States, corn, the ceremony continued to remind farmers of the historical struggle for control of the land for purposes of planting that had been carried out between the settlers and the wilderness—and the Indians.

The corn harvest, while an exuberant celebration of natural plenitude, evokes the history of pioneer life, including the expropriation and exploitation of Indian lands, crops, and agricultural technique. While the indigenous peoples of New England and the Chesapeake regions were first described as successful clearers of the land and planters of grain, by the time of the War of Independence the settlers had seized the lands and learned the crop technology from the Indians, but did not celebrate the presence of these peoples who had supplied them with their subsistence in the earliest days.

On the plantation tobacco, cotton, and indigo were the

crops most central to the economic lives of the planters. But corn was the original crop that made the settlements possible, and it remained the most important food resource. It continued to provide the basic foodstuffs for the farm families' subsistence, whether on the family farm of the plain folk of the South or on the plantation.

As James Battle Avirett pointed out with regard to the plantation as both a social and an economic enterprise: "There was a time in the old Southern plantation life that all roads led to the corn house." He proceeded to note that there was "a common saying among the servants" that he heard as a boy in the 1840s: "Nigger make de co'n; hog eat de co'n and nigger eat de pig."[28]

In Old World agricultural celebrations, the focus is invariably upon the crop being raised and harvested. Consequently, the crop itself is commonly featured in some dressed-up ornamental form in the festivities marking the end of the hard work. The work animals wear braided flowers or grasses, or the crop itself is rendered in decorated form like a corn dolly. The last leaf or the last load is carried from the field to the celebration site and paraded, accompanied by a good deal of singing, dancing, joking, and so on.

Since there were several other major crops raised in the New World, the question arises why this crop, Indian corn, was the one chosen to celebrate. It was neither the major product of the plantation nor the primary food consumed during the festive meal. Moreover, maize itself is strongly identified with frontiers, boundaries, and the margins of the plantation community, with the cattle and slaves—and, of course, with Indians.

The first settlers realized that they could not survive without the help of the Indians, and especially their corn. A number of the earliest reporters on first contact noted that the Indians had already developed an admirable corn-based agricultural system. William Wood, for instance, in his tract of 1634, *New England's Prospect,* exclaims that the Indians plant corn with such expertise that "they exceed our English husbandmen, keeping it so clear with their clamshell hoes as if it were a garden rather than a corn field, not suffering a choking weed to advance his audacious head above their infant corn or an undermining worm to spoil his spurns. . . . Their corn being ripe they gather it, and drying it hard in the sun convey it to their barns, which be great holes digged in the ground. . . ."[29]

Similarly, farther south, Thomas Hariot sent back word of the Indians' agricultural abilities, in his *Brief and True Report of the New Found Land of Virginia* of 1588. Like

Wood's treatise, this was directed at prospective "investors, farmers, and well-wishers of the project of colonizing and planting." Its depiction is of a garden spot redolent of golden age possibilities. He notes that the ground does not have to be manured, but only the upper crust need be broken with a long-handled hoelike tool with which the Indian farmers cut down the weeds. One or two days later, they set out their plot, beginning in one corner and by making "a hole with a pecker." Into each hole they put four grains, "about an inch apart, taking care that they do not touch one another," which they then cover. The picture he provides is of naturally rational farmers, who plant in rows and use the "spare ground" between the planted corn to grow other crops. The harvest he reports is five times that of England![30]

In the earliest accounts, Indians were depicted as splendid agriculturalists. But as the settlers' needs for cleared land became more pronounced, the indigenous peoples were progressively relegated to the condition of trees: seen and treated as naturally occurring obstacles to plantation success. Like the native forests, in the settlers' minds they came to represent the wilderness condition, and were virtually erased as their lands were confiscated. Yet their presence remained inscribed in maize agriculture as long as that crop provided the means by which the settlers could maintain themselves at the margins of the wilderness.

Francis Jennings has argued that early in the colonial enterprise it became important in both northern and southern settlements to deny the agricultural skills of Indians, thereby portraying them as wilderness dwellers, indeed as wandering, unlanded non-persons.[31] As Samuel Purchas, the Renaissance travel writer, came to call them, the Indians were "unnaturall Naturalls" who because of their purported murderous ways could "scarcely" be called "Inhabitants."[32]

The production of Indian corn, then, carried with it a vocabulary of production and preparation historically associated with frontier subsistence, and with the earliest cultural interactions with American Indians. It maintained the ambiguous status of a crop of frontierspeople and, by extension, of other people on the margins. It was a sign at once of the plenitude of the land and of the lower-status creatures among whom it was first found, and those for whom it was now designated as fodder or food. Yeoman farmers and planters continued to eat corn products—in fact, corn bread and other corn products remained an important feature of their cuisine, especially throughout the South. But corn was regarded as inferior to other grains, as it was heavy, more difficult to ship than other grains, and not as readily refined in preparation for yeast-raised breads.

Strangely, the very characteristics of Indian husbandry that most appealed to Thomas Hariot—the rational use of the space between the corn hills—came to be regarded more critically by later agricultural observers. The Indians' mixture of crops seem to them evidence of chaotic practices. "It was not an agriculture that looked very orderly to a European eye accustomed to monocultural fields," William Cronon has written in commenting on such accounts. "Cornstalks served as beanpoles, squashes sent their tendrils everywhere, and the entire surface of the field became a dense tangle of food plants."[33]

On the plains and elsewhere in the Middle West the crop was to take a different place in the agricultural economy. But in areas in which it was planted as a crop secondary to tobacco, cotton, or wheat, Indian corn remained the most sturdy of all—first in, last reaped, susceptible to being used in multiple ways.[34] The association with wilderness and social license continues to be carried by those red or black or

multicolored ears still called "Indian corn" on the general
market today, and which are still used to decorate our por-
tals during the high season of autumn, as symbols of the
bountiful harvest. Moreover, the focus on the red ear was
taken directly from the Indian ceremonies celebrating the
properties of corn.[35] Throughout the original colonies, such
apparently off-colored ears were markers of license—especially sexual activities.

Such reports continued to be produced for prospective
European settlers. The first description of the corn shucking
in the South was made early in the nineteenth century by

the English farmer William Faux.[36] Writing for those interested in American agricultural practices, Faux pointed to the
distinctive features of the shucking. "Corn shucking means
plucking the ears of Indian corn from the stalk, and then
housing it in cribs, purposely made to keep it in, for winter
use." Both the crib and the crop itself were American developments. He continues, noting that the technique of
growing and harvesting the crop is also sufficiently distinct
to bear notice: "The stalk is left in the field; the leaves, while
half green, are stripped off, and tied up in bundles, as hay
for horses and cattle, and good food it is, much resembling
in form the flags in English marshes." The celebratory dimensions of the corn-shucking event seem to have been sufficiently familiar that he simply mentions that "the hawkey
supper commenced; all seemed fun, created by omnipotent
whiskey."[37]

The observers often noted in detail the actual practices
and the factors of geography and climate. For instance, John
Bradbury, early in the nineteenth century, wrote of an English farmer who had moved to America: "the succession of
crops and the mode of culture vary much from what he has
experienced in England, and . . . a differently modified climate, and, a sun more nearly vertical, greatly change the
order of things to which he has been accustomed." He went
on to note that the rye was harvested in June, the wheat
soon after that, and then oats and grass, then potatoes, and
finally the "Indian corn."[38]

"Corn" was the generic term for all grain crops in Great
Britain. The designation "Indian corn" marked the indigenous plant; it was also called "maize." As it could be cut
and stacked in the field for later processing, Indian corn
often became the last crop to be harvested completely. The
rhythm of the Old World agricultural year did not fully apply

to the new climatic situation or to the soil conditions encountered by the settlers. Indian corn did not have to be harvested quickly at the end of a short growing season. Rather, it could be shocked (stacked in clumps, the stalks resting on each other) and left for future gathering, or it could be brought into the pen or barn and shucked at a later time when there was more leisure.

A number of accounts of frontier life detailed how the corn was raised. David Barrow from Georgia, for instance, reported the ways in which working the corn in the fall led up to the corn shucking. "The first work toward gathering the corn is to strip the stalks of their blades. . . ." which was done in late summer. Here the blades were pulled by hand from the stalks, at which time the worker tied them together, which then "constitutes a 'hand.' " After a day or two of curing, the hands were then further tied into bunches and either left in the field or thrown into the fodder loft.

This left the stalks with the ears on them in the field, where they sat until late October or November, growing "hard and dry." "If Georgians, . . . had nothing to gather in the fall but the corn," Barrow mused, "we might spend the whole fall gathering it." However, cotton was the cash crop here and thus "most of this season must be devoted to gathering and preparing it for market." "King Cotton is a great tyrant, and unless you are a willing and ready subject, he will make you suffer." Cotton had to be picked at a particular moment in its growth. The boll is particularly resistant to manipulation, and those who had to pick it came away with hands bloody from the encounter. Whatever was picked had to be carried in a sack slung around the neck.

Corn, by contrast, was not a demanding crop, since it might be cut at any time and left in the field. The corn needing shucking would accumulate until all the other crops had been harvested. Many farmers and planters would wait until the winter rains set in, and did the shucking in the barn with the hands that were then available. A large effort was expended in organizing the shucking, turning out the needed number of shuckers, and cooking the food. The corn shucking demonstrated the neighborhood's ability to muster the hands necessary to carry out the enormous amount of shucking with dispatch, so that the supper could then be enjoyed. Thus, the communal shucking of the corn was not crisis work, but rather the final act in the harvesting of the grain which provided the basic food resource for slaves and domestic animals. It occurred after the intense gathering of the cotton or tobacco. The shucking signaled the onset of relief from the need to work long hours in the field. Harvesting

cotton was a task that demanded enormous physical effort which became especially onerous when the picking had to be carried out by everyone—men, women, and children— and in a short burst of time. The shucking, then, stood in dramatic contrast, from the perspective of the workers. Says Barrow: "Out of these conditions has sprung the corn-shucking; and it has grown into importance, even more as a social than as an economic feature. . . ."[39]

The ceremony of the corn shucking could be carried out in a more leisurely fashion, during slack time or even when it was raining. Structurally, corn took the place of the grain crop in Great Britain which had provided the "last leaf"— the grain which, when reaped, was woven into the *corn dolly,* the *neck* or *queen,* to be used as a symbolic device recognized in the community as heralding the onset of *the harvest mell, the hawkey, kern,* or *harvest home* ceremony. In the American South, Indian corn was left in the fields until late October or even mid-November before it was shucked. If there was a climax harvest in the South, then, it was tobacco or sugar, not corn. The corn husking was not a harvest in the British sense, as the ears were not brought into the yard or the barn until the other crops had been gathered.

As a kind of "found food," corn was strongly identified with wilderness plenitude, and by extension with other wild food sources, especially the pigs and cows that roamed the Southern grazing lands.[40] Ironically, this process of ordering life, the landscape introducing "civilization" itself into the settlements, was made possible by the settlers' learning relevant domestic practices from the indigenous peoples. These techniques included methods not only for sowing the crop but for clearing the fields quickly and easily, by girdling the trees and planting between the resulting stumps; for planting

Indian crops, such as squash, pumpkin, gourds, and maize, in an Indian manner; and for preparing these foods in Indian style. When speaking of the plenitude to be found in the New Eden, this indigenous element was described as part of nature, to be taken for granted and seized upon and made orderly.

The corn shucking was carried on throughout the South, not only on the plantation but among the plain folk farmers as well. It went on regardless of whether the labor was provided by slaves. Moreover, a number of reports tell of blacks and whites shelling the corn together, as well as sharing many of the same customary practices at the shucking.[41]

Unfortunately, descriptions of the shucking among Southern yeoman farmers alone are sparse. Those that have come to notice suggest that while there are a number of similarities between the ways whites and blacks celebrated, the slaves performed with greater spirit, invoking different performance activities, and carried them out in a different style.[42]

For instance, in his reminiscences James Love described a white corn shucking as a gathering around the corn pile where a good deal of tomfoolery would take place along with the work. Much mention is made of the search for red ears, for which some prize was designated, and little contests between "nearby mates to see who could get his ears of corn out quickest."[43] Beyond this, the most memorable feature of the event for Love was the huge outdoor supper that was prepared and consumed. The meal was cooked in the wash kettle, for the ordinary kitchen lacked equipment large enough to prepare food for the crowd. The shucking was done by the men, the cooking by the women. "There were no stoves then," he recalled, therefore "all the cooking had to be done over open wood fires." This put a major burden on the women, "as hard a task" as could be found and one which could hardly have been "more disagreeable . . . in preparing a feast."[44]

F. D. Srygley also reported a relatively sedate tradition from Tennessee. The event began in mid-afternoon and went far into the night. As with the plantation celebrations, there was a good deal of artificial illumination, from pine-knot lanterns and lightwood fires. People of all ages participated, for the small boys were charged with keeping the fires going, and with sweeping the shucks into the fodder pens.[45] Srygley also described a contest between teams which, as in the plantation accounts, were led by captains who chose the sides and were responsible for whipping up the enthusiasm of their group. While the contest seems to have stirred up a good deal of irritation, and sometimes some fighting, there is no indication that the work was coordinated, nor that singing was in any way a part of the practice.[46]

The other major description of the event among whites also came from a frontier and border area—in this case Kentucky—and was written by Dr. Daniel Drake, in one of the fullest reminiscences of agricultural life in the early nineteenth century.[47] His description of the shucking records one facet of his fascination with the whole process of corn production on the frontier; for, as a boy, he played a number of roles in the cultivation process.

In Drake's part of the South, as in Srygley's, they chose captains and sides. And like Srygley, Drake remembered the drinking, the little tricks the shuckers played in finding creative ways of "cheating," and the fighting that broke out between the two sides during the contest. Additionally, he notes that "the victorious captain, mounted on the shoulders of some of the stoutest men, with the bottle in one hand and his hat in the other, was carried in triumph around the vanquished party amidst shouts of victory which rent the air."[48]

Among the features of the celebration that were shared by blacks and whites were the time of year chosen, late fall; the organization of participants around the corn pile, often into two teams; the contest, with its tomfoolery; the frenzied search for the red ear, and the ample supper afterward. While the shucking seems to have been regarded as fun, the reports of the practice among the plain folk indicate more a concern with demonstrating community resourcefulness than festive abandon.

James Lamar makes just such a point when he openly compares the practices of slaves and plain folk. "During the early years" in his area of Georgia, the workers "were all white people and the corn-shuckings were comparatively tame."[49] After describing the cutting of the corn from the stalk and its gathering in the lot near the corn house, Lamar notes that as on plantations which had slaves, invitations were sent out to the neighbors for the shelling and the feast to follow. He proceeds: "The parties would gather about dark, take their places at the corn pile, and, while the work went steadily on, would chat and joke, and chew tobacco, and tell anecdotes." Some of the young men attempted to sing songs they had recently heard, but there was no concerted singing. As the pile diminished, someone might suggest having a race. At this, the pile was divided, and two sides arranged themselves and went at the task with greater intensity. After the last ear was shucked, the host was raised on the shoulders of "some powerful man," the others all getting in line behind them, and carried around the house and indoors to the feast table. At this point, the hilarity ceased while the host made a speech of welcome and thanks, and they fell to eating. So this report contains more of the features of the shucking that were described in the slave plantation literature: the chairing and speechmaking, in addition to the contest and the feast.[50]

Lamar also tells of one evening in the late 1830s when the shucking did not proceed as usual. His father had made the usual preparations for the yearly holiday, and the neighbors had come into the yard and begun shucking, when suddenly, about eight-thirty, they heard "from the top of a long high hill two miles to the east, the sound of the negroes singing. . . ." One of the neighbors said he had told a slave at the mill that day that a shucking was to take place, and he supposed the man "sends word to one and another, and so gets up a company of twenty or thirty who of their own violition [sic] came to the corn-shucking."

As the singing grew nearer, the shucking stopped. "In due time the negroes arrived singing at the very top of their voices, marched right into the lot, surrounded the corn pile, signaled the white men away and took their places."[51] Lamar described the shucking by the slaves that followed, underscoring their tremendous energy as they sang and worked.

Thus, there were clearly observable differences of spirit and organization of work and play between the slaves and the white yeoman farmers. But the common features of the division of the pile and the consequent contest, the drinking and the occasional fights all serve to distinguish the Southern style of shucking from the husking bee held in the North and the old Northwest.

While husking became the activity around which the event was organized in both the North and the South, the setting, the tempo, the approach to the work, and the celebration afterward differed significantly. In the Southern corn shucking, the power relationships of slavery itself were dramatized through scenes in which slaves sang as they worked, engaged in what was taken to be joyful competitive work and play activities, and were rewarded for their labors with food and a good time. In this as in so many other features of practice, the Northern husking and the Southern shucking differed. While both were held at night under artificial illumination, the husking was held in the barn, the shucking was carried out in the plantation yard, out of doors. Participants in both regions felt the thrill of finding the first red ear, but its discovery and the awarding of the prize were marked in different fashions.

In the North, the affair was a modest one, circumscribed by the fact that it had to be held indoors. The kinds of food and the number of dishs prepared were considerably more modest in the North. To be sure, people in both regions celebrated with extensive socializing, drinking, eating, and other forms of merrymaking.

The Southerners added the shucking contest, with its division of the shuckers into two groups. From this developed the election of the captains, who displayed leadership in both work and entertainment. Finally, the ceremonial speeches delivered by the masters and the captains to each other were unique to the Southern corn shucking. Through the addition of these, the English countryside tradition of the harvest home was transformed into a slaves' holiday.

That the harvest celebration managed to survive in New England is a matter of some note. The revulsion revealed in Cotton Mather's comments expressed the typical Puritan attitude toward English country pastimes which had become a part of the official church calendar that involved mumming, masking, or revelry of any sort, especially if the baiting of animals was called for. All such practices were regarded as evidence of deceitful worldliness of the sort they associated with the Roman Catholic Church. As Alice Morse Earle summarized the matter, with direct reference to Christmas: "The very name smacked to them of incense, stole, and monkish jargon."[52]

In the South, corn filled a different niche in the agricultural economy than elsewhere, and was produced for other purposes than the crops at the center of the related Old World harvest customs. More, in the transatlantic journey, a number of major alterations occurred in the Old World harvest practices. The grain around which the ceremony developed was a New World crop, cultivated in different climates and soils, and carrying a different technology of sowing, cultivation, reaping, and preparation as food and fodder. Within the growing year, each of these cultivating activities found a slightly altered place in the agricultural economy.

The Southern corn shucking enables us to see two Old World traditions—the European and African—coming together under frontier conditions. Equally significantly, the crop itself, and the techniques of its cultivation, harvest, and preparation as food, were indigenous. Like so many festivals, the plantation corn shucking can be understood as a dialogue of the cultural vocabularies of the many people who come together to mark the passage of life.

CHAPTER FOUR

Festive Spirit in the Development
of African American Style

Rooted though it may have been in English celebrations and pioneer frolics, the plantation corn shucking was animated by the style, spirit, and social and aesthetic organization of sub-Saharan Africa. This was widely recognized, in fact, by Southerners such as David Barrow, who explained that from his perspective the event was "peculiarly suited to the negro genius," involving a set of stylistically distinctive expressive talents."[1]

But more than exhibiting a distinctive style of celebration, the corn shucking reflected an attitude toward the relationship between singing, dancing, work, and celebration that was carried over from the sub-Saharan world. "Africans rely on music to maintain the happiness and vitality of their social worlds," John Miller Chernoff points out. "In Africa, music helps people to work, to enjoy themselves, to control a bad person or to praise a good one, to recite history, poetry, and proverbs, to celebrate a funeral or a festival, to compete with each other, to encounter their gods, to grow up, and fundamentally to be sociable in everything they do."[2] The corn shucking brought this complex of functions together in a unique way.

In large areas of West and Central Africa under the hoe, cooperative group labor was traditionally employed, and these practices were continued throughout Afro-America, in Brazil, Haiti, Cuba, the anglophonic and francophonic West Indies, and on the mainland United States. The important twentieth-century collector of Afro-American songs Harold Courlander, says, "Even . . . where men gather to work for pay, the old patterns of work have nevertheless continued. The rhythmic use of tools, the sense of community, and responsive singing have remained significant elements in these patterns."[3]

Certain kinds of labor encouraged team endeavor, especially those in which movement and tools were used in unison and created regular sounds which could be incorporated into the music. Reaping different crops called for distinct

techniques—gang cutting for crops such as corn (when taken on the stalk and shocked in the fields) and cane; more care and greater individual attention, for others, especially the delicate tobacco leaf. Cotton stood somewhere in between, for it involved individual picking effort, but this was often done by the row, sometimes involving a picking competition which was followed by a barbecue.

The slaves organized themselves in gangs not only in the shucking but on the roads going to and from their tasks. As they moved they sang, in the same kind of call-response fashion that is found in the corn shucking. The songs collected in connection with the corn shucking bespeak the Afro-Americans' excitement in working, competing, eating, and dancing together. They also continually comment upon the world the slaves saw around them, poked fun at the actions and attitudes of certain planters and other powerful whites, and expressed their shared anger at the agony they found in being "sold off to Georgia," and other inequities.

The merriment of the slaves at the corn shucking not only involved "getting happy" in the most immediate sense but also "keeping up the spirit." The songs were a record not of the contentment of the slaves but of the value they placed on experiencing the intense moments of life together. Happiness was not a condition, as Frederick Douglass pointed out in discussing slave songs in his autobiography, but the expression of intense feelings as they were experienced by the whole group moving together in common purpose.[4] The expression of the experience of the spirit as it descended upon the group is an important concept to bear in mind considering how African style was maintained in events such as the shucking. Morton Marks has pointed out that in many areas in which there are large numbers of people descended from slaves the styles of expression become more deeply imbued with African stylistic characteristics as celebrations become more intense.[5]

A stylistic alteration occurred in the corn shucking itself as the contest heated up, and again after the feast when the fiddle came out and the dancing began. Many outside observers, such as Charles Lanman, recognized the way in which the spirit caught the hands at some point during the shucking, bringing their performance in both song and work to a high pitch. At the moment the shuckers saw that the contest was coming to an end, Lanman says, there "commences a mingled sound of shouting and singing voices, which presently swell into a loud and truly harmonious chorus . . . and the husking scene is in its prime." He continues enthusiastically, "The very fires seem elated with the singular but interesting prospect which they illumine, and shoot their broad sheets of flame high into the air. Song follows song, in quick succession, and in every direction piles of beautiful corn seem to spring out of the earth. . . ."[6] In so many of the eyewitness accounts, the singers' various ways of playfully cutting in and out of the singing and competing in loudness and within invention increased the general level of intensity and involvement.

This spirited breaking out was especially pleasurable to slave masters. As one ex-slave indicated, the best dancers were rewarded for their efforts in "the strut," one of the competitive dances held at the end of the slave dances. Because of her prowess, this young lady "was taken from one plantation to another and entered in dancing contests with other slaves, while her own [master] wagered on the outcome with other owners."[7]

Recognizing the time and place in which performance, contention, and risk taking were encouraged, the hands took

advantage of the opportunity to express themselves in their own style. They found occasions in which they could present themselves both as subservient to the master of the plantation and yet they themselves were "masters of ceremonies."

Far from simply imitating the festive forms of their masters, the hands established a point in the performance in which they crossed the threshold between their everyday world and fully entered into the experience of the celebration. Almost always, what followed this opening illustrated the African American genius for festive invention. Says Samuel Kinser in his recent history of African American celebrations: "The slaves, given entrance to the plantation mansion and plied with good food and drink, did not content themselves with effusive thanks, but performed sly, satiric songs and skits about the lords' and ladies' behavior."[8] In performing such skits, simply through the act of mimicry or some other form of grotesquerie, they created a world of imitational possibilities that became a part of the cultural process of breaking out.

The corn shucking was held at that time of year when, by tradition, the slaves had license to go about the country-side. The time of the harvest when the slaves' "toil is pushed to the utmost," as John Pendleton Kennedy noted, was when they enjoyed a time of recognized privileges.[9]

With the first frost, the hog killing commenced, and from that point on through the corn-shucking season and on to the major slave holiday, Christmas, the requirement for passes to travel on the roads at night between plantations seems to have been relaxed in many places. Indeed, the sing-ing of corn songs itself appears to have been understood as signaling the time of license. George Brewer of Alabama put it this way: ". . . if the familiar sound of a number of negroes singing corn songs at one place was heard, any negro man or boy felt he had a right to go . . ."[10] Thus late autumn became a season for celebrations by slave and master alike, reaching its peak at Christmas. Slaves and masters exhibited gregarious behavior, the masters permitted slave marriages, exchanged gifts with the slaves, and exhibited themselves in their most magnanimous guise.

Planters knew about the nighttime activities taking place. They created a force of police, night *patrollers,* who were to instill fear of getting caught without a pass on the part of the slaves. Gladys-Marie Fry has documented, from the blacks' perspective, the effort made to keep the slaves at home through official and unofficial means, and the methods by which the slaves sidestepped such inhibitions.[11] Slave meetings took place after dark: the religious meetings out-of-doors, rendezvous between lovers, and dances. The de-

liberate slowdown implied in the much-quoted slave proverb "Come day, go day, / God send Sunday" is only one expression of the division of the worlds of the masters and that of slaves.[12] For instance, there was a widespread feeling among the slaves that the daytime hours, sunup to sundown, might belong to Old Master, but sundown to sunup belonged to themselves.

Many observers reflected on the vitality and reservoirs of enthusiasm the slaves drew on in seizing the nighttime hours. In 1797, a reporter to the *American Museum,* a journal directed specifically at taking an inventory of cultural resources in the new country, noted of the slave's life: "His time for repose and eating never exceeds eight hours in the twenty four. . . . But instead of retiring to rest, . . . he generally sets out from home . . . [walking great distances to a dance] in which he performs with astonishing agility, and the most vigorous exertions, keeping time and cadence, most exactly, with the music of the banjor [sic] . . . until he exhausts himself, and scarcely has time, or strength, before he is called forth to toil next morning."[13]

Both religious and entertainment "steal aways" were carried on at night, their noises "contained" within an inverted vessel, usually a pot, put near the door to cover the sound, or so they thought, so that they would not be caught by the night patrollers.[14] Social and religious practices were organized in the same manner and used the same devices to coordinate the power of the group. There are many indications that a radical distinction between sacred and secular occasions makes little sense in Afro-American practice, especially on occasions such as a harvest ceremony. Indeed, a number of observers note that the songs sung while working were often spirituals.[15]

Wherever slaves worked together they transformed the work through song, even when they were separated from

each other in the fields. This fact was noted by many visitors reporting on life in the South. The account of the slaves' singing by the Swedish visitor Frederika Bremer is one of the most famous, and justly so: "These songs have been made on the road; during the journeyings of the slaves; upon the rivers, as they paddled their canoes along or steered the raft down the stream; and in particular, at the corn-huskings. . . . They sing impromptu whatever is uppermost in their heart or in their brain . . . peculiarly improvisations, which have taken root in the minds of the people, and are listened to and sung to the whites. . . ."[16]

Few observers of slave life failed to notice the importance of call-and-response singing. Many other accounts give a closer analysis of how the songs and the singing were produced. All focus on the sense of power produced by the overlapping of the leader's voice with the voices of the chorus as they engaged with each other antiphonally. Planter-journalist David Barrow, for instance, says of the "corn-song" that it "is almost always a song with a chorus, or to use the language of the corn-shuckers, the 'gin'r'ls give out' and the shuckers 'drone.' " He points out that the "songs are kept up continuously during the entire time the work is going on," thus maintaining a high level of involvement of everyone within hearing distance.[17]

Many of the accounts of white reporters go into extraordinary detail about the singing and dancing form often referred to in discussions of Afro-American culture as *apartplaying,* in which a central performer interacts in counterpoint or some other contrasting mode with the rest of the performing group.[18] Both work and play forms feature a ring in which individuals step to the center of the group, to whom the rest of the performers then respond playfully.

Exactly this organization can be seen in the way in which

the corn captains interact with their side. In the accounts of the forming of the corn pile, the coming together of the slaves in the yard, the election of the captain, and the organizing of the rest of the shuckers around the pile in such a way that the captain can lead them in their efforts, the captain's leadership is related by slave and master alike, not only in the respect due him but in his ability to lead the singing from the center of the ring.

This ring comes to represent the ideal of a community bringing itself into being through the chanter-response performance. The big voices and the master improvisers of the quarters take their place at the center of the ring (in this case, the pile) and call for the response of their fellow workers and players.

Letitia Burwell's remembrance of the singing is typical: "Selecting one of their number—usually the most original and amusing, and possessed of the loudest voice—they called him 'captain.' " This figure then "seated himself on top of the pile—a large lightwood torch burning in front of him, and while he shucked, improvised words and music to a wild 'recitative,' the chorus of which was caught up by the army of shuckers around."[19]

Through the exhortation of the captains and their lieutenants, the shucking was brought to a climax, a point announced not only in the winners' shouts of exultation, but in the consequent seizure of the host planter. The chairing of the master served as a kind of marker dividing the shucking proper from the feast and dance: ". . . master took a jug er licker 'roun' and got dem tight and when dey got full, dey would histe master up and toat him 'roun' and holler, then the fun started and dey would play de old gourd an' horse-hair dance . . . ," remembered George Strickland of his slave years in Alabama.[20]

For the slaves, the driving force of the occasion was the feast and the dance afterward. There is no evidence that the dancing which took place was in any way unusual; but the descriptions of the slaves' dancing contained in these accounts provide some of the fullest information on record of their traditions of dance.

Like the corn-shucking contest, the dance was organized around a ring, and featured multimetric music, now embellished with the playing of musical instruments, each with its own special tones and rhythmic responses. Nancy Williams, an ex-slave, describes one such instance. Before these dances, the master would send some of his men to the mill to get boards, and they would make a "gra' big platform an' brung it to de house for to dance on. Den come de music, de fiddles an' all dem other things."[21]

The platform dance floor was an especially important part of the proceedings if dancing was to take place in the yard. Not only did it raise the dancers to a position in which the onlookers on the portico might better see them, but the sound of dancing on the boards conveyed the multimetrical effects. The sound of feet dancing flat against the boards was amplified by the enclosed space beneath the platform that operated like a sound baffle.

John Wyeth provides some of the nicest insights into these practices. The slaves "did not relish dancing on the ground, in the manner of the American Indians," which fact he explained as resulting from "the negroes' instinctive love of rhythm. . . ." That is, "the shuffle of the feet, in many instances unshod . . . could not be heard as distinctly on the ground as on a plank floor or a tight puncheon"—this latter referring to the flattened and smoothed surface of a split log used in cabin floors. "When the negroes would dance a pas de deux, a tight puncheon was selected and the two danced forward and back on this single slab." Wyeth also notes the use of a wagon bed for a dance floor, as it "made an excellent sounding-board."[22]

The pat of the feet on the dancing boards was mentioned by a great number of observers, often in combination with the patting of other parts of the body. The most complicated rhythmic effects might be achieved even without instrumental accompaniment, in the performance routine commonly called "Patting Juba." (Juba, a common African personal name, seems to have become a generic name for a comic performer in the South.) In a sense, such patting became the signature of Afro-American performance style, for, through clapping hands, patting legs, arms, and armpits, snapping fingers, and other such rhythmic effects and countereffects, an individual could use his or her whole body to create multiple rhythms simultaneously.[23] Thus, an individual could recapitulate through complicated comic gestures many of the core features of black performance style.[24]

Clapping was a form of accompaniment for singing or dancing that did not require any instruments. The term most commonly used by the slaves for clapping was *patting*. In its common Anglo-American usage, "patting" refers to the gentle striking or stroking of the open hand on some other part of the body for purposes of reassurance and encouragement. As a term for bringing the two hands together, "patting" is more unusual, being confined to the babytalk of "pattycake," which of course refers to the patting of the hand against the dough.

"Patting" had another association for slaves: as Gladys-Marie Fry noticed, "the murmured phrase 'patter de pat, patter de pat' . . . was used to warn fellow slaves of the presence of patrols in the neighborhood." She perceives that "pat" was a strong word made all the more powerful "by enabling the speaker to play upon . . . multiple meanings."[25]

Patting created a field of rhythm in which each performer responds to a basic beat. By doubling or tripling the time, breaking each beat into doublets or triplets, a performer produced a rolling effect that played against the master pulse without necessitating an actual change in the basic meter.

The effects of patting may be as varied as a drum orchestra, and as in such a group, the variety is produced by counterposing different meters and timbres. As Bessie Jones explained the practice to Bess Lomax Hawes in their *Step It Down,* patting involved not only bringing the hands together to make a sound, but cupping them to produce a variety of pitches. Additionally, each part of the body that was slapped—side, chest, cheek, top of the head, and leg—could produce a variety of pitches depending on how the hand was cupped.[26]

Of patting at dances, John Wyeth says that those not actually playing banjo or fiddle were considered "accompanists who 'patted' with the hands, keeping accurate time with the music."[27] Bessie Jones thought of the patting not as a sign of encouragement or accompaniment so much as part of the music itself. And when only patting was available, it was referred to as the music for dancing.[28]

The Southern poet Sidney Lanier was also fascinated by patting: "I have heard a Southern plantation 'hand,' in 'patting Juba' for a comrade to dance by, venture upon quite complex successions of rhythm, not hesitating to syncopate, to change the rhythmic accent for a moment, or to indulge in other highly specialized variations of the current rhythms."[29]

Lewis Paine pointed out some other rhythmic and textural features of patting, noticing that the foot is brought down in response to "regular time" even while "the hands are

struck lightly together, and then upon the thighs." This cre-
ates a "most curious noise, yet in such perfect order, it fur-
nishes music to dance by."[30] In fact, there is good reason to
suppose that as the patting developed among the attending
group, a number of counterrhythms were established by others patting.[31]

The thickening of the metrical texture produced by the
presence of cross-rhythms encouraged the competitive spirit
during these dances. Wyeth says that "when two danced
alone, whether of the same sex or not, the object seemed to
be to determine which could outdo the other." This was
encouraged by the other dancers, of course. "As the 'steps,'
or gyrations and contortions, not only of the body and the
legs, but of the arms and hands, grew more violent and
rapid," the patting and the shouts of praise and encouragement, even criticism would be heard. The contest would
proceed "until at last one of the contestants gave up and the
victor was hailed as the 'best man.' "[32]

This competitive motive underscores the importance of
cutting, or setting strong alternative stylistic challenges to
one another. The more alternative beats were introduced,
the greater were the metrical resources available to the individual and the group in their responsive elaborations. As
Wyeth noted, the hips, legs, arms, and hands might all take
on their own separate rhythms, playing off against each
other, just as the individual dancer would play off from the
other dancers.

Against this heating up was counterposed the coolness of
the dancer's head, a stylistic feature which became most
clearly elaborated in the so-called *cakewalk*. Also called the
walkabout or the *strut*, this was one of the most celebrated
of competitive dances, primarily because it made its way
into the blackface minstrel show. But as the black entertainer

Tom Fletcher heard from his grandfather, the cakewalk began as "the chalkline walk." After the boards were laid down "for an impromptu stage before the verandah so the guests could have a good view of the proceedings," the dancers would appear, displaying themselves in a "straight walk on a path" chalked onto the boards. Along this line, the "dancers made their way with a pail of water on their heads." The judging would be based on which couple stood straightest and spilled the least amount of water.

Such descriptions are found in abundance in the ex-slave narratives. Of one slave well known for his dancing abilities, an ex-slave recalled that "everyone around would try to best him." The contest, like the contest Fletcher's grandfather described, turned on the dancer's holding a container of water on the head while performing tricks with the rest of the body, especially the feet, making them "go like triphammers and sound like snaredrums. He could whirl around and such, all the movement from his hips down."[33]

The chalk-line or cakewalk dance[34] was only one of a very

great many that were described as emerging from the slave holidays. The most common dance forms, the ring dance, the jig, and the reel, appear to have been adaptations of European forms, but in fact only the names were borrowed, at least for the jig. As Levine noticed, "While slaves often learned the dances of the whites—the quadrille, the reel, the cotillion, and even the waltz—their own dance style remained distinctive."[35] More than this, the way in which the body is organized and articulated in black dance is radically different from European-style dancing.

In European social dancing the body is maintained as a single unit of behavior. Integrity is asserted with a strongly unified torso. The shoulders are set back and the center of balance is located at the sternum—thus emphasizing the sexual points of differentiation between the man's chest and the woman's bosom.

The African and African American organization of the body differs most profoundly in locating the center of gravity at the hips. Movement is initiated from that area and emanates outward to the shoulders, arms, and hands, and the knees and feet, which play off against the pulse established by the hip movements. The centrality of the hips produces the sense of strong sexuality in African American dance.

With knees bent and the flat foot beating its own set of rhythms, the other parts of the body play against the metrical pulse system originating in the hips. This produces what Laurence Levine refers to as "the basic characteristic of African dance, with its gliding, dragging, shuffling steps, its flexed, fluid bodily position," which are "opposed to the stuffily erect position of European dancers. . . ."[36] Thus the flexibility and fluidity in black dancing arises from the division of body at the pelvis, with the upper body playing against the lower much as individual dancers or singers play-

fully oppose themselves to the rest of the performing community.

Much of European social dance involves asserting, testing, and maintaining one's balance, through adroitness in executing the steps. The placement of the arms and the hands complements the foot movements. Raising the hands above the head or placing them on the hips calls attention to the footwork that is being carried out, and the tests of agility or balance which are being put into action.

Not only is the carriage of the torso sustained by a return to a set attitude, a standing in place at the beginning and ending of an elaborated figure, but this ordering is socially articulated as well, for most of the European-derived dances called for pairs dancing in contraposed lines or in sets. The male dancer leads, the female follows; the male leans back slightly when partnering a female, who herself leans slightly forward, placing her very balance in the hands of her partner.

While slave dancing tested balance, the site of order was at the head and not the torso. This is most evident in the chalk-line and cakewalk dances. The body flexes at the hips, with the feet commonly kept flat on the ground. Forward movements tend toward shuffling if the feet remain on the ground; otherwise they gravitate toward leaps with the legs held parallel and knees bent to the side or back; and the torso moves ever lower to the ground as the aesthetic environment gets heated.

While some of the slave dances adopted the organization into couples, this was far from the norm. Illustrations of slave dancing as well as written accounts make it clear that anyone could get up and dance, and that there was no imperative to form couples before entering the dance. And even where couple dancing occurred, the degree of contact between the partners was limited. Far from providing the sustaining spirit of the dancing, slave couple-dancing appears to have constrained the impulse to improvise and compete. The more common adaptation from European dance forms was the counterposed couple, in which each partner could playfully relate to the other while responding to the same rhythmic impulses as they faced each other.

Slave dancing called for a more spontaneous and individually stylized body response to the multimetric sounds produced by the musicians and the patters. Says the ex-slave Aunt Cicely Cawthon, remarking on the dance after the shucking, "After they got through, the fiddler would start to fiddling and they would ring up in the old-time square dance." Lest it be presumed that the slaves were organizing themselves in sets, such as one finds at balls, she continues: "Everybody danced off by themselves. Just let your foot go backward . . . and then let your foot go forward and whirl around. Men, too, danced that way. . . ."[37]

The great virtuoso dances called for the dancer to openly imitate some stylized movement observed in nature or in social life. So we find in the cakewalk a mimicry of the white cotillion through an exaggeration of European-style walking, parading, and dancing, with the hypercorrect throwing back of the shoulders and head, and the exaggerated forward march of those white swells on parade. Other dances featured imitations of the movements of animals or birds, as in the Turkey Trot or the Pigeon Wing.

The slaves themselves often described such dancing as a cutting or breaking move, terms surely derived from African or African American sources, as this usage is not found in English until the interaction with slaves and their music and dance. "Cutting" may refer simply to a cutting up, a breaking away from the group, with the dancer making a bid for attention as he "shows his stuff" or she "makes her motion" to the others. Cutting also means entering into playful competition, a stylized practice which, as discussed above, stands at the center of the black aesthetic.

Breaking is also a distinctively African American term, connoting the same sense of transformation as the cutting, with a greater emphasis on the strangeness of the alteration. The use of the term *breakdown* to refer to the customary slave dance was common in the South from the early nineteenth century. The word may have come from the harvest season itself, for the act of cutting the ear from the stalk was referred to as *breaking down the corn*.[38] "Breakdown" enters vernacular American English as references to the kind of dance associated with the slave holidays. Almost certainly this usage achieved its primary meaning from the *breaking down* or *away* that occurred at the end of many slave dance routines, such as "Patting Juba," in which one dancer asserted himself or herself with such astonishing virtuosity that everyone else began to watch, to pat along, and to lend encouragement.

Robert Cantwell has recently suggested that the extremely fast-paced dance found in American (white) country music which is called the breakdown developed from "the African practice of annealing rhythms to melodies. . . ." Specifically, the African aesthetic draws attention to the possibility of constant rhythmic alteration, or as the jazz man puts it, *running changes*. The simplest way of doing this, and the way most easily adopted by whites, is to take the square orientation of European dance music, commonly structured in 4/4 meter, and to move the accent away from the on-beat, at the end of the third beat, onto the second and fourth beats, that is, the off-beats, thus producing syncopation. Says Cantwell, referring to tunes that begin as European dances and were adapted to New World rhythmic imperatives, "Generally speaking the reel became a breakdown when the rhythm accent shifts from the third to the second and fourth beats."[39]

Syncopation is only one way in which the dissociation of rhythm from meter informs black singing and dancing, giving it the sense of ongoing rhythmic exploration and experiential openness. One performer ordinarily would carry the beat—often playing at the bottom of the register, on a drum, a boom-box, a washtub. Equally often, near the one maintaining the central meter would be a second performer playing against him, sometimes even on the same instrument, as in the case of the slave fiddler whose second man beat straws in counterrhythm on the same strings on which the fiddler carried his syncopated melody. David Barrow described this trick: "The performer provides himself with a pair of straws about eighteen inches in length, and stout enough to stand a good smart blow." These straws, he notes, are carefully chosen, usually from a sedge broom. The performer uses them "in the manner of drum-sticks, that portion of the fiddle-strings between the fiddler's bow and his left hand serving as a drum." Just as in a noisy environment the drumbeat is the only thing the dancers can hear, so the fiddle sticks' counterrhythms carried: "One of the first sounds which you hear on approaching the dancing party is the *tum tee tum* of the straws, and after the dance begins, when the shuffling of feet destroys the other sounds of the fiddle, this noise can still be heard."[40]

The ring play often noted as a slave practice, both in the evening's entertainments and at the dances, provides the clearest and simplest illustration of many of the most important features of African American style. Says Bessie Jones, the great teacher of these plays in recent times: "One gets in the middle of the ring, and they all clap and sing, . . . and it go on until you get to each one . . . each player, then, having a turn in the middle." Bess Lomax Hawes goes on to describe what this means in practice: "The center player in a ring play . . . stands alone to make his statement by dance or 'acting,' usually within the context of courtship play." Not that courtship was carried on in the same manner as in the British and American singing game tradition, with couples moving together around the circle. Rather, in the Afro-American pattern, the play provided an opportunity to display each player's "romantic availability" alone; at the end of each turn, the player "picks out not so much a partner as a successor."[41]

However, Jones and Hawes are quick to point out, "there is little paired or coupled action." Rather, each player is encouraged to show off in some way, either through some kind of individualized dance step ("show me your motion"), or through strutting, teasing, flirting, and wiggling, with everyone else clapping, commenting, and joking in support. This is the point. For while the player is at the center he or she is never alone; rather there is constant commentary and support provided by the ring: "The ring play [is] the ultimate opportunity for personal reassurance, for feeling the warmth and support of a tight-locked and indestructible circle within which [each] could act out . . . feelings without any fear of rejection or shame."[42]

In at least one area of the South, coastal Georgia, the ring dance was, in fact, strongly associated with both harvest and a sense of the sacred. "Dance roun' in a ring. We has a big time long bout wen de crops come in an evrybody bring sumpin tuh eat wut they makes an we all give praise for the good crop and then we shouts an sings all night. An wen the sun rise, we stahts tuh dance."[43]

The ring organization, with its implied sense of community, and with its emphasis upon the active involvement of everyone potentially playing against or apart from the ring, may offer a folk-mapping of the ways in which the world was brought together by African Americans in celebrations of life's continuities. Roscoe Lewis makes a related point in his survey of the Virginia ex-slave materials: "Slave celebrations were regarded by whites, who allowed them to take place, as innocent pleasures, though harvest festivals had existed for centuries in Africa before blacks had arrived in North America." He continues in this vein: "The dances at festival time on Virginia plantations usually represented vital aspects of religious expression. In that context, festivities and work were combined at corn-shucking time, with specific kinds of work an inspiration to slave creativity."[44]

The ring plays were accompanied by dance-instruction songs, in which the lyrics describe what is to be danced. These songs were part of the process of *calling*. Like the captain's singing, it was designated by this name, as was the antiphonal singing referred to by African Americans as *call an' 'sponse*.[45]

In African and African American responsive style, there is a high degree of overlap between individual voices and physical movements. Each person's voice and body calls attention both to itself and to the ways in which the individual is related to the overall group effect. Each performer sings and dances, facing inward toward a common point, contrasting his or her actions with those emerging from within the circle.

Here a position of real importance may be granted the person who finds himself or herself in the center, for each participant is called upon to help in the project of keeping up the spirit. In this style of oppositional entanglement, winning or losing is not as important as getting and keeping the spirit, through the leader's mastery. His leadership enables his followers to have an intense life-affirming experience together. The way of organizing group activity, of playing each part of the body and of the individual against the whole, establishes that special sense of vibrancy that has continued to fascinate outside observers of black performances and celebrations to this day.

CHAPTER FIVE

Signifying Leadership on the Plantation

The ability to improvise, to make rhymes and to lead while entertaining, was highly valued by planter and slave alike. The good rhymer might use his wits to confront others in situations which otherwise would have resulted in whipping. There are many stories on this theme, from both slaves and planters. One, from the Virginia ex-slave Cornelius Garner, suggests the usefulness of this ability.

One day Charlie saw ole Marsa comin' home wid a keg of whiskey on his ole mule. Cuttin' 'cross de plowed field, de old mule slipped an' Marsa come tumblin' off. Marsa didn' know Charlie saw him, an' Charlie didn't say nothin'. But soon arter a visitor come an' Marsa called Charlie to de house to show off what he knew. Marsa say, "Come here, Charlie, an' sing some rhymes to Mr. Henson." "Don' know no new ones, Marsa," Charlie answered. "Come on, you black rascal, give me a rhyme fo' my company—one he ain't heard." So Charlie say, "All right, Marsa,

I give you a new one effen you promise not to whup me." Marsa
promised, an' den Charlie sung de rhyme he done made up in
his haid 'bout Marsa:

> *Jackass rared,*
> *Jackass pitch,*
> *Throwed ole Marsa in de ditch.*

Well, Marsa got mad as a hornet, but he didn't whup Charlie,
not dat time anyway. An' chile, don' you know he used to set
de flo' to dat dere song? Mind you, never would sing it when
Marsa was roun', but when he wasn't we'd wing all roun' de
cabin singin' 'bout how old Marsa fell off de mule's back. Charlie
had a bunch of verses:

> *Jackass stamped,*
> *Jackass neighed,*
> *Throwed ole Marsa on his haid.*

Don' recollec' all dat smart slave made up. But ev'y'body sho'
bus' dey sides laughin' when Charlie sang dat las' verse:

> *Jackass stamped,*
> *Jackass hupped,*
> *Marsa hear you slave, you sho' git whupped.*[1]

This kind of satiric invention has been noted of slave
singers as early as Nicholas Cresswell's observations before
the Revolution. After visiting a "Negro Ball" on May 29,
1774, he notes: "In their songs they generally related the
usage they have received from their Masters or Mistresses
in a very satirical style."[2]

John Pendleton Kennedy describes a rhymer, old Carey,
"a minstrel of some repute," in his novel of early Virginia
life on the plantation, ". . . [L]ike the ancient jongleurs,"

Kennedy notes, Carey "sings the inspirations of his own muse, weaving into song the past or present annals of the [planter's] family." When asked to sing, "the bard" produces a song directed at the hero of the novel who is involved in a courtship. Carey sings:

> *The rich man comes from down below,*
> *Yo ho, yo ho.*
> *What he comes for I guess I know,*
> *Long time ago.*
> *He comes to talk to the young lady,*
> *Yo ho, yo ho.*
> *But she look'd proud, and mighty high,*
> *Long time ago.*[3]

Slaves could gain some advantage in encounters with their masters by drawing on their abilities to improvise wittily. And in such situations, they often used irony to launch moral commentary at certain figures who made claims for themselves as agents of benevolence.

In the shucking, the slaves seized upon the season, anticipating whatever liberties the harvest might encourage. At these times, performers might emerge as leaders. One able to command through an ability to use his wits would find himself at the center of the festivities. These figures were first among equals in the organization of the activity. The captains as the originating leaders of the singing, and the fiddlers and callers as the driving force of the dancers, served as models of leadership. As improvisers and exhorters in song, these people were the leaders of the revels. In this dimension, they partook of the great African bardic tradition in which the poet performs a number of social services for individuals and the community in general. As a moral commentator, the bard may point to wrongdoers within society. Or, as praise-singer, he may amplify the deeds of a king or a hero. And finally, bards enter into singing combats which often draw heavily on devices of exhortation and moral scorn.

The songs and speeches recorded from the corn-shucking accounts do not reveal how these capabilities were learned and maintained in the plantation setting. The regard for improvisation is evident, especially in the use of aggressive rhyming and allusive song-making by plantation men-of-words. But, more broadly, a system of wily and allusive suggestion, operating through indirection and parodic imitation, has been noticed often in Afro-American folklore throughout the United States and in the trans-Caribbean region. The tradition of topical play is featured in song-making contests such as the calypso tent and samba school competitions, the tap-dancing and break-dancing face-offs, and the great battles of the stick-fighters in Trinidad and Brazil.

In its more everyday uses, this competitive and allusive play is present wherever slanging matches arise, especially at markets where the *higgler* women hold forth, and wherever the men hang out, rhyming or joking with each other, playing the dozens, ragging, playing at the game of 'busin' (abusing), or jiving. It is heard whenever someone is eloquently *talking sweet* or aggressively *talking bad,* a range of expression referred to as "signifyin(g)."[4]

Commonly, signifying word play has been regarded as defensive, allusive behavior in the face of otherwise overpowering societal forces. (Indeed, Br'er Rabbit stories are often interpreted simply as models for coping under surveillance on the plantation, a perspective that does not account for many features of these tales.)⁵ But these signifying practices could become very pointed and particular. The Reverend T. C. Thornton, an ex-slave, after discussing the topicality of the songs which were improvised by the captains, gives us a song of this sort, concerned with the irony of a preacher forcing his slaves to work on Sunday:

L. *The parson says his prayers in church.*	c. *It rain, boys, it rain.*
L. *Then deliver a fine sermon.*	c. *It rain, boys, it rain.*
L. *He cut the matter short, my friends,*	c. *It rain, boys, it rain.*
L. *He say the blessed Lord send it.*	c. *It rain, boys, it rain.*
L. *Now's the time for planting bacco.*	c. *It rain, boys, it rain.*
L. *Come, my negroes, get you home.*	c. *It rain, boys, it rain.*
L. *Jim, Jack, and Joe and Tom.*	c. *It rain, boys, it rain.*
L. *Go draw you plants and sell them out.*	c. *It rain, boys, it rain.*
L. *Don't you stop a moment, boys.*	c. *It rain, boys, it rain.*
L. *'Twas on a blessed Sabbath day.*	c. *It rain, boys, it rain.*
L. *Here's a pretty preacher for you.*	c. *It rain, boys, it rain. . . .*⁶

One notorious Georgia planter, Bill Mattox, liked to tell of the song his slaves used to sing about him. Once when he heard someone singing it he asked the singer who was the subject of the song. The singer replied, "Marster, . . . ain't you nebber heared of old Bill Mattox! 'Dats de meanest man dey is!"⁷

Verbal play directed at a powerful figure is perhaps the keynote of African American expression. As Charles Joyner has noted, such lore emerges from the "African tradition of indirection" through which the doings of humans are commented upon in a condemnatory way.[8] The notion of employing song or rhyme for making oral commentary came directly from the various African cultures from which the slaves were taken. Singers attack pride and vainglorious pretension wherever they see it, especially in the doings of those in power.

Says John Miller Chernoff, surveying the literature on song making: "In general, African song lyrics . . . are especially concerned with moral and ethical pretensions in whatever form these unsociable qualities appear. . . . Such songs serve as vehicles of the mobilization of authoritative community values." Chernoff continues: "In many African societies, someone with a grievance may hire a songwriter to prepare a song which states the problem; a song may exceed the boundaries of social propriety without giving offense. . . ."[9] The musician, and especially the bardic improviser, is invested with moral authority within the compass of the songs, in which he must demonstrate "insight into deep issues" as he plays "certain moral roles which our society delegates to other professions."[10]

Many features of the performance of the corn-shucking captain seem to arise from the bards of sub-Saharan Africa. Here I draw on Karin Barber's insightful work on the Yoruba form of bardic allusion, the *oriki* praise poetry, for an understanding of how improvisation achieves its power.[11] By drawing on Barber's work, I am not arguing that the role of the captain was introduced into slave practice from Yoruba tradition; rather, that it had roots in bardic forms found throughout those areas of West and Central Africa from which the slave population originated.

Says Barber:

A corpus of oriki is a collection of discrete and disparate epithets belonging to or attributed to a subject, whether a person, a lineage, or an *orìsa* ("god") or an object or natural phenomenon. Oriki are accumulated over time, often composed by different people, in reference to different events or qualities. Individuals collect them over a lifetime; lineages and towns, over a much longer period. There is considerable latitude in the process of transmission, for although certain core elements are carefully retained, each successive performer, in the process of stringing the epithets together into a performance, selecting, varying and adding to them, puts his or her own stamp on the material. A present-day performance is thus a palimpsest of elements, which originated from different sources at different moments in time, each bearing the undetectable imprint of its individual history of transmission.[12]

Barber notes that the form is by its nature fragmentary, composed of elements strung together, yet autonomous both in memory and realization in performance. The oriki are recognizable both as allusive references from past singings, and as newly brought-together strings of honorifics. They are cryptic formulations of the characteristics of individuals, of occasions, and even of events, resembling riddles in their apparent obscurity, but understandable to the community. Many of them are associated with the most common and sacred stories of the community, the *itan,* and are understood by the community as allusions to these important doings. "The mode of being historical, then," Barber maintains, "is to trap and embalm a feature of social experience—sometimes an event, more often a personality, a communal characteristic or a value—in a dense, heavy and cryptic form."[13]

These praises live on the interest provided by their very disjunctive qualities; they surprise and delight in their random combinatory character. While every Yoruba knows some of these oriki, the great singers are entrusted with their power through their ability to combine them successfully.

All bardic composition centers not only on the deeds of the great warriors, though such epics are to be found in Africa, and in some abundance. The bard in this tradition is not commonly a singer of tales but an adept at verbal confrontation, operating through various forms of disjunction, or, as Barber calls them, "the never-resolved textual confrontations that are continually arising and falling behind as the performer moves on."[14] These songs of praise and complaint feed on disconnected images, promising only a never-ending sense of confrontation, scrutiny, a celebration of life through a danced-out scream.

Unlike a Western poet, the bard is not known for a finished product which encapsulates an experience or describes an event; rather, she or he is called upon to maintain a sense of openness of composition. As Barber puts it of the oriki singers, "lack of closure is highly desirable; the performer wants precisely to give the impression that she could go on forever, that . . . her own powers to invoke . . . are limitless."[15] This is eloquence in the oldest sense, drawing on the enormous funds of remembered deeds and memorable stories as they reflect on the problems of the present. The great singer, then, had a fund of fragmentary reference on which to draw, and asserted his or her rhetorical skills through stitching these fragments together, much as great orators draw on proverbs and other quotations of past wisdom, fables, and exemplary tales.

In sub-Saharan cultures, license to make such essentially *heated* compositions—individualized and personally directed songs—emerges from the midst of the more rational and considered situation of the surrounding group of singers displaying themselves through their responsiveness. That is, the call-and-response pattern maintains the balance of the group, countering the potential "heating up" of the bardic individualized commentary with the "cool," morally responsive answering energies of the chorus. Thus, as Robert Farris Thompson describes the stylistic contract being entered into by the community, "Call and response is a means of putting innovation and tradition, invention and imitation into amicable relationship with one another."[16] While the Yoruba oriki may involve primarily praise epithets, bards elsewhere in African traditional politics had a similar repertoire of satirical fragmentary devices as well. Parody, burlesque, and derision are all forms of heated discourse. Making fun of someone in song or dance is heated discourse; the community response cools down any unbalancing move such an invention might call forth.

At the corn shucking, the captain found that the event itself provided license for "singing the master," commenting on his presence in praise or jest.

> *Old marster shot a wild goose . . .*
> *Ju-ran-zie, hio ho.*
>
> *It wuz seben years fallin'.*
> *Ju-ran-zie, hio ho.*
>
> *It was seben years cookin'.*
> *Ju-ran-zie, hio ho.*
>
> *A knife couldn't cut it.*
> *Ju-ran-zie, hio ho.*
>
> *A fork couldn't stick it.*
> *Ju-ran-zie, hio ho.*[17]

The earliest observers noted how this event provoked singing at the expense of Old Master or his guests. One such reporter, James Kirke Paulding, observed: "The Negroes have a great number of songs, of their own composition, and founded on various little domestic incidents. . . ."[18] George Tucker's firsthand description of the shucking from late in the eighteenth century, in *The Valley of the Shenandoah*, points out that the slaves' songs are directed at the planter in "gratitude for his kindness, thanks for his goodness, . . . and, now and then, a little humorous satire."[19] Indeed, this stark alternation of praise and jest, topical comment and sentimental observation, is present in the actual texts reported in the shucking and other tasks.

Just as certain slaves came to be elected captain on the basis of their ability to improvise, others came to local renown for their skill in making fun of "Old Marster" by describing ways to get out of trouble with him. The ex-slave accounts are filled with accounts of the fear slaves experienced because of brutal encounters with members of the night patrol, called *patterrollers* by the slaves.

These night riders were as disliked by the masters as they were feared by the slaves, for they usurped certain property rights to the point of occasionally maiming or killing the masters' slave properties. As Gladys-Marie Fry has shown, the slave reminiscences contain a wealth of information about the ways in which individual slaves outwitted the night patrollers by sending warnings to each other, or figuring a way out if caught.[20] One slave song that served as a record of this encounter, in fact, was the ubiquitous "Run Nigger Run, Patterroller Catch You":

> *De sun am set—dis nigger am free,*
> *De colored gals he goes to see;*

> *I hear a voice cry, "Run, dad, fetch you!*
> *Run, nigger run, or de M.P.'ll catch you!!*[21]

This song was turned into an entertainment routine in which the slaves acted out the numerous ways they had developed to spread the word that the night riders were in the vicinity. Here is one example:

> *Run, nigger, run; patter-roller catch you;*
> *Run, nigger, run; it's almos' day;*
> *Run, nigger, run, patter-roller catch you;*
> *Run, nigger, run; you'd better get away.*
> *Dis nigger run; he run his best;*
> *Stuck his head in a hornet's nest.*
> *Jump'd de fence and run frew de paster;*
> *White man run, but nigger run faster.*[22]

and another:

> *I fooled Old Master seven years,*
> *Fooled the overseer three.*
> *Hand me down my banjo,*
> *And I'll tickle your bel-lee.*[23]

The earliest reports by white reporters dwell on how the song leaders seemed to improvise their songs, the anchoring effect of the refrain repeated by all, and in the way in which the singers passed on this role as they grew tired or ran out of invention. The first extensive description of a shucking comes from George Tucker's *Valley of the Shenandoah,* which though published in 1824, is situated in 1796. The "corn songs" which Tucker notices "have a small smack of poetry" to them. While not carried away by the songs' poetic features, he is moved by the musical abilities of the singers:

The air of these songs has not so much variety or melody, and requires not more flexibility of voice than they all possess, as they all join in the chorus. Some one . . . strikes up, and singly gives a few rude stanzas, sometimes in rhyme, and sometimes in short expressive sentences, while the rest unite in chorus, and this he continues, until some other improvisatore relieves him.[24]

For some, virtuosity of the lead singers consisted in their amazing ability to make sense and maintain metrical restraints while improvising. As one commentator put it, "it is curious to see how they get over any difficulty about adapting their unequal lines to the tune." He continues: "If the verse be too short, some word is dwelt upon until the measure of time is filled—if there be more than enough, the redundant syllables, sometimes to the number of three or four, are run rapidly through one note."[25]

Poet-observers of the shucking and other slave improvisations were fascinated by their freedom from the usual European notion of metrical constraints. Edgar Allan Poe seems to have been especially interested in the subject. A number of his correspondents sent him observations concerning the slaves' abilities to depart from regular meter in such a way that they seemed to create an "irregular" rhythm, but a rhythm that at least one observer, Beverley Tucker, noticed never hindered their ability to return to the rhythmic center of the activity: "The beat is capriciously irregular; there is no attempt to keep time to *all* the notes, that then it comes so pat and so distinct that the cadence is never lost." He depicted a flexible attitude toward meter, in which "the time of the bar must be the same, no matter how many notes are in it."[26] This kind of metrical adventurousness is more fully spelled out in singing and dancing unfettered by the call to shuck, and emerges in all its fullness in the slave dances held after the feast.

By aligning himself with metrical impulses, a leader encourages others to follow. He is not responsible for maintaining the beat once it has begun. For once established, the pulse proceeds on its own, and he and the others respond to it playfully but forcefully, pulling against it, bending it, commenting on its social and moral necessity.

This playful responsiveness encourages an experience of difference within a dynamically contained whole. Difference is played out through engaging with the dominant figure in the display by contesting him, even competing with him. This is most fully seen in the shucking contest, which in effect is not really an antagonistic encounter but an outgrowth of the creative tension between principals in song. Contrasts in voices animate the singing, giving it dramatic interest because of the contest involved.

To the white reporters, these contrasts made the event seem to explode with sound, for though the songs are recorded in European-style leader-response format when put into print, in fact the leader not only *gives out* the song, but as the rest come in with the chorus he sings over, under, and through their response. They support each other—he provides them with the initiating and sustaining move, they maintain the common meter and then move out and against it. They encourage each other to play against the central tune or text, commenting upon it in piping falsetto or guttural growl, interposing themselves as individuals even as each contributes to the overarching effect of the whole.

The song itself is hardly improvised. The captain draws upon songs which are traditional to the event or to accom-

panying work activities in general. Songs with the same refrains and tunes as corn shuckings are found in cotton-
loading and hoeing songs and sea shanties (including the
songs above, "Ju-ran-zie," "Long Time Ago," and "It Rain,
Boys, It Rain"). By drawing upon songs already known to
the group, the captain can rely upon the supporting voices
and launch his topical remarks without having to key them
in any way to the meaning of the refrain.

This dislocation between the refrain and the lines between
led a number of observers to comment on the apparent ran-
domness of the remarks. For instance, a "gentleman" who
sent back a report to the *The Family Magazine* in 1836 was
fascinated by the gap between the poetic capacities of the
leader and his ability to stick to the subject. He notes that
atop the corn pile "sat a person, selected for his skill in
improvisation," who sang out a line to which the others
responded with a chorus. However, he muses, "The poet
seemed to have no fixed object in view, but to sing. He passed
from one subject to another without regard to connexion."
He illustrates his point:

> *Oh, Jenny, gone to New-town*
> CHORUS: *Oh, Jenny gone away!*
> *She went because she wouldn't stay,*
>   *Oh, Jenny gone away!*
> *She run'd away, an' I know why,*
>   *Oh, Jenny gone away!*
> *For she went a'ter Jones's Bob,*
>   *Oh, Jenny gone away!*
> *Mr. Norton, good ole man,*
>   *Oh, Jenny gone away!*
> *Treats his niggers mighty well,*
>   *Oh, Jenny gone away!*[27]

And this song actually has a good deal more consistency of subject than many of the others reported from the corn shuckings. In this regard, Houston Baker's analysis of the way in which blues lyrics are constructed effectively describes the continuum from the great African bardic traditions of disjunctive improvisation through the corn shucking and other work songs and jigs, to the present: "Like a streamlined athlete's awesomely dazzling explosions of prowess, the blues . . . erupts, creating a . . . playful festival of meanings. Rather than a rigidly personalized form, . . . [these songs] offer . . . a nonlinear, freely associative nonsequential meditation. . . ."[28] The blues, like corn songs, draws on conventions of improvisation, tunes and rhetorical devices already recognizable to its responsive audiences. The use of such conventional patterns both ties the improviser to a form and liberates him or her to introduce new observations, often ones emerging from the immediate situation. Like the tra-la-la nonsense refrain, the repeated conventional lines in the responsive singing liberates the improviser to maintain the flow of song and to seize on matters that come to his or her notice for spontaneous comment.

In the corn shuckings, the captain was constantly being tested in terms of his ability to maintain his position, not only by the other captain but by other team members who could cut in; it was not regarded as any failure on his part when he gave up this role, for after all, he had propelled the performance into being, and established it. He could continue to lead and command, then, by giving over as well as calling out.

Indeed, in the classic formulation of the African responsive singing and dancing, once the master meter and melodic line is established, the leader may simply let the ensemble maintain itself while he falls silent, or simply grunts or laughs or finds some way other than simply singing words to maintain the flow of sound. This opens up the performance for the cutting move, in which somebody else takes over the melodic and metric leadership.

The virtuoso performer himself will call for responsive virtuosity on the part of others in the group. Indeed, a great performer will bring along a friend, sometimes called his *cutting man* or *cutty*, to ensure that someone will lead off.

The structure of the songs, pivoting about the repeated lines of the chorus, anchors the commentary of the leader, freeing him up to improvise upon whatever comes to his notice. This includes praise, scandalizing, and commenting on the activities taking place or soon to come. The improviser's muse is not restricted to specific topics in any order. His improvised lyrics indicate his ability to respond to the audience and to draw upon the present situation. The following song, for instance, clearly called on the singer to use the chorus, "shucking ob de corn," as a steadying refrain, while he took note of those present on that occasion.

> *Eugene hab good whiskey,*
> *Makes de niggers bery friskey,*
> > CHORUS: *shucking ob de corn.*
> *Oh, ho! de niggers jolly!*
> *See dah, de pretty Polly!*
> > CHORUS: *shucking ob de corn.*
> *Dar are Jake, he sits beside her,*
> *Will she hab dat big black spider?*
> > CHORUS: *shucking ob de corn.*
> *Jeff's so mad, he look like tunder—*
> *O-o-o-o! who dat hit me wid de corn day?*
> > CHORUS: *Jeff, he trew dat corn.*[29]

This technique of rhyming on the situation of those present, including the significant white folks sitting on the veranda, emerges in a number of reports.

> *Dere's Mr. Travers lub Miss Jinny;*
> *He thinks she is us good us any.*
> *He comes from church wid her er Sunday,*
> *Un don't go back ter town till Monday.*
> *Hooray, hooray, ho! [etc.]*

> *Dere's Mr. Lucas lub Miss Treser,*
> *Un ebery thing he does ter please her;*
> *Dey say dat 'way out in Ohio,*
> *She got 'er plenty uv de rhino.*
> *Hooray, hooray, ho! [etc.]*

> *Dere's Marster Charley lub Miss Bettie;*
> *I tell you what—he thinks her pretty;*
> *Un den dey mean ter lib so lordly,*
> *All at de Monner House at Audley,*
> *Hooray, hooray, ho! [etc.]*

> *Dere's Marster Wat, he lub Miss Susan;*
> *He thinks she is de pick un choosin';*
> *Un den dey gains de marriage station,*
> *He take her to de ole plantation.*
> *Hooray, hooray, ho! [etc.]*

> *Dere's Marster Clarence lub Miss Lizzy;*
> *Dressing nice, it keeps him busy;*
> *Un where she goes den he gallants her,*

Er riding on his sorrel prancer.
Hooray, hooray, ho! [etc.][30]

Alternatively, the song maker might, at one and the same time, describe some of the activity of the occasion while commenting ironically on the plight of the slaves:

Shuck corn, shell corn,
Carry corn to mill.
Grind de meal, gimme de husk;
Bake de bread, gimme de crus';
Fry de meat, gimme de skin;
And dat's de way to bring 'em in.[31]

Such songs, gently chiding the company of whites, seem to have been common.

De ladies in de parlor,
Hey, come a rollin' down—
A drinking tea and coffee;
Good morning ladies all.

De gemmen in de kitchen,
Hey, come a rollin' down—
A drinking brandy toddy;
Good morning, ladies all.[32]

The antiphonal structure of the corn-shucking song, then, not only embodies the very way in which the work is organized. By centering and coordinating the group's combined energies, the singing empowers the captain to speak for the group and to make whatever commentary he might wish to make on the proceedings, on slave life in general, and on the nonsensical goings-on he has noticed in Big House life.

One ex-slave, the Reverend I. M. Lowery, expresses the importance of these chosen leaders' role: "It was considered no little honor to be elected captain of a corn-shucking company." Lowery remembered that the captain wore his badge of office on his hat, "and everybody—white and colored—did him honor."[33] He points out that the election of the captains was the first order of business, and then "these captains selected their companies from the crowd present." Such military references are found in other descriptions too. Garnett Andrews, for instance, describes the antics of a "General" who moves at the top of the pile, "to encourage his soldiers."[34]

These practices maintained an African-style system for paying homage to leaders, including expressions of regard for them as military commanders, which was indicated by placing the captain within the power circle, elevating him through a physical and spiritual lifting technique, and amplifying his power through the responsive working and singing. The captain was both the leader of men and the exhorter, the singer of praise and scorn. Power of the big-voiced sort continued to be highly valued and used as the basis for choosing leaders within black communities.[35]

Mary Banks describes some of the ways in which honor was paid to the captain. She describes "an important conference" held by the home slaves before the event on her father's plantation concerning who should become the leaders. After some confabulation, one slave, Talbot, is chosen, "whose duties it will be to make a speech and conduct the ceremonies generally, though leading the singing is considered the most important feature of the occasion." Two of the other slaves then "conduct him to the place of honor" by joining their hands together to make a "cat-saddle" seat upon which Talbot sits. He is then "trotted around the pile three times, the carriers keeping time to a kind of monotonous dirge sung by the company," after which they stop, and "give a long swing with their arms" which provides him with "considerable impetus" which he translates into a jump into the center of the corn pile, accompanied by cheers. From this perch he proceeds to make a speech, demonstrating the "dignity of leadership, . . . the importance of his position."[36]

White observers saw this process as analogous to choosing up sides for a sport.[37] Inasmuch as the event puts into practice the slave sense of community, the election of the captains also revealed the existence of a system of leadership. Similar kinds of election celebrations are found in other slave and free Negro communities, in which the honor in the election for the slaves is clearly indicated. As William Van Deburg noticed of these elections, they were an indication that the captain was not so much "looked upon as the 'planter's man' . . . able to rule over them, [as] he was considered by the slaves to be one of them."[38]

Election to the position of captain seems to have been based in great measure on an ability to use words effectively.[39] Dr. John Wyeth describes how personal appeals might be made through the use of eloquence. "On these occasions extraordinary liberties were permissible, and not infrequently, as the white people of the premises were listening, the bold leader would by suggestion open the way for a holiday, or a barbeque, or a dance, or extra Christmas vacation, when they visited relatives and friends on other plantations. For example:

> *Marster an' Mistus lookin' might fine—*
> *Gwine to take a journey; gwine whar day gwine;*
> *Crab-grass a dyin', de sun in de west—*
> *Saturday's comin', nigger gwine to rest."*[40]

Eloquence and the ability to perform effectively were talents through which enabled slaves could raise themselves out of the ranks of the field hands, sometimes rising to positions of trust, both on and off the plantation. This possibility was clearer with the other central performers in the corn shucking, the fiddler and dance caller.

While the American square dance is in the main an elaboration of European contra or set dancing such as the reel or the quadrille, the practice of calling the figures in rhyme almost certainly originated on the plantations. As John Szwed and Morton Marks noticed, "The dance calls . . . were different from their European counterparts: more than mere directions, they took the shape of rhymed 'raps,' adding rhythmic subtlety and humor that helped the spirit of both the dancer and band alike."[41]

Such calling emerged from the practice, exhibited most clearly in the ring play, of singing about the movements while carrying them out, as if the dancing instruction was both coded into the song and used to amplify the dances' effects. Szwed and Marks relate this, in general, to the "Black square dance- and reel-calling" which, they argue, "are part of the Afro-American dance instruction tradition which extends from 'Ballin' the Jack' to 'The Twist' and beyond [songs which tell the dancers what to do next] . . . at least partly rooted in the older tradition in which African master drummers signal and direct dancers."[42]

The planter-journalist David Barrow, in his article on the

Georgia corn shucking, tied the introduction of the caller to the black style of performing the cotillion: "The "caller-out," though of less importance than the fiddler, is second to no other. He not only calls out the figures, but explains them through the performance." Barrow notes his abilities: "He is never at a loss. 'Genman to de right! . . ."[43]

On this point the ex-slave accounts of the dance after the shucking are even more instructive. "There were two fiddlers amongst us. . . . They'd have a big barbecue for folks from miles around and had coffee and chicken and turkey and dancing and fiddling all night. Come daybreak they were just going good. Us niggers danced back to the quarters and called:

> All eight balance, and all eight swing,
> All left allemond, and right hand grind,
> Meet your partner and promenade, eight,
> Then march till you come straight.
> First lady out to couple on the right,
> Swing Mr. Adam and swing Miss Eve,
> Swing old Adam before you leave,
> Don't forget your own—you you're home.[44]

The runaway slave Solomon Northup gives a full rendering of the privileges accorded a fiddler in his autobiography. Of fiddling, he says, "It introduced me to the great houses—relieved me of many days' labor in the field—supplied me with conveniences for my cabin—with pipes and tobacco, and extra pairs of shoes." More than this, it provided him with a name, a place of honor in the plantation community among both slaves and masters, making him friends among people who otherwise would never have noticed him.[45]

Northup's experience was by no means unique. As the scholar of plantation life Leslie Owens pointed out, "Fiddlers and songsters whose skills had been sharpened by practice in the quarters were in demand at social gatherings, playing at these events gained them privileges they might otherwise not have had."[46] Dena Epstein amplifies this: "These obscure musicians at times achieved what would have been a professional status if their earnings had remained in their own hands. Many of them earned a reputation for excellence that extended for miles around."[47]

The music that was being played was not African, though the tunes were made uniquely Afro-American as they were rendered by slaves.[48] The fiddler played a European instrument, bending it to his own aesthetic purpose, yet working within the constraints of the intensely melodic as well as metrically layered tradition. The caller, even when he erupted into rhymes, developed upon essentially European figures, while mixing in some African American turns. However, both the captain and the fiddler-caller were placed in a position to mimic and call out whites in their audience, and thus to make jokes at their expense for the slaves' pleasure.

Thus the corn shucking, along with the Saturday night dances and the other permitted entertainments, provided an occasion in which the slaves not only could enjoy themselves but were encouraged to do so in their own style. In the process, traditional features of African eloquence and improvisation in speech, song, and dance provided the basis for the development of an Afro-American aesthetic system which has been maintained to this day.

That whites were drawn to these occasions is manifest. That they themselves began to imitate their slaves at play is also clear. To explain this imitation will be the burden of the final chapter.

CHAPTER SIX

Powerful Imitations

The slave holidays left traces on American life that went far beyond the corn-shucking accounts. From the observation and imitation of such practices emerged the minstrel show, with its blend of eccentric costumes, blackface makeup, and a musical ensemble that included fiddles, banjos, tambourines, and bones. The minstrel show was such a popular form of entertainment from the time of its emergence in the 1840s and its theatrical vocabulary so caught the American imagination that it has persisted to this day. One can see this lineage run from the wizard oil show, vaudeville entertainments, in Mardi Gras and the Philadelphia Mummers Parade, even to radio and television shows as diverse as "Amos and Andy," "Grand Ole Opry," "The Jack Benny Show," "The Ed Sullivan Show," and "Hee-Haw."

The examples are endless. The black skiffle and jug bands of the early twentieth century were descendants of minstrel music, and (just to show how far out the historical string can run) the Beatles began their career as an English skiffle band. So, too, the mountain string band emerged from the blackface stage, and in its wake, the bluegrass band: making them white imitations of a blackface imitation of a plantation musical group.[1]

The minstrel or blackface show was more than an attempt to depict the playful doings in the plantation yard and the slave quarters. It was confected from a great number of theatrical traditions, using its own rendering of the rags-and-tatters costume and the sometimes blackened visage characteristic of (among other such figures) Harlequin in the commedia dell'arte. Indeed as the historian of the minstrel stage Robert Toll has shown in *Blacking Up*, the blackface show brought together elements of many entertainment forms during the earliest period of its development after 1825, and continued to assimilate other theatrical impulses throughout the remaining hundred years in which it was the preeminent American form of music hall entertainment.[2]

In the early years of this country, being on the move was a fact of life, and this was reflected in the development of various kinds of traveling entertainments. Theatrical circuits arose which sent performers to even the smallest frontier outposts. The nineteenth century was an era of touring performers as well as traveling variety shows, a time when the greatest Shakespearean actors, operatic virtuosos and other musicians, and ballet dancers made their fame and significant fortunes touring in the new republic.[3] It was also the age that developed the variety show, burlesque, the freak show and other rarees, the circus, and touring historical dioramas. And of these performances, none was more popular nor more quintessentially American than the minstrel show.

Why the blackface entertainment arose at precisely the period in which slavery was the center of national confrontation will never cease to challenge observers of American culture, just as it did during its heyday on the American stage. The most positive interpretations underscore the fact that observers of that period recognized the form as a truly indigenous development: for example, the antislavery spokesman Horace Greeley put it in the same cultural position as the development of opera in Italy, both being expressions of "the peculiar characteristics" of native genius.[4] Many of those seeking to identify unique American cultural forms, such as Mark Twain, Walt Whitman, and Margaret Fuller, recorded their enthusiasm for this indigenous development, a position satirized by J. K. Kinnard, the " 'Salt Fish Dinner' Correspondent" of *The Knickerbocker Magazine,* even while he limned many unique features of this form of entertainment.[5]

The corn-shucking reports formed part of the body of scenes and sketches of plantation life that became an important feature of the literary and dramatic life of the new nation. Not only in diaries and travelers' reports, but in novels and on the stage, Americans found the plantation South a compelling *mise en scène.* This popular interest had already produced, by the end of the first quarter of the nineteenth century, the beginnings of the blackface minstrel entertainment. The fully developed blackface show emerged in the middle of the nineteenth century, featuring "authentic" slave performances brought from the plantation yard into the theater.

It is tempting to regard this movement of the plantation yard into the center of our theatrical landscape as a simple derogation of the plantation as a place of backward people living in rustic simplicity. However, the blackface show was much more than a theater of nostalgia. It represented an ardent effort to bring to the stage studied imitations of slave styles of singing and dancing and celebrating. In so doing, it brought to the nation's attention the very concept of racial and cultural difference, making black-style expression into a vocabulary of social commentary. How else could a form of entertainment be interpreted when everyone on the stage but one performer, Mr. Interlocutor, was portrayed as black, and when he continually played straight man to those portraying slave—and thus was often the butt of laughter?

Onstage, the position of the slave was apparently depoliticized. The blackface figure seemed to ratify antiblack sentiment by presenting blacks as happy but worthless figures, a perspective represented onstage by Mr. Interlocutor. But in drawing on slave form of expression, the blackface entertainment undercut such an apologist political position by celebrating the abilities of blacks to create and to entertain. And most importantly, it continually humanized the situation of slave life even if it created the baleful image of the happy and frivolous slave. In this process, the minstrel-stage entertainment confounded American notions of self and other, for the very success of the form placed American actors of all sorts in the position of agreeing to play black even as the system of enslavement was being subjected to moral scrutiny.[6]

In the middle of the Civil War, a Northern performer described the minstrel show as "our only original American Institution," knowing that it had already been accepted as such in England and throughout Europe. As Toll observed, "To some mid-nineteenth century Americans, it was 'The only true American drama' or an 'American National Opera' even while, to most observers, it could easily be derogated as simply 'nigger minstrelsy.' "[7]

Mark Twain brought his complicated and unreflexive response to blackface to bear in his autobiography, referring to it as setting "a stand and a summit to whose rarefied altitude . . . other forms of musical art may not hope to reach." He continued: "[T]he first Negro musical show I ever saw . . . must have been in the early forties. It was a new institution. In our village of Hannibal we had not heard of it before and it burst on us as a glad and stunning surprise." He went on to describe the event in detail, including its gag men or end men with their "coal-black hands and faces" and costumes which were "an extravagant burlesque of the clothing worn by the plantation slave of that time; not that the rags of the poor slave were burlesqued, for that would not have been possible; . . . it was the form and color of his dress that was burlesqued."

These plantation figures played against Mr. Interlocutor, a figure "clothed in the faultless evening costume of the white society gentleman, [who] used a stilted, courtly, artificial and painfully grammatical form of speech." The proceedings were structured around the contrast between the extravagant rags and wild gestures and slanging of the end men and the hypercorrect dress and speech of this master of ceremonies. As Twain described it, Mr. Interlocutor not only introduced the topics which the end men would joke about, but he organized the proceedings in such a manner that early on the gag men would have a loud argument: "a delightful jangle of assertion and contradiction . . . a quarrel [which] would grow louder and louder and more and more energetic and vindictive, and the two would rise and approach each other, shaking fists and instruments and threatening bloodshed." This figure, "the courtly middleman," would then find himself caught between them, and would act the peacemaker, urging them "to observe all the proprieties—but all in vain, of course." After a pitched battle, "the house shrieking with laughter all the while, at this happy and accurate imitation of the usual and familiar Negro quarrel, . . . the pair of malignants would gradually back away from each other."[8]

In the minstrel show, jokes would fly, and the middleman would continue to attempt to maintain order. While the master of ceremonies seemed to instigate the activity, his authority was constantly tested, not only in the fights between the blackface figures, but in the jokes that were often directed at his starchy obtuseness to the end men's witty turns of phrase. The audience laughed as much at Mr. Interlocutor's inability to control things as it did at the fractured speeches and the eccentric dances of the end men. Occasionally, a song would break out, and perhaps a solo dance, with the other members of the troupe playing the banjo or tambourine or bones which they had carried onstage. At the end of this virtuoso exhibition, the whole group would form a ring and do the strut or cakewalk, aping the walk of the high-born, breaking out into a boisterous finale which brought down the curtain on the first act.

Clearly, the minstrel show developed from outsiders' observations of the corn-shucking event and other slave holidays. For not only were the instruments, the songs, and the dances said by the performers to have been learned from observation and imitation of slaves, but the mock fights which the middlemen tried to control projected the very details of the plantation social order which could be seen in the accounts of the corn shucking. The dominant position of the white man was constantly subverted in the humor of those dressed in elegant rags delivering their lines in elevated imitations of black talk. The minstrel show at its inception elaborated the principles of imitation already in place on the plantation and elsewhere in the South where masters and their slaves were found together.

In the midst of the Civil War, on August 2, 1862, Mary Chesnut chuckled to her diary that that night at a party, "Senator Semmes of Louisiana danced a hoedown for us: a Negro corn-shucking, heel-and-toe fling with a grapevine twist and all." Everyone gathered was able to put aside the cares of the war for the moment: "Martha Levy applauded heartily and cried, 'The Honorable Senator from Louisiana has the floor.' "[9] By this time, playing black was one of the conventional ways in which whites might amuse each other on social occasions of many sorts. It is reasonable to assume from Mrs. Chesnut's diary that the senator was simply drawing on the vocabulary of the blackface minstrel entertainments. For by 1862, this form of variety theatrical entertainment had been fashionable as a popular entertainment in the North and South for over fifteen years. Moreover, individual white performers in blackface had been carrying on such stage displays for three times that long.

But the phenomenon of white Southerners imitating blacks in performance predates even the earliest development of the blackface entertainments. The earliest reports of whites dancing in slave style, in fact, come from the period of the American Revolution. And, by the mid-1820s, when such imitations first appeared on the stage through the development of blackface entertainments, the slave owners themselves and their families had been carrying on in a similar manner for their own entertainment for some time.

Not only did slaves provide the music for the entertainments of Old Master and his family and friends, but the planters included imitations of slaves dancing their distinctive jigs at the end of their cotillions. In one report, Nicholas Cresswell, a visitor to Virginia in the mid 1770s, noted that at the end of the Twelfth Night Ball he attended "[a] couple gets up and begins to dance a jig (to some Negro tune) others comes and cuts them out. . . ." Cresswell regards the practice as barbaric, "more like a Bacchanalian dance than one in polite company."[10]

Others noted these imitations of black jigs at this period, including one much-reprinted account by Andrew Burnaby of a similar fancy ball in Virginia: "Towards the close of an evening, . . . it is usual to dance jigs," a practice originally initiated in couple formation but which calls for individuals cutting in. Then Burnaby noticed that "the dances seemed without any method or regularity," though he proceeded to describe their method and their regularity:

. . . a gentleman and a lady stand up, and dance about the room, one of them retiring, the other pursuing, then perhaps meeting in an irregular fantastical manner. After some time, another lady gets up, and then the first lady must sit down, she being, as the term is, cut out; the second lady acts the same part which the first did, till somebody cuts her out. The gentlemen perform in the same manner.[11]

If whites were imitating blacks, this was hardly a radical departure from what court dancers had been doing for some time in England and elsewhere in Europe: adapting "country" (that is, peasant) dance forms into more genteel formulations for use in the court and in other upper-class company.

The very vocabulary of the slave jig bespeaks an opening up of the senses for whites, whose dances are otherwise described in terms of elegance achieved and order enacted with grace. The jig introduces a dizzying quality for the dancers and a means of carrying apparently nonsensical virtuoso dancing by individuals. As performed by slaves and imitated by young master and mistress, the jig in this view, was a kind of show-off dance, derived in good part from the spirit of the contests found at slave dances.

Here a feature of white imitations of blacks first asserts itself, a feature which has remained a part of "mainstream American" culture for a very long time. Through this imitation, whites seized license to dance alone, each dancer simply responding to the rhythms of the music. This is a white interpretation of the "apart-playing" of the slave ring play or dance, without adopting or recognizing the black convention in which the dancer at the center of these show-off occasions relied on the support of the circle of dancers.

The imitations went both ways within the plantation world. While the white dancers found themselves freed up by dancing the black jig, the slaves imitated their masters' movements in a different manner. "Us slaves watch the white folks' parties when the guests danced a minuet and then paraded in a grand march," reported an ex-slave eighty years and more after the fact. "Then we'd do it too, but we used to mock 'em every step. Sometimes the white folks noticed it but they seemed to like it," she went on.[12]

During the antebellum period the pattern was that individual whites learned to imitate a slave style of dancing, and developed it into a virtuoso routine; while the slaves *took off*[13] on their masters as a group. Not until the 1840s did the blackface groups build the larger group effects of the slave entertainments into the minstrel show, when four "Ethiopian" blackface virtuosos performed together as "The Virginia Minstrels."

Blackface minstrelsy, by legend, had begun twenty years before, with studied imitations of specific black figures by white actors developing their stage routines. The first of these, Thomas D. Rice, while on tour in 1828, reportedly observed an old Negro groom dancing in Cincinatti. From this man he learned not only the tune that was to make his reputation, "Jump Jim Crow," but a series of dance gestures that may have been dictated by the groom's physical disabilities. With his right shoulder deformed and his left leg gnarled, the old man did an eccentric dance while singing "Weel about and turn about and do just so; / Ebery time I weel about I jump Jim Crow."[14]

Rice costumed himself in garb borrowed from a free Negro porter who worked out of the hotel in which he was staying in Pittsburgh. As legend had it, the porter, Cuff, "who won a precarious subsistence by letting his open mouth serve as a mark for boys to pitch pennies into, at three paces" as well as carrying trunks to and from the riverboat landing, was prevailed upon to come to the theater with Rice and lend him his clothes for the performance. "Rice, habited in [the] old coat forlornly dilapidated, with a pair of shoes composed equally of patches . . . , and wearing a coarse straw hat in a melancholy condition of rent and collapse over a dense black wig of matted moss, waddled into view." When he sang and danced as Jim Crow, "the effect was electric." Meanwhile, Cuff was sitting backstage in his semidressed state, and he heard the whistle of the next steamer. Trying to get the attention of the performer so that he might retrieve his clothes and get about his usual business, he was finally forced to thrust his head through the curtains and say, "Massa Rice, Massa Rice, must have my clo'se . . . STEAMBOAT'S COMIN'!!" As another chronicler of minstrelsy put it, "The incident was the touch, in the mirthful experience of that night, that passed endurance." In fact, as he reported it, the routine caused such an excess of laughter that the show could not proceed.[15] Rice developed this scene and character into a set piece for the stage, and went on to receive international renown for the portrayal.

The chance encounter with a specific black person in a specified place was a commonplace story for blackface performers to tell as a way of explaining how they first developed their comic characters and routines.[16] Even before "Jump Jim Crow" made it onto the stage, the first great American-born actor, Edwin Forrest, developed such an encounter with a Negro into a dramatic sketch. As Constance Rourke relates the story in her classic *American Humor:*

In the early '20's, . . . the southern plantation Negro was drawn on the stage in Cincinnati by young Edwin Forrest. Made up for the part, Forrest strolled through the streets, where an old Negro woman mistook him for a Negro whom she knew; he persuaded her to join him in an impromptu scene that evening. This little sketch seemed unimportant, but Forrest had studied the Negro character; he inaugurated a tradition for faithful drawing.[17]

Forrest, like Rice and other stage personalities of that generation, was primarily interested in developing memorable stage characters, whether because of their moral depth or their eccentric comic potential. As the American variety theater developed, eccentric characters made their way more and more onto the stage, eventuating in the imitation of a number of comic arguments, speeches, and specific Afro-American dances. In this way, the ring shout, the buck and wing, the essence (the ancestor of the soft-shoe, and the turkey trot, among others, were introduced as popular dance forms.[18] Further humorous sketches were developed from encounters with street vendors and workers on the levees along the Mississippi, as well as from observing slaves in the quarters on plantations.

One minstrel performer, Ben Cotton, argued for the authenticity of his act thus: "I used to sit with them in front

of the cabins, and we would start the banjo twang-
ing . . . their voices would ring out in the quiet night air in
their weird melodies. They did not understand me. I was the
first white man they had seen who sang as they did; but we
were brothers for the time being and were perfectly happy."[19]
More dramatically, the blackface entertainer Eugene Strat-
ton, known as the "Whistling Coon," upon being asked
about a particularly beautiful tune he had sung, said, "You
see that young man over there? . . . He was a slave, and the
song you have just heard was one they used to sing upon
their plantation. He hummed it over to me and I have set it
to music."[20]

These are tales of random encounters by entertainers who
themselves were peripatetic outsiders. The authenticity of
the material itself became an important feature of presen-
tation for these singers and dancers wearing blackface. Often
Irish, and therefore subject to marginal status themselves
in mid-nineteenth-century American life, these entertainers
found in black culture an abundance of stylized ways of
acting, singing, and dancing by which they could establish
themselves as performers.

By the end of the nineteenth century such authenticating
stories had become almost conventional, so often had the
theme been embellished upon by the most successful writers
of the time: Joel Chandler Harris, Lafcadio Hearn, Mark
Twain, and George Washington Cable. All of them could
make righteous claims to have learned major portions of
their repertoires from specific black performers.

Consider the case of Harris, the bastard son of an Irish
itinerant field worker and a Georgia seamstress, who was
throughout his life painfully bashful and extraordinarily ret-
icent about his personal life. Yet he was far from timid in

making claims for his ability to collect the Br'er Rabbit tales from the lips of blacks: "Curiously enough, I have found few negroes who will acknowledge to a stranger that they know anything of these legends," he avers. "Yet to relate one of these stories is the surest road to their confidence and esteem. In this way . . . I have been enabled to collect and verify the folklore included in this volume."[21]

Harris's friend Mark Twain walked this road as well. An important part of his public persona had to do with his Southern forebears and his personal connection with his maternal uncle's plantation. In his public appearances, he read a number of the Uncle Remus tales, at first giving credit solely to Harris's researches, but later resuscitating a figure from his childhood, Uncle Dan'l, who he remembered as telling the very same tales as Harris reported in his books: "I know the look of Uncle Dan'l's kitchen as it was on the privileged nights, when I was a child," Twain recalled, "and I can see the firelight playing on their faces and the shadows flickering on the walls . . . , and I can hear Uncle Dan'l telling the immortal tales which Uncle Remus Harris was to gather into his books and charm the world with. . . ."[22] Eventually, Twain was to admit that the slave suffered from something like lockjaw, but his repertoire grew more immense as slave lore became ever more popular as material. Uncle Dan'l's repertoire came to include the spirituals as sung by the Fisk Jubilee Singers, whom Twain met when touring Switzerland.[23] Throughout the nineteenth century, then, a brush with slaves at play and an absorption of elements of their lore from direct observation became a way of establishing one's credentials as a vernacular artist, whether on the minstrel stage, the lecturer's platform, or the written page.

The first two stock characters who embodied the essence of the minstrel stage entertainment were stage eccentrics, outsized figures derived from observation but rendered in outlandish garb and grotesque gesture. These were Zip Coon, the Dandy, and Jim Crow, the black bumpkin, the former from the city, the latter from the plantation.

One writer who was both fascinated and repelled by such figures and by the national and international appeal of black-face minstrelsy was J. K. Kinnard, the " 'Salt Fish Dinner' Correspondent" to *The Knickerbocker Magazine*. Detailing the requisite factors that would go into the formation of a national literature, Kinnard emphasized that "poetry should smack strongly of the locality in which it is written." Tongue in cheek, he suggests that therefore young poets should be kept at home to ensure that their productions preserve their sense of place. But, he insists, we already have such bards in our midst, "James Crow and Scipio Coon." "What class," he asks, "is most secluded from foreign influences, receives the narrowest education, . . . and mixes least with any class above itself? Our Negro slaves to be sure!"

He notices a further irony: "Messrs. Crow and Coon could not be spared from the hoe, but they might be introduced to the world by proxy!" That is, the blackface minstrel show was but an imitation of slave performances, their speechmaking, singing and dancing styles, and an enactment of their most private scenes of courtship and the breaking up of their families. "And thus it came to pass, that while James Crow and Scipio Coon were quietly at work on their masters' plantations, all unconscious of their fame, the whole civilized world was resounding with their names."[24] But, in fact, Jim and Zip's names were well known on the plantation.

The ironies of the situation were not lost on the slaves themselves. As one ex-slave, Isaac Williams, exclaimed in discussing the many troupes of white minstrels, the claim of providing "exact delineations of negro character and plantation sketches and scenes . . . is like a counterfeit bill to a real one." He went into just how plantation life gave birth to the set of scenes that found their way to the minstrel hall stage: "When our masters had company staying with them, they would often collect all their slaves for a general jubilee frolic," Williams explained. Banjo pickers would be called upon to "play all their fancy jigs and liveliest tunes for the jolly dance." Everyone from the quarters would be put on exhibit, "little boys and girls, old men and women, as well as the maidens and youths. . . ." The best performers would be given their special due, and then everyone would join "in a grand run around, all-off-to-Georgia style, and twenty-five cents was given to the best dancer of a regular break down."[25]

While it is true that the minstrel shows were a white rendering of slave life, there were some black performers who took part in them. The most famous of these was the black dancer "Juba" (the stage name of William Henry Lane), who not only performed on the same stage as blackface entertainers but received top billing. With four white minstrel men, Juba was featured in a show in New York City in 1845.

There he came to the notice of Charles Dickens, who describes his dancing in some detail in his *American Sketches* of 1842. He begins: "The corpulent black fiddler, and his friend who plays the tambourine, stamp upon the boarding of the small raised orchestra in which they sit, and play a lively measure." He proceeds to describe the regular dancing

which occurs in this place: "Five or six couples come upon the floor, marshalled by a lively young Negro, who is the wit of the assembly, and the greatest dancer known. He never leaves off making queer faces, and is the delight of all the rest, who grin from ear to ear incessantly." The dancing proceeds with a good deal of courting behavior on the part of the young dancers. "Every gentleman sits as long as he likes to the opposite lady, and the opposite lady to him, and all are so long about it that the sport begins to languish, when suddenly the lively hero dashes in to the rescue. Instantly the fiddler grins, and goes at it tooth and nail." Juba brings "new energy in the tambourine; new laughter in the dancers; new brightness in the very candles." He goes through his extensive repertoire of styles: "Single shuffle, double shuffle, cut and cross-cut, snapping his fingers, rolling his eyes, turning in his knees, presenting the backs of his legs in front, spinning about on his toes and heels like nothing but the man's fingers on the tambourine." The effects are dazzling, for he seems to dance "with two left legs, two right legs, two wooden legs, two wire legs, two spring legs— all sorts of legs and no legs—what is this to him? And in what walk of life, does man ever get such stimulating applause as thunders about him, when, having danced his partner off her feet, and himself too, he finishes by leaping gloriously on the bar-counter and calling for something to drink, with the chuckle of a million counterfeit Jim Crows, in one inimitable sound."[26]

With his customary insouciance, Dickens casts light not only on the dancer but on the imitational process taking place in this theatrical entertainment. If he underscores the grotesque features of the costumes, the gestures, the dance itself, this is not simply in reaction to the presence of black entertainers, but reflects the degree to which the conventions of the minstrel stage had affected the ways in which black performers presented themselves.

As an indication of how complicated the problem of authenticity and imitation had become by this time, the playbill announced that Juba would "give correct Imitation dances of all the principal Ethiopian Dancers in the United States. . . . After which he will give an imitation of himself— and then you will see the vast difference between those that have heretofore attempted dancing and this WONDERFUL, YOUNG MAN." Juba, in his short career, made a triumphal

tour of New England along with the other most famous jig dancer of his age, John Diamond. Throughout this tour they staged dance contests like cutting competitions, with Juba winning regularly.[27]

Juba came to prominence during that period of entertainment history when individuals continued to be featured in variety entertainments. In February 1843, a significant shift occurred in the minstrel tradition as four blackface performers—Billy Whitlock, Frank Pelham, Dan Emmett, and Frank Brower—pooled their talents, billing themselves as "The Virginia Minstrels." Says Toll of this development, "To improve the coordination of the show they arranged their chairs in a semi-circle, with the tambourine and bones players on the ends; to give the performance the aura of a real party and to provide continuity, they interspersed comic repartee between their otherwise unconnected songs and dances."[28] All that remained was the introduction of Mr. Interlocutor as the sober middleman in these proceedings, for the form of the blackface show to be fully worked out.[29]

Thus the conventions of the performance developed from the variety format to one with a more dramatic buildup. The performers all trooped onto the stage, led by Mr. Interlocutor. When they were assembled, he would say, "Gentlemen, be seated," and then would instigate a comic routine, introducing the performers as they took their solo spots. All of this culminated, in the last portion of the show, in the performers' breaking out of the semicircle to form a ring for the great walkaround, strut, or cakewalk. This last was the seal that a real frolic was being reenacted, one ostensibly reflecting the way things were done in the plantation yard itself.

A number of other Afro-American entertainers became well known for their minstrel portrayals, but none was as important as Juba. After the Civil War, several troupes of black performers endeavored to represent plantation life realistically, such as Haverly's Minstrels and the various groups featuring Billy Kersands. These troupes made claims for the authenticity of their representation by referring to the shows as "Plantation Pastimes," "Plantation Revels," or "Plantation Frolics." Or, as one touring group of white the-

atrical performers advertised themselves, they featured the
"Sports and Pastimes of the Virginia Colored Race."[30]

If the advertisements for the shows are any gauge, after
the Civil War there was an ever-greater attempt to reenact
these scenes with an actual assemblage of rag-headed and
banjo-playing cottonpickers and corn shuckers. At that time,
"Uncle Tom's Cabin" had become a set piece in the variety
show repertoire, and it was surrounded by scenes of plantation revelry purporting to be realistically rendered.

Both the corn-shucking accounts and the minstrel show
dramatized plantation scenes and styles, elaborating upon
the idea of the American South as the locus of pastoral
simplicity. They built upon the region's image of itself as a
land of plenty. They contrasted figures playing the roles of
black men and white. The corn-shucking accounts made by
whites are full of the same sense of wonderment and amusement at the exotic performance behaviors. Conventional
stage representations of plantation life first appeared on he
minstrel stage, then in traveling shows such as *Uncle Tom's
Cabin* and, finally, late in the nineteenth century, at national
and international expositions.[31]

In the records of the corn shucking and other slave holidays one can recognize the genesis of the process of appropriation which was to become the dominant strand of American popular culture. The blackface entertainment developed the beginnings of a system of encouraging strangeness for its own sake, within the bounds of an entertainment. In this system African Americans have remained cast as the strangers in our midst, the exotics. But as contemporary black performers continue to assert and to remind us, blacks will not simply take a place as entertainers in American life. In their performances, as in the performances of their slave forebears, they remain active moral commentators on life as they see it taking place before them.

It is not necessary to see the corn shucking and the accompanying performance styles as reflections of anything other than cultural resistance and resiliency. This is not a record of African Americans' retaining any special kind of naturalness nor some direct access to deeper truths. African American singers, preachers, and bards do not see American life more clearly than anyone else. In every culture figures develop who compose and perform on the basis of received conventions and agreed-upon fictions. Afro-American performances are just as cliché-ridden and as limited by stereotypic portrayals as anyone else's. But one of the realities of American life is that certain features of African American performance style will remain strange and alluring to those outside the culture. Not least among such features is the making of hard social commentary on recurring problems of life, often through cutting and breaking techniques—contentious interactions continually calling for a change of direction, with alterations expressed in rhythmic, tonal, textural, and other kinds of figures.

Simply fighting through to understandings of the primordial exuberance and the historical continuities of African American culture unlocks a message of cultural vitality in the face of adversity that should provide food for the soul for some time. We do not have to make heroes out of the purveyors of this tradition. It should suffice to give them honor and applause.

Coda:
Freedom Mighty Sweet

To the extent that the hands enjoyed and anticipated corn shuckings and the other slave holidays, it can be argued that these events were successful attempts on the part of benevolent planters to rationalize the continuation of slavery in the face of pressures for manumission. The plantation records do in fact tell of the surprise of many slaveholders on finding that their hands left them as soon as the opportunity arose. Twenty-five years after emancipation, the Southern writer James Lane Allen remembered the following exchange with a continuing sense of wonder:

Christmas was . . . the time of holiday merrymaking, and the "Ketchin' marster and mistiss Christmus gif' " was a great feature. One morning an aged couple presented themselves.

"Well, what do you want for your Christmas gift?"

"Freedom! Mistiss."

"Freedom! Haven't you been as good as free for the last ten years?"

"Yaas, mistiss; but—freedom mighty sweet!"[1]

What could explain this major misapprehension, and how do similar misunderstandings in the same form repeatedly continue to arise?

The pattern is clear at least in its outlines: African Americans have found that the integrity of their sense of community and self-value is sustained through celebrations which knit together the past and the present, and which use the deepest traditions of African behavior to articulate their sense of mutual engagement in life. This ethos emerges clearly in prayer meetings and religious services, but is equally present on nonsectarian occasions as well, from rap sessions to rap concerts. Performers and entrepreneurs of every color see the power of these improvisatory practices and recognize the viability—and salability—of the forms. And so the African American community continues to maintain not only the great tradition of the praise- and scandal-singing wordsmith but the approach to performance that is morally informed and which draws upon the participation of all present.

Performers in this tradition know that they may be playing to two audiences simultaneously—the black community and the white hipsters or weekend trippers. They are willing to imitate others as well as to hold themselves up for imitation. Black performers constantly recognize that the very performance that is conventional within the black community will be seen as strange, as pleasurably exotic to the hipster. Thus they operate out of a kind of double consciousness, knowing that they are called upon to present an image which will be interpreted as exotic to the outside world and not to the blacks in the audience. Furthermore, the exotic features, simply because of their cultural strangeness, not only fulfill the stereotypical images held by whites, but are appropriated

by the hipster segment of the audience, whose stylistic imitations isolate the style from its community-reinforcing context and make it available for commodification and public consumption. Moreover, the black performer knows that under those marketplace conditions, the role of playing black is available to the singer or dancer, for him and the hipsters in his audience to experience a sense of cultural liberation.

The cultural critic cannot discount these motives in coming to an understanding of why whites have imitated blacks in so many ways over the last few centuries. The motives of the Southern white dancers who engaged in the black jig at the end of their formal dances are not that removed from those of the white bluesman, rapper, or break dancer.

Indeed, the cultural dynamic driving American public culture produces aficionados of stylistically alternative performances—like the "moldy figs" who followed traditional jazz or the hipsters who identified themselves with beebop style; individuals who in their tasks or performances adopt a distinctly Afro-American style. The very existence of such followers depends upon the maintenance of these styles even as new ones are created by performers within black communities.

But the proceedings when the community comes together in celebration, cannot be made available for exploitation. In the heated-up performances of the great black bardic singers, musicians, and dancers, the technique of the breakdown or breakout developed a stylistic turn which carried the participants to another state of being. Whenever this occurred (and still occurs) the style became more deeply African— more layered with alternative metrical pulses, more highly textured and colored, and emotionally more engaged.

That such intensification of the celebratory experience

occurred in the corn shuckings can hardly be doubted. By their own account, the onlookers witnessed and were dazzled by the transformation, even if they often were mystified or even appalled by it. Pulling together the many voices, meters, styles, and enthusiasms of the participants stunned the onlookers, who were forced to recognize the totality of the experience even as they could not always comprehend its character.

The African American genius begins, then, with the ability to draw into a performance almost any instrument, any object, any stylized gesture. This technique of festive incorporation was a power move no less than those developed by the pageant state processions in Elizabethan England and throughout Europe in the Renaissance. Just as those states consolidated the vocabulary of power of the peoples they conquered and colonized, so in the African and Afro-American techniques of festive display, power objects and styles are represented, imitated, paraded forth, and fused within a larger whole to demonstrate the protean capabilities of the representative performers. If the theater-state makes the pageantry subordinate to the larger political and economic concerns of those who govern in the Western world, in African American life the festival is transformed into a world unto itself, in which the celebration of community wholeness is manifested primarily within the performance or ritual.

Afro-American festive drama draws on the vocabulary of the economic and political spheres, but for purposes of bringing together the whole community in some sense of common moral or spiritual purpose.

Nothing is more bothersome to African Americans than the performer who operates for his or her own benefit and glorification—"profiling," "showboating," or whatever. Mastery of the conventions of oral performance in song or speech remains especially valued and feared. The ability to shout praise or abuse remains deeply feared and venerated, and the bardic man-of-words continues to be given a special place within the black community. While not necessarily a heroic leader of men, the shouter is recognized for his power to gain the group's attention and thus to galvanize opinion and even unite them in a common moral perspective on a certain point. In Africa, commonly, the shouters lent their abilities to singing the praises of heroes and kings. But these potent men-of-words could be found at places where ordinary people converged, like the market—where in many places they continue to hold forth.

I am not arguing that such a talent is unique to African and Afro-American display activities. I simply am trying to account for a pattern of African American performance vitality which is still manifest throughout Afro-America, and which continues to produce great and righteously scornful performers whose social commentary is couched in brilliant and skillful aesthetic gestures—to be once again commodified and seized upon by white performers and used for different moral and aesthetic purposes.

NOTES

Introduction

1. Robert Darnton, *The Kiss of Lamourette: Reflections on Cultural History* (New York: Norton, 1990), pp. 342–43.

2. Greg Dening, *History's Anthropology: The Death of William Gooch* (Lanham: University Press of America, 1988), p. 27.

3. John Fanning Watson, *Methodist Error, or Friendly Christian Advice to those Methodists Who Indulge in extravagant emotions and bodily exercises* (Trenton, N.J.: D & E Fenton, 1819), pp. 30–32.

Chapter One
"Ain't You Gwine to the Shucking of the Corn?"

1. The reports from which this description is taken are all contained in Appendix One, where a bibliography of the reports is provided.

2. Sara Colquitt, in *The American Slave: A Composite Autobiography,* 20 vols., ed. George P. Rawick (Westport, Conn.: Greenwood Press, 1972), vol. 6, p. 89. (Ala.).

3. Henry A. Woods, "A Southern Corn-Shucking," *Appleton's Journal* (Nov. 12, 1870), p. 571.

4. Charles Lanman, *Haw-He-Noo: Or Records of a Tourist* (Philadelphia: n.p., 1850), p. 142.

5. Francis Fedric, *Slave Life in Virginia and Kentucky* (London: Wertheim, McIntosh and Hunt, 1863), p. 47.

6. Ibid.

7. Ibid.

8. Booker T. Washington, *Story of the Negro* (New York: Doubleday, Page, 1909), vol. 1, pp. 159–60.

9. Jethro Rumple, *A History of Rowan County, North Carolina* (Salisbury, N.C., n.p., 1881), pp. 171–72.

10. Lanman, *Haw-He-Noo,* p. 142.

11. Mary A. Livermore, *The Story of My Life* (Hartford, Conn.: A. D. Worthington, 1897), p. 334.

12. Quoted in Lynne Fauley Emery, *Black Dance in the United States from 1690 to 1970* (New York: National Press Books), pp. 113–14.

13. Livermore, *The Story of My Life,* pp. 332–33.

14. John Allen Wyeth, *With Sabre and Scalpel* (New York: Harper, 1914), p. 57.

15. Washington, *Story of the Negro,* p. 159.

16. George E. Brewer, "History of Coosa County, Alabama" (ms. in Alabama Department of Archives and History, Montgomery, Alabama), p. 197.

17. Mingo White, in Rawick, *The American Slave,* vol. 6, pt. 1, p. 419.

18. John Spencer, in *Weevils in the Wheat: Interviews with Virginia Ex-Slaves,* ed. Charles L. Perdue, Jr., Thomas E. Barden, and Robert K. Phillips (Charlottesville: Univ. of Virginia, 1975), pp. 278–79.

19. C. L. Walker, in *The Frank C. Brown Collection of North Carolina Folklore* (Durham: Duke Univ.), vol. 4, p. 236.

20. William Wells Brown, M.D., *My Southern Home, or the South and Its People* (A. G. Brown and Co., 1880), pp. 92–93.

21. Garnett Andrews, *Reminiscences of an Old Georgia Lawyer* (Atlanta: J. J. Toon, 1870), pp. 10–11.

22. Livermore, *Story of My Life,* p. 335. For other similar detailed accounts, see James Battle Avirett, *The Old Plantation: How We Lived in Great House and Cabin Before the War* (New York: Neely, 1901), pp. 141–42; John Cabell Chenault, *Old Cane Springs: A Story of the War Between the States in Madison County, Kentucky,* rev. and suppl. Jonathan Truman Dorris (Louisville: The Standard Printing Co., 1937), pp. 44–46; *New York Sun* (November 11, 1895), repr. in William S. Walsh, *Curiosities of Popular Customs and of Rites, Ceremonies, Observances and Miscellaneous Antiquities* (Philadel-

phia: Lippincott, 1907), p. 278; Mrs. R. H. Marshall, "A Negro Corn-shucking," ed. David J. Winslow, *Journal of American Folklore* 86 (1973), 61–62 (from Laurens, S.C., 1852). Many of the accounts, in fact, indicated that the groups were recognizable by their voices or the ways in which they sounded their way, through the blowing of wooden bugles, pan pipes, or some other identifiable sound.

23. Chenault, *Old Cane Springs*, p. 46.

24. James S. Lamar, *Recollections of Pioneer Days in Georgia* (n.p., 1828).

25. Daniel Drake, M.D., *Pioneer Life in Kentucky* (Cincinnati: Robert Clarke, 1870), pp. 54–55.

26. Avirett, *The Old Plantation*, p. 143.

27. Drake, *Pioneer Life in Kentucky*, p. 55.

28. Joel Chandler Harris, *Uncle Remus and His Friends* (Boston: Houghton Mifflin, 1882), p. 201.

29. David C. Barrow, "A Georgia Cornshucking," *Century Magazine* 24 (1882), 874.

30. Rev. I. M. Lowery, *Life on the Old Plantation in Ante-Bellum Days* (Columbia, S.C.: The State Company, 1911), p. 97. See also Andrews, *Reminiscences*, p. 11: "the general, sticking a cornshuck in his hat by way of distinction. . . ."; John Van Hook, in Rawick, *The American Slave*, vol. 8, pt. 4, p. 81 (Ga.): "the generals would stick a peacock feather in their hats and call the men together and give their orders."

31. Barrow, "A Georgia Cornshucking," p. 874. Note the orthographic alterations which occur at the points at which the slaves are being quoted. This technique was followed throughout the plantation literature as a means of demonstrating, on the one hand, the familiarity between the reporting whites and the performing blacks, and on the other, the attempt on the part of blacks to produce standard English, and their continued inabilities to do so. While these orthographic vagaries continue to carry reminders of the racist attitudes of many of the reporters, I have refrained from altering them, for not only the corn-shucking customs but the documents reporting them are, after all, the object of my study.

32. Lewis N. Paine, *Six Years in a Southern Prison* (New York: 1851), p. 181. See also Prince Johnson, in Rawick, *The American Slave*, suppl. 1, vol. 3, p. 1173 (Miss.); Jake McLeod in Rawick, vol. 3, pt. 3, p. 160 (S.C.) (" 'point two captains"); Drake, *Pioneer Life in Kentucky*, pp. 54–55 (describing what was probably a group of whites

shucking in competition, he simply noted that two men or boys "constituted themselves, or were by acclamation declared captains" and later said, "two men were chosen"; his description is almost certainly of white frontiersmen, in any case); Letitia M. Burwell, *A Girl's Life in Virginia Before the War* (New York: Frederick A. Stokes Co., 1895), p. 131 ("selecting one—usually the most original and amusing and possessed of the loudest voice."); *New York Sun* ("two captains were appointed . . .").

33. Spencer, in Perdue et al., *Weevils in the Wheat,* p. 278.

34. *New York Sun.* James Lee Love, "Recollections," in James Lee Love Papers, 1860–1864 (Univ. of North Carolina Library), vol. 14 (April 1863), pp. 29–30, provides a description of this operation in the context of a shucking. See also Nicholas P. Hardeman, *Shucks, Shocks and Hominy Blacks: Corn as a Way of Life in Pioneer America* (Baton Rouge: Louisiana State Univ., 1979), for a survey of this technology.

35. Charles R. Bagley, in *The Frank C. Brown Collection of North Carolina Folklore,* vol. 4, p. 230.

36. Lamar, *Recollections,* p. 19.

37. Avirett, *The Old Plantation,* p. 144.

38. Marinda Brown in Rawick, *The American Slave.* See also F. D. Srygley, *Seventy Years in Dixie* (Nashville: Gospel Advocate Co., 1891), pp. 288–89; Luke E. Tate, *History of Pickens County, Georgia* (Atlanta, 1935), pp. 63–64.

39. Lina Hunter, in Rawick, *The American Slave,* vol. 4, pt. 2, pp. 266–67 (Ga.). See also *New York Sun* in William S. Walsh, *Curiosities of Popular Customs* (Philadelphia: Lippincott, 1907), p. 278; Hugh Johnson, "Old Times in the South Contest," ms. in the Clarence Poe Papers (Raleigh, N.C.: North Carolina State Archives, sent in the 1950s, from Reidsville, N.C.). Penny Thompson remembered the reward as "two fingers of peach brandy," Rawick, vol. 5, pt. 4, pp. 104–5 (Tex.).

40. Quoted in Eugene D. Genovese, *Roll, Jordan, Roll: The World the Slaves Made* (New York: Pantheon, 1974), p. 318.

41. Lamar, *Recollections,* pp. 23–24.

42. Ibid., pp. 27–28.

43. S. M. Holton, in *Frank C. Brown Collection,* p. 234.

44. Paine, *Six Years in a Southern Prison,* p. 181.

45. Srygley, *Seventy Years in Dixie,* p. 289; Drake, *Pioneer Life in*

Kentucky, p. 55; another fight is described by Barrow, "A Georgia Cornshucking," pp. 876–77.

46. Barrow, "A Georgia Cornshucking," p. 876.

47. Such tactics might have led to fighting, though fisticuffs are more often reported among white huskers than black shuckers. But see Harry Smith, *Fifty Years of Slavery in the United States of America* (Grand Rapids: West Michigan Printing), 1891, pp. 62–63. As the white planter F. D. Srygley remembered of a group of Southern whites who engaged in a corn-shucking contest in black style, the fights were more conventionally spontaneous and playful than dangerous. "Sometimes," he noticed, "determination of both parties to win in the race, would lead to charges of unfairness, angry recriminations. . . ." The ears would fly through the air, and sometimes there was even "a general fisticuff." Each man, of course, would bravely stand his ground. Ultimately, "such fights were fierce, but short, and when they ended every man resumed his place at the corn-heap and proceeded with his work, with renewed energy, without any feeling of malice or fear of an enemy in his heart. . . ."

48. Quoted in Emery, *Black Dance in the United States,* p. 114.

49. Paine, *Six Years in a Southern Prison,* pp. 181–82.

50. Ida Henry, in Rawick, *The American Slave,* vol. 7, pt. 1, p. 134 (Okla.).

51. Mary Ross Banks, *Bright Days on the Old Plantation* (Boston: Lee and Shepherd, 1882), p. 131.

52. Alberta Ratliffe Craig, "Old Wentworth Sketches," *North Carolina Historical Review* 11, no. 3 (1934), 184–205. See also *New York Sun* in Walsh, *Curiosities of Popular Customs,* p. 280; Jake McLeod in Rawick, *The American Slave,* vol. 3, pt. 3, p. 160 (S.C.); Andrews, *Reminiscences;* Lydia Wood Baldwin, *A Yankee Schoolteacher in Virginia* (New York: Funk and Wagnalls, 1884), pp. 22–26; Barrow, "A Georgia Cornshucking," p. 876.

53. Letitia M. Burwell, *A Girl's Life Before the War* (New York: Frederick A. Stohes Co., 1895), p. 132.

54. Lamar, *Recollections,* p. 28.

55. Rumple, *A History of Rowan County,* p. 172..

56. Love, "Recollections," p. 30.

57. Livermore, *Story of My Life,* p. 334.

58. Avirett, *The Old Plantation,* pp. 146–47.

59. Chenault, *Old Cane Springs,* p. 49.

60. Fedric, *Slave Life in Virginia and Kentucky,* pp. 50–51.

61. Lanman, *Haw-He-Noo,* p. 144.

62. Nettie Powell, *History of Marion County, Georgia* (Columbus, Ga.: Historical Publishing Co., 1931), p. 33.

63. William Cullen Bryant, *Letters of a Traveller* (New York: G. P. Putnam, 1850), pp. 87. For more extensive descriptions of the dancing, see Barrow, "A Georgia Cornshucking"; Hugh Johnson, "Old Times in the South Contest"; Lanman, *Haw-He-Noo;* Woods, "A Southern Corn-Shucking."

64. William Wells Brown, *My Southern Home, or the South and Its People,* p. 95.

65. Banks, *Bright Days,* p. 132.

66. Fedric, *Slave Life in Virginia and Kentucky,* p. 48

67. Samuel Alexander Hamilton, "The Civil War Journal of Dr. Samuel A. Harrison," ed. Charles L. Wagandt, *Civil War History,* 13 (May 1967), 136.

68. Nicey Kinney, in Rawick, *The American Slave,* vol. 13, p. 30; and *Lay My Burden Down: A Folk History of Slavery,* ed. B. A. Botkin (Chicago: Univ. of Chicago, 1945), p. 82.

69. Barrow, "A Georgia Cornshucking," p. 876.

Chapter Two:
Orders Within Order: Cavalier and Slave Culture on the
Plantation

1. Emily Burke, *Pleasure and Pain: Reminiscences of Georgia in the 1840's* (Savannah: The Beehive Press, 1979), p. 40.

2. Sarah Fitzpatrick, in *Slave Testimony,* ed. John Blassingame (Baton Rouge: Louisiana State Univ., 1977), p. 639. From an interview of 1938 in the WPA ex-slave narrative collection.

3. W. J. Cash, *The Mind of the South* (New York: Vintage, 1941, repr., 1963), p. ix.

4. Ibid., p. 51.

5. Bertram Doyle, *The Etiquette of Race Relations: A Study in Social Control* (New York: Schocken, 1971; reissue of 1937 ed., intr. Arthur Sheps).

6. Eugene D. Genovese and Elizabeth Fox-Genovese, *The Fruits of Merchant Capital: Slavery and Bourgeois Property in the Rise and Expansion of Capitalism* (New York: Oxford Univ., 1983); and

Elizabeth Fox-Genovese and Eugene D. Genovese, "The Cultural History of Southern Slave Society: Reflections on the Work of Louis P. Simpson," in *American Letters and the Historical Consciousness: Essays in Honor of Lewis P. Simpson,* ed. J. Gerald Kennedy and Daniel Mark Fogel (Baton Rouge: Louisiana State Univ., 1975), pp. 16–41.

7. Gerald Mullin, *Flight and Rebellion: Slave Resistance in Eighteenth Century Virginia* (New York: Oxford Univ., 1972), p. 3.

8. For the development of the upcountry in terms of population growth, see Rachel N. Klein, *Unification of a Slave State: The Rise of the Planter Class in the South Carolina Backcountry, 1760–1808* (Chapel Hill: Univ. of North Carolina, 1990), pp. 1–45 passim, esp. p. 2. See also the suggestive comments on population changes and their effect on slave life in Philip D. Morgan's "Slave Life in Piedmont Virginia, 1720–1800," in *Colonial Chesapeake Society,* ed. Lois Green Carr, Philip D. Morgan, and Jean Russo (Chapel Hill: Univ. of North Carolina, 1988), ppa. 464–79. For an overarching view of the role of cotton in the development of the plantation as an economic site, see Gavin Wright, *The Political Economy of the Cotton South: Households, Markets, and Wealth in the Nineteenth Century* (New York: Norton, 1978), pp. 12–15. I am not arguing that the corn shucking was found only in cotton-growing areas. Rather, the rise of cotton seems to mark the era in which the region had sufficient capital to increase the labor force.

9. For the demographic changes for at least one major Tidewater or low-country area, the Chesapeake region, see Allan Kulikoff, *Tobacco and Slaves: The Development of Southern Cultures in the Chesapeake, 1680–1800* (Chapel Hill: Univ. of North Carolina, 1986), pp. 335–51.

10. This is hypothesized by Stephen Innes, "Fulfilling John Smith's Vision: Work and Labor in Early America," in *Work and Labor in Early America,* ed. Stephen Innes (Chapel Hill: Univ. of North Carolina, 1988), p. 41. We see this changed perspective clearly in the records of one representative planter, Landon Carter, though he was surely more influenced intellectually by arguments for scientific agriculture than most. See also Drew Gilpin Faust, *James Henry Hammond and the Old South: A Design for Mastery* (Baton Rouge: Louisiana State Univ., 1982), pp. 105–34.

11. See Philip D. Morgan, "Task and Gang Systems: The Organization of Labor on New World Plantations" in Innes, *Work and Labor*

in Early America, pp. 188–220; Peter Wood, *Black Majority: Negroes in Colonial South Carolina from 1670 to the Stono Rebellion* (New York: Knopf, 1974); Charles Joyner, *Down by the Riverside: A South Carolina Slave Community* (Urbana: Univ. of Illinois, 1984), pp. 127–41. Two recent and valuable works on the limits of slave autonomy are Peter Kolchin, *Unfree Labor: American Slavery and Russian Serfdom* (Cambridge, Mass.: Belknap Press of Harvard Univ., 1987) and Robert W. Fogel, *Without Consent or Contract* (New York: Norton, 1989), pp. 169–98.

12. James Battle Avirett, *The Old Plantation: How We Lived in Great House and Cabin Before the War* (New York: F. T. Neely, 1901), p. 146. These were also movable in the European agricultural calendar. Avirett's notice is simply an indication that from the planter's perspective, the agricultural worker continued to employ a different sense of marking time than did his master.

13. Says Mechal Sobel, *The World They Made Together: Black and White Values in Eighteenth-Century Virginia* (Princeton: Princeton Univ., 1987), p. 53, "For both the English and the African farm worker, the harvest was a time of joy, a time to overeat, to drink, and to express feelings of personal and communal accomplishment and well-being."

The actual process of agriculture entered into the lives of the planters and their families somewhat less than it did the field hands, a fact registered in the ways by which the year was marked out. Sobel does not refer here in any depth to the corn shucking, but rather to harvest activities in general. That I disagree with the general direction of Sobel's argument will become evident.

14. Philip Fithian, quoted in Rhys Isaac, "Evangelical Revolt: The Nature of the Baptists' Challenge to the Traditional Order in Virginia, 1765–1775," in *Shaping Southern Society: The Colonial Experience,* ed. T. H. Breen (New York: Oxford Univ., 1976), p. 251.

15. Isaac, "Evangelical Revolt," in Breen, *Shaping Southern Society.*

16. Breen, intr. remarks to Isaac, p. 111.

17. The literature on the slaves' Christmas is abundant. For this literature, see especially Harnett T. Kane's popular overview, *The Southern Christmas Book* (New York: Crown, 1957). Modern scholarly discussion of plantation culture, including the slaves' holidays, begins with Kenneth M. Stampp, *The Peculiar Institution: Slavery in the Ante-Bellum South* (New York: Vintage, 1956), p. 169. The most thorough and still the most stimulating discussions of the subject of slave hol-

idays is Eugene Genovese, *Roll, Jordan, Roll: The World the Slaves Made* (New York: Pantheon, 1974), pp. 575–79. See also, John Blassingame, *The Slave Community: Plantation Life in the Antebellum South* (New York: Oxford Univ., 1979), rev. ed., p. 107. The discussion in David Kenneth Wiggins's dissertation, "Sport and Popular Pastimes in the Plantation Community: The Slave Experience" (Univ. of Maryland, 1979), pp. 303–14, is unusually full, drawing predominantly on the accounts given in *The American Slave: A Composite Autobiography,* vol. 21, and the supplement, vol. 21, ed. George P. Rawick (New York: Greenwood Press, 1972).

18. Lucy Breckinridge, *Lucy Breckinridge of Grove Hill: The Journal of a Virginia Girl, 1862–1864,* ed. Mary D. Robertson (Kent, Ohio: Kent State Univ., 1979), pp. 87–88. See Genovese, *Roll, Jordan, Roll,* pp. 476–81, for a record of other such wedding scenes.

19. Bertram Doyle, *The Etiquette of Race Relations,* pp. 18–33. Classic accounts from the plantation literature include: Susan Dabney Smedes, *Memorials of a Southern Planter* (New York: Knopf, 1965), p. 64; and Robert Manson Myers, *A Georgian at Princeton* (New York: Harcourt, Brace Jovanovich, 1976), pp. 4–6. See also Genovese, *Roll Jordan, Roll,* pp. 194–98.

20. James Boyd, in Rawick, *The American Slave,* vol. 4, pt. 1, p. 118 (Tex.).

21. Philip Fithian, *Journal and Letters of Philip Vickers Fithian, 1773–1774: A Plantation Tutor of the Old Dominion,* ed. Hunter Dickenson Farish (Charlottesville: Univ. of Virginia), pp. 37, 88, 201. Cf. John Michael Vlach, "The Yard," in his *Beyond the Big House,* forthcoming. My thanks to John Vlach for calling this material to my attention and for assisting me in developing this idea.

22. Mary Boykin Chesnut, for instance, reflecting upon the killing of some white neighbors by slaves during the Civil War, observed that ". . . nobody is afraid of their own negroes . . ." in spite of the savagery of those elsewhere: "I find everyone, like myself, ready to trust their own yard." *Mary Chesnut's Civil War,* ed. C. Vann Woodward (New Haven: Yale Univ., 1981), pp. 211–12.

23. David Hackett Fischer, *Albion's Seed: Four British Folkways in America* (New York: Oxford Univ., 1989), pp. 267–68. See also Henry C. Forman, *The Architecture of the Old South: The Medieval Style, 1585–1650* (Cambridge, England: Cambridge Univ., 1948), pp. 122–27.

24. Burke, *Reminiscences,* p. 36.

25. Dell Upton, "Black and White Landscapes in Eighteenth Century Virginia," in *Material Life in America: 1600–1860,* ed. Robert Blair St. George (Boston: Northeastern Univ., 1988), p. 367.

26. Ibid., pp. 363–64.

27. St. George, intr. remarks to Upton, pp. 357–66. Rhys Isaac analyzes one observation of the power display commonly involved simply in going to church, in his article "Ethnographic Method in History: An Action Approach," *Historical Methods* 13 (1980), 56: "A dramatic pattern is evident: . . . Firstly . . . the line drawn by status. . . . Secondly, an age distinction. . . . Thirdly . . . there was the ever recurrent division of the sexes." He concludes: "Those who proudly played the male part of gentlemen by their entrance into the church were supremely those who played the patriarchal part in the churchyard, before and after, when they issued invitations to dine."

28. St. George, *Material Life in America,* p. 357.

29. Upton, "Black and White Landscapes," pp. 364–65.

30. In such a landscape, as John Vlach has suggested, the yard is a contested area predominantly ceded to the occupations of slave artisans and to the servants. John Michael Vlach, "The Yard," in his *Beyond the Big House: Ethics and Behavior in the Old South* (New York: Oxford Univ., 1982).

31. Isaac, "Ethnographic Method," p. 55.

32. See here Bertram Wyatt-Brown, *Southern Honor.* That their wives were also called upon to condescend in similar style cannot be doubted; after all, they were called upon to run the household in a similar fashion. The human details of deferential interaction among and between women is detailed in Elizabeth Fox-Genovese, *Within the Plantation Household: Black and White Women in the Old South* (Chapel Hill: Univ. of North Carolina, 1988), pp. 228–34. She suggests, but does not explicitly argue, that journal keeping and correspondence entered into the system of manners by which these attitudes were played out by Southern women. Also, see Nell Irvin Painter's introduction to *The Secret Eye: The Journal of Ella Gertrude Clanton Thomas, 1848–1889,* ed. Virginia Ingraham Burr (Chapel Hill: Univ. of North Carolina, 1990), p. 23.

33. Frederick Douglass, *My Bondage and My Freedom* (New York: Miller, Orton & Mulligan, 1855), pp. 97–98. See also Nehemiah Caulkins in Dena J. Epstein, *Sinful Tunes and Spirituals: Black Folk Music to the Civil War* (Urbana: Univ. of Illinois, 1977), p. 178.

34. Faust, *James Henry Hammond,* p. 103. See also Joyner's account

of slave life in the Waccamaw River area of South Carolina, *Down by the Riverside*, p. 133.

35. Rosa Stark, in *Bullwhip Days: The Slaves Remember—An Oral History*, ed. James Mellon (New York: Avon, 1988), p. 136.

36. Mullin, *Flight and Rebellion*, p. 19.

37. Carl Bridenbaugh, *Myths and Realities: Societies of the Colonial South* (New York: Atheneum, 1969), p. 24.

38. Susan Bradford Eppes, *Through Some Eventful Years* (Gainesville: Univ. of Florida, 1968), p. 12.

39. See Wyatt-Brown, *Southern Honor*, chap. 2.

40. Isaac, "Ethnographic Method," p. 57.

41. Allan Kulikoff, *Tobacco and Slaves: The Development of Southern Culture in the Chesapeake, 1680–1800* (Chapel Hill: Univ. of North Carolina, 1986), p. 11.

42. The most thorough study of Afro-American worship is Albert J. Raboteau's *Slave Religion: The "Invisible Religion" in the Antebellum South* (New York: Oxford Univ., 1978), pp. 68–75. See also Genovese, *Roll, Jordan, Roll*, pp. 232–34; Joyner, *Down by the Riverside*, pp. 160–61, and his extensive notes on the practice, pp. 305–6; Epstein, *Sinful Tunes and Spirituals*, pp. 278–87; Blassingame, *The Slave Community*, pp. 134–35; Sterling Stuckey, *Slave Culture: Nationalist Theory and the Foundations of Black America* (New York: Oxford Univ., 1987); Harold Courlander, *Negro Folk Music, U.S.A.* (New York: Columbia Univ., 1963), pp. 194–200; Eileen Southern, *The Music of Black Americans: A History* (New York: Norton, 1971), pp. 160–63; and Lawrence Levine, *Black Culture and Black Consciousness: Afro-American Folk Thought from Slavery to Freedom* (New York: Oxford Univ., 1977), pp. 37–38.

43. Kulikoff, *Tobacco and Slaves*, p. 12.

44. Ibid.

45. At least this is suggested by some of the corn-shucking accounts in which the prodigality of the master and his family were exclaimed upon by the house servants; but these accounts are reported by whites raised on the plantation.

46. Daniel Blake Smith, "In Search of the Family in the Colonial South," in *Race and Family in the Colonial South*, ed. Winthrop D. Jordan and Sheila L. Skemp (Oxford, Miss.: Univ. of Mississippi, 1987), p. 32.

47. Daniel Blake Smith, *Inside the Great House: Planter Family Life in Eighteenth-Century Chesapeake Society* (Ithaca: Cornell Univ.,

1980), p. 22. See also Rhys Isaac, *The Transformation of Virginia, 1740–1790;* Philip D. Morgan, "Three Planters and Their Slaves: Perspectives on Slavery in Virginia, South Carolina and Jamaica, 1750–1790," in *Race and Family in the Colonial South,* ed. Jordan and Skemp, pp. 37–79; Jan Lewis, *The Pursuit of Happiness: Families and Values in Jefferson's Virginia* (Cambridge, England: Cambridge Univ. Press, 1983); Jane Turner Censer, *North Carolina Planters and Their Children, 1800–1860* (Baton Rouge: Louisiana State Univ., 1984); and Steven M. Stowe, *Intimacy and Power in the Old South: Ritual in the Lives of the Planters* (Baltimore: Johns Hopkins, 1987).

48. Morgan, "Three Planters and Their Slaves," pp. 39–40.

49. Eugene Genovese, "The Southern Slaveholders' View of the Middle Ages," in *Medievalism in American Culture,* ed. Bernard Rosenthal and Paul E. Szarmarch, Medieval and Renaissance Texts and Studies (Center for Medieval and Early Renaissance Studies, State Univ. of New York at Binghamton, 1989), pp. 31–32. The relationship between the new sentimentalism and this attraction to medievalism has not yet received much discussion, perhaps because the attraction to things medieval during this period was so ubiquitous. For the story of the attraction of these notions in North after the war, see T. J. Jackson Lears, *No Place of Grace: Antimodernism and the Transformation of American Culture, 1880–1920* (New York: Pantheon, 1981).

50. Genovese, *Roll, Jordan, Roll,* p. 344. For an explication of the details of the reciprocal, but far from equitable or even commensurate, features of the exchange system of sentiments between black and white women, see Fox-Genovese, *Within the Plantation Household,* pp. 146–86.

51. Morgan, "Three Planters and Their Slaves," p. 78.

52. Mary Boykin Cheṣnut, *A Diary from the South,* ed. Ben Ames Williams (Boston: Houghton Mifflin, 1949), p. 122.

Chapter Three:
An American Version of Pastoral

1. I have pursued this argument at greater length in "The Language of Festivals: Celebrating the Economy," in *Celebrations,* ed. Victor W. Turner (Washington, D.C.: Smithsonian Institution, 1975), pp. 161–77.

2. See Christina Hole, *A Dictionary of British Folk Customs* (Lon-

don: Paladin, 1978), pp. 138–39. David Hoseason Morgan, in *Harvesters and Harvesting, 1840–1900* (London: Croom, Helm, 1982), conveniently brings together the British literature on harvesting, including the harvest home ceremony, pp. 151–81. For an especially full rendering of one local version of the event, see W. H. Long, "An Island 'Hooam Harvest,' in *A Dictionary of the Isle of Wight Dialect* (London and Isle of Wight: Reeves and Turner, G. A. Brannon, 1886), pp. 109–23.

3. Henry Bourne, *Antiquitates Vulgares, or the Antiquities of the Common People, giving their account of their opinions and ceremonies* ("printed by J. White for the author, Newcastle upon Tyne, Eng.," 1725). Bourne, according to the *Dictionary of National Biography*, was born in 1696 and died at the age of thirty-seven in 1733. The son of a tailor, he had been recognized for his talents by the local gentry, and sent to Cambridge, where he received the B.A. in 1717 and the M.A. in 1724. His book, *Antiquitates Vulgares,* was published in 1725, and formed the basis for all subsequent dictionaries of English country practices.

4. Thomas Tusser, *Five Hundred Points of Good Husbandry* (New York: Oxford Univ., 1984), p. 122; in his emendations of 1717, Richard Hillman says: "He that is the Lord of the Harvest, is generally some stay'd sober working Man, who understands all Sorts of Harvest work. . . . If he be of able Body, he commonly leads the Swarth in reaping and mowing."

5. As Dorothy Hartley, in *Lost Country Life* (New York: Pantheon, 1979), p. 179, describes him, " 'The Harvest Lord' was a subordinate employee . . . a capable, experienced man and, if the owner was wise, a man known to be reasonably 'well thought of and firmly authoritative.' "

6. For a survey of the custom, under the term "Easter Lifting," see Hole, *A Dictionary of British Folk Customs,* pp. 99–100. This is not to argue that the tradition is solely English in origin, for similar practices are found in the central and southwestern Bantu groups in Africa, from which many slaves derived.

7. Cotton Mather, "Advice from the Watchtower," Boston, 1713, quoted in George Lyman Kittridge, *The Old Farmer and His Almanack* (Boston: William Ware, 1904), pp. 172–73. See also Cotton Mather, Benjamin Colman, and Benjamin Wadworth's broadside on this question and others associated with drinking and revelry, "A Testimony Against Evil Customs," Boston, 1719.

8. Ned Ward, "A Trip to New-England with a Character of the Country and People, both English and Indians," London: 1699, p. 11, repr. in *Five Travel Scripts Commonly Attributed to Edward Ward* (New York: Columbia Univ., 1933).

9. "The Ames Diary," *Dedham Historical Register*, vol. 2, 1891, quoted from C. F. Adams, *Three Episodes of Massachusetts History* (Boston: Houghton Mifflin, 1894), vol. 2, p. 791, as well as Kittredge, *The Old Farmer*, p. 172.

10. J. A. Leo Lemay, "The American Origins of 'Yankee Doodle,' " *William and Mary Quarterly*, n.s. 3 (1976), pp. 447–51.

11. *Memoirs of Madame de La Tour du Pin*, ed. and trans. Felice Harcourt (New York: McCall Publishing, 1971), p. 278.

12. Ibid.

13. William Dawson Johnston, *Slavery in Rhode Island, 1775–1776*, Providence, R.I., 1894, p. 30; quoted in T. R. Hazard, "Recollections of Olden Times," *Providence Journal* (October 1877), p. 119.

14. Rear Admiral Bartholomew James, Navy Records Society, 1896, p. 193; quoted in Kittredge, *The Old Farmer*, p. 168.

15. Joel Barlow, "The Hasty Pudding," *The Oxford Book of American Poetry*, ed. F. O. Mathiessen (New York: Oxford Univ., 1950), pp. 41–47. For "red ear" as a tag for festive license, see Mary Helen Dohan, *Our Own Words* (New York: Penguin, 1975), p. 112; Mitford Matthews, *A Dictionary of Americanisms* (Chicago: Univ. of Chicago, 1951), p. 1374. John Greenleaf Whittier also wrote of this event in its Yankee form in 1850, in "The Corn Song," and a number of New England village memoirs well into the twentieth century record the custom; see, for instance, R. E. Gould, *Yankee Boyhood* (New York: Norton, 1950), pp. 132–33.

16. William S. Walsh, *Curiosities of Popular Customs* (Philadelphia: J. B. Lippincott, 1907), p. 277.

17. *The Political Works of James I*, ed. Charles H. McIlwain (Cambridge, Mass.: Harvard Univ., 1918), p. 27.

18. "A Declaration of Sports," in *Minor Prose Works of King James VI and I*, ed. James Craigie and Alexander Law (Edinburgh: Scottish Text Society, 1982), pp. 217–42. The editors provide an introduction that situates the issuing of this declaration and clarifies the politics of culture concerning these sports.

19. In addressing the problem of dispelling the influence of the Puritans in Jacobean and Carolingian England, the court seized upon the

customs of the countryside as embodying the ideal working out of a modus vivendi between the classes. The Anglican Church continued to observe the occasions and spirit of earlier agrarian religious practices, and related them to analogous Christian precedents. The Stuarts used the attitude of the English Church, under Archbishop Laud, to rationalize the economic and social system in which the landowner provided the land and tools which enabled his laborers to feed their own families in addition to his. This system was dramatized through the cyclical progression of seasonal festivals, when people of all classes came together to celebrate, through feasting and merriment, their mutual dependence.

I am not arguing that the American Cavaliers subscribed to the entire complex of ideas purveyed by James I or Archbishop Laud, only that the complex of features revolving around the idea of the Cavalier originated with that age and their prosecution of an argument.

20. Leah Marcus, *The Politics of Mirth (Chicago:* Univ. of Chicago, 1986), pp. 6–7.

21. Richard Price, *Observations on the Importance of the American Revolution* (London: n.p., 1785), pp. 57–58; Leo Marx, *The Machine in the Garden: Technology and the Pastoral Ideal in America* (New York: Oxford Univ., 1964), p. 105.

22. Drew R. McCoy, *The Elusive Republic: Political Economy in Jeffersonian America* (Chapel Hill: Univ. of North Carolina, 1980), p. 85.

23. Slaves were drawn into occasions on which their doings would be involved in the wagerings of their masters. This is a subject which arises in black stories a good deal, especially in the Master-John stories, which commonly turn on Old Master's compulsion to gamble, a character flaw which could be turned to the slave-trickster John's benefit. See Richard M. Dorson, *American Negro Folktales* (New York: Fawcett, 1967), pp. 131–36, and *Afro-American Folktales: Stories from Black Traditions in the New World,* ed. Roger D. Abrahams (New York: Pantheon, 1985), pp. 263–94. Important insights into these and related trickster tales can be found in Gladys-Marie Fry, *The Night-Riders in Black Folk History* (Knoxville: Univ. of Tennessee, 1975); John W. Roberts, *From Trickster to Badman* (Philadelphia: Univ. of Pennsylvania, 1989); and Lawrence W. Levine, *Black Culture and Black Consciousness: Afro-American Thought from Slavery to Freedom* (New York: Oxford Univ., 1977), pp. 389–92.

24. Richard Bushman, "High Style and Vernacular Cultures," in *Colonial British America,* ed. Jack P. Greene and J. R. Pole (Baltimore: Johns Hopkins, 1984), pp. 371–72.

25. As noted in Chapter Three, Christmas was the most universally celebrated festivity. Puritan New England, which overtly rejected this calendar, carried over one event from English practice: Pope's (Guy Fawkes) Day. See the early discussion by William De Loss Love, *The Fast and Thanksgiving Days of New England* (Boston: Houghton, Mifflin, 1895); and the following more recent work: Susan G. Davis, *Parades and Power: Street Theater in Philadelphia* (Philadelphia: Temple Univ., 1986), p. 76; Paul A. Gilje, *The Road to Mobocracy: Popular Disorder in New York City, 1763–1834* (Chapel Hill: Univ. of North Carolina, 1987), pp. 25–30; and David Cressy, *Bonfires and Bells* (Berkeley: Univ. of California, 1989), pp. 204–6. See Alice Morse Earle, *Customs and Fashions of Old New England* (New York: 1893), pp. 228–30.

26. Cressy, *Bonfires and Bells.*

27. "Report of the Journey of Francis Louis Michel from Berne, Switzerland to Virginia, October 2, 1701–December 1, 1702," trans. William J. Hinke, *Virginia Magazine of History and Biography,* 24 (1916), 32. Cf. Mary Newton Stanard, *Colonial Virginia: Its People and Customs* (Philadelphia: Lippincott, 1917), pp. 136–37. Stanard relates this merriment to the shucking: "A similar festival for the negroes, which was held throughout Virginia until the War between the States and doubtless began far back in the colonial period, was the corn-shucking." She places the event as a traditional October celebration, in which the hands "of a neighborhood gathered at each plantation in turn," and after the work and the eating, there was much "laughter and song, antics and buffoonery which would make a modern minstrel show appear tame. . . ."

28. James Battle Avirett, *The Old Plantation* (New York: F. T. Neely, 1901), p. 139.

29. William Wood, *New England's Prospect,* ed. Alden T. Vaughan (Amherst: Univ. of Massachusetts, 1977), p. 113.

30. Thomas Hariot, *A Brief and True Report of the New Found Land of Virginia, directed to the investors, farmers, and well-wishers of the project of colonizing and planting there.* London, 1688, repr. in *The New World: The First Pictures of America,* ed. Stefan Lorant (New York: Duell, Sloane and Pierce, 1946), p. 244.

31. Francis Jennings, *The Invasion of America: Indians, Colonialism and the Cant of Conquest* (New York: Norton, 1975), pp. 58–84.

32. Quoted in ibid., p. 81.

33. William Cronon, *Changes in the Land: Indians, Colonists and the Ecology of New England* (New York: Hill and Wang, 1983), p. 43.

34. Ibid., pp. 43–44. Grady McWhiney, *Cracker Culture: Celtic Ways in the Old South* (Tuscaloosa: Univ. of Alabama, 1988) describes a number of such irregular agricultural habits in the South (such as allowing animals free range in the planted field), reporting them as evidence of Celtic disregard of rational planting practices.

35. See, for instance, the report of a ceremony in Arthur C. Parker, *Parker on the Iroquois,* ed. William Fenton (New York: Syracuse Univ., 1968), pp. 31–33. Says Parker: "When harvesters find a red ear all the harvesters give the finder for his or her own use two ears of corn with the husk pulled back ready for braiding. The red ear is called 'King Ear.' . . ." The significance of the red ear in Indian culture is first noticed in Samuel Sewall's journal, September 1712, where it was used by the Indian chief Joe Oenoe to signal the acceptance of a treaty. See Mitford, *A Dictionary of Americanisms on Historical Principles* (Chicago: Univ. of Chicago, 1951), p. 1374.

36. William Faux, *Memorable Days in America* (London: W. Simpkin and R. Marshall, 1823), p. 211.

37. Ibid.

38. John Bradbury, "Travels in the Interior of America, 1809–11," in *Early Western Travels, 1748–1846,* ed. Reuben Gold (Thwaites, Cleveland: Arthur H. Clark, 1904), vol. 5, p. 310.

39. David C. Barrow, "A Georgia Cornshucking," *Century Magazine* 24 (1882), 873.

40. For a paean to corn and corn culture that details this perspective, see Nicholas P. Hardeman, *Shucks, Shocks and Hominy Blocks: Corn as a Way of Life in Pioneer America* (Baton Rouge: Louisiana State Univ., 1979), pp. 20–34. Howard Russell's excellent *A Long, Deep Furrow: Three Centuries of Farming in New England* (Hanover, N.H.: University Presses of New England, 1976), pp. 39–46, provides an overview of the early reception of corn in that region. I have not been able to find a similar survey for the situation in the South. Corn was also identified with frontier subsistence, with the need to come to

terms with a new land and its new (and frequently uncivilized) ways, and thus with the ambivalent relationship between settlers and denizens of the wild, human and animal.

41. See Celia M. Benton, "Corn Shuckings in Sampson County," *North Carolina Folklore* 22 (1974), 131–39, for reminiscences of the social occasion involving segregated blacks and whites.

42. The most extensive descriptions of the shucking involving only white plain-folk farmers are in James Lee Love, "Recollections," in James Lee Love Papers, 1860–1864, Univ. of North Carolina Library, vol. 14, April 1863, pp. 29–30; James S. Lamar, *Recollections of Pioneer Days in Georgia* (1828), pp. 21–28; F. D. Srygley, *Seventy Years in Dixie* (Nashville: Gospel Advocate Co., 1891), pp. 288–89; and Daniel Drake, M.D., *Pioneer Life in Kentucky* (Cincinnati: Robert Clarke, 1870). Of these, only the first two come from east of the Appalachians.

43. Love, "Recollections," p. 29.

44. Ibid., p. 30.

45. Srygley, *Seventy Years in Dixie,* p. 288.

46. Ibid., p. 289.

47. Drake, *Pioneer Life in Kentucky,* pp. 44–60.

48. Ibid., p. 55.

49. Lamar, *Recollections,* p. 28.

50. One should not presume from this that the contest with its organization around captains is an invention of whites. The slave practice may have preceded the actual introduction of slaves into the event in Lamar's area.

51. Lamar, pp. 21–28.

52. Alice Morse Earle, *Customs and Fashions in Old New England* (New York: 1893), p. 215.

Chapter Four:
Festive Spirit in the Development of African American Style

1. David C. Barrow, "A Georgia Cornshucking," *Century Magazine* 24 (1882), 873–78.

2. John Miller Chernoff, *African Rhythm and African Sensibility: Aesthetics and Social Action in African Musical Idioms* (Chicago: Univ. of Chicago, 1981), p. 167.

3. Harold Courlander, *Negro Folk Music U.S.A.* (New York: Columbia Univ., 1963), pp. 91–92. See also Lawrence Levine, *Black Culture and Black Consciousness* (New York: Oxford Univ., 1977), pp. 208–17. The scholarship on slave work patterns fails to take these matters of traditional organization into consideration. It has been presumed that gang labor was regarded as onerous by slaves and observers alike. The reports of slave labor, read in combination with more recent ethnographic observation, suggest that from the slaves' perspective gang organization was perhaps the more valued way of working. Perhaps gang organization seems least desirable insofar as it carried with it the connotation of being supervised by the overseer, driver, captain, or boss. Just as the slaves came to regard the corn shucking (should it be held) as their time, one should not discount their own input as to how the event was organized and carried out. See Philip D. Morgan's argument regarding the gang versus the task orientation for slave labor on the various New World plantations; he summarizes the relevant studies in his "Task and Gang Systems: The Organization of Labor in New World Plantations" in *Work and Labor in Early America,* ed. Stephen Innes (Chapel Hill: Univ. of North Carolina, 1988), pp. 188–220. Morgan does not consider the African style of team labor, accepting without question that ganging was only a form of surveillance imposed by the masters. Morgan's major point, that gang or task work orientation seems to emerge from the characteristics of the crop in production, seems to be illustrated in some interesting ways if the corn shucking arises primarily in areas of cotton cultivation as a way of punctuating that rendering of the agricultural year.

4. Frederick Douglass, *Narrative of the Life of Frederick Douglass, an American Slave,* ed. Houston A. Baker, Jr. (New York: Penguin, 1982), pp. 57–58. The keeping up of the spirit is best illustrated in the "ring shout" of slave religious practice. Albert J. Raboteau has made the fullest survey of the reports of this practice, in his *Slave Religion: The Invisible Institution in the Antebellum South* (New York: Oxford Univ., 1978), pp. 68–75. John A. Lomax and Alan Lomax, in *Folksong, U.S.A.* (New York: Duell, Sloan and Pearce, 1947), p. 335, reported a ring shout in Louisiana in 1934, and compared it to similar counterclockwise holy ring dances elsewhere in the black New World. Alan Lomax and a number of others have observed ring shout churches still worshiping throughout the South. I have learned a good deal from my student Jonathan David, who has been studying one group of "bands" in Maryland since 1980, and

who has made a number of reports on his work at scholarly meetings which he has shared with me. See also Levine, *Black Culture and Black Consciousness*, pp. 37–38; Sterling Stuckey, *Slave Culture: Nationalist Theory and the Foundation of Black America* (New York: Oxford Univ., 1987), pp. 53–64; Genovese, *Roll, Jordan, Roll*, pp. 134–35; Courlander, *Negro Folk Music U.S.A.*, pp. 194–200. The form of worship was so widely observed in the nineteenth century that each of these surveys identifies a number of eyewitness reports.

5. Morton Marks, "Ritual Structures in Afro-American Music," in *Religious Movements in Contemporary America*, ed. Irving Zaretsky and Mark P. Leone (Princeton: Princeton Univ., 1974), p. 110.

Referencing musical forms in African and African American festivities (most of them, in fact, from urban areas), Marks tells us that they obey a ritual structure. At the point of greatest interpenetration of styles, voices, timbres, and metrical pulse systems, the participants are conveyed into and out of the deepest kind of spiritual experience. This seems to occur at a point in which a departure from one state of being to another is experienced, often in common by many members of the group of celebrants, through a "breaking out" or "breaking down" or "getting happy." According to Marks, "one of the defining features of Afro-American rituals is the alternation or switching between European and African forms," a switch that is interpreted by nonblack observers as going from " 'order' to 'making noise.' " He concludes that "social meaning is generated through the alternation and interplay among a set of codes and channels of communication, and that one social meaning consists of statements of cultural identity." This deepening of experience would seem to be one of the most important features of the corn shucking, as it certainly was in the religious ring shouts, on the plantation. The level of emotional involvement was sufficiently different culturally that white observers discussed it a great deal, seeing in it something savage and therefore frightening, but enormously attractive at the same time.

6. Charles Lanman, *Haw-He-Noo: Or Records of a Tourist* (Philadelphia: n.p., 1850), p. 143.

7. Marshall Stearns and Jean Stearns, *Jazz Dance: The Story of American Vernacular Dance* (New York: Macmillan, 1968), p. 22. The "strut" was another name for the cakewalk.

8. Samuel Kinser, *Carnival American Style: Mardi Gras at New Orleans and Mobile* (Chicago: Univ. of Chicago, 1990), p. 73. Whenever slaves were encouraged to develop such festive worlds, Kinser

nicely points out, "slavery for black people . . . turned out to be a point of transfer, not a dark, impenetrable wall." See also Stearns and Stearns, p. 22.

9. John Pendleton Kennedy, *Swallow Barn, or a Sojourn in the Old Dominion* (New York: Putnam, 1854, first published in 1832), p. 454.

10. George E. Brewer, "History of Coosa County, Alabama" (ms. in the Alabama Department of Archives and History, Montgomery, Alabama), p. 197.

11. Gladys-Marie Fry, *Night Riders in Black Folk History* (Knoxville: Univ. of Tennessee Press, 1975), esp. pp. 93–109.

12. This proverb emerges as one of the commonplaces in minstrel songs and speeches, an indication of how widely it was known and how deeply associated with slaves; see, for instance, the song in *Nigger Melodies* (New York: Nafis and Cornish), pp. 97–98.

13. *American Museum* 1, no. 3 (1787), 215–16. For another such account from the same era, see John Bernard, *Retrospections of America, 1797–1811* (New York: 1887), p. 206, as well as the report in *Swallow Barn* by John Pendleton Kennedy, p. 454.

14. See Dave Lowry, in *Weevils in the Wheat: Interviews with Virginia Ex-Slaves*, ed. Charles L. Perdue, Jr., Thomas E. Borden, and Robert K. Phillips (Charlottesville: Univ. of Virginia, 1975), p. 198, for an account of such noise containment at a dance. As one slave, quoted in Levine, *Black Culture and Black Consciousness*, put it, "All the noise would go into that kettle. . . . They could shout and sing all they wanted to and the noise would go outside" (p. 42); Levine's footnote on p. 454 provides a great many references in the ex-slave narratives.

15. For some time, writers on Afro-American secular singing have underscored the essential unity of the aesthetic in both worlds. Scholars such as John Szwed, Charles Keil, and Lawrence Levine have gone further and argued that the bright and energetic surface features of popular entertainment forms should not blind us to the potential ritual significances to be found there, especially in live performances; see John Szwed, "Musical Adaptation among Afro-Americans," *Journal of American Folklore* 82 (1969), 112–21; Charles Keil, *Urban Blues* (Chicago: Univ. of Chicago, 1966), chaps. 4–5; and Levine, pp. 234–39. Levine provides a number of other references.

It has become a commonplace in discussions of black culture to focus on the musicians' relationship to each other, the ways they play against each other in ensemble groups. This structure is clear in jazz and has come to be best known in relation to that set of musical styles. We understand the importance of the improviser within such ensembles in the same light. I am suggesting that we can see precisely the same set of aesthetic practices in place a century and more before jazz and blues performances came into being. And percolating through all of these secular styles is a vision of the performing world akin to the religions, in terms of the profundity of the experience both for the performers of the music and the participants responding to it.

16. Frederika Bremer, *Homes of the New World* (New York: Harper, 1853), p. 370.

17. Barrow, "A Georgia Cornshucking," pp. 874–75.

18. The term is first used by Robert Farris Thompson in "An Aesthetic of the Cool: West African Dance," *African Forum* 2, no. 2 (Fall 1966), 93–94. Thompson draws on the profile of African social and musical organization Alan Lomax first gave in "Song Structure and Social Structure," *Ethnology* 1 (1962), 425–51, and elaborated on in "The Homogeneity of African–Afro-American Musical Style," in *Afro-American Anthropology: Contemporary Perspectives* (New York: The Free Press, 1970), pp. 181–202.

19. Letitia M. Burwell, *A Girl's Life in Virginia Before the War* (New York: Stokes, 1895), pp. 131–32.

20. George Strickland, in *The American Slave: A Composite Autobiography,* ed. George P. Rawick, suppl. series 1, vol. 1, p. 398.

21. Nancy Williams, in Perdue et al., *Weevils in the Wheat,* p. 318.

22. John Wyeth, *With Sabre and Scalpel* (New York: Harper, 1914), pp. 60–61.

23. See Dena J. Epstein, *Sinful Tunes and Spirituals: Black Folk Music to the Civil War* (Urbana: Univ. of Illinois, 1977), pp. 141–44, for a survey of the places in which Juba was reported in the nineteenth century.

24. Courlander, *Negro Folk Music U.S.A.,* pp. 191–92; Eileen Southern, *The Music of Black Americans: A History* (New York: Norton, 1971), pp. 168–69.

25. Fry, *Night Riders,* p. 85.

26. Bessie Jones and Bess Lomax Hawes, *Step It Down: Games, Plays, Songs and Stories from the Afro-American Heritage* (Athens, Ga.: Georgia Univ., 1972), pp. 14–24. They demonstrate the simplest way of clapping as it was found in one Sea Island, Georgia, tradition—the patting game played to infants. Each of the following syllables represents a separate clap: "Tom, Tom, Greedy Gut, Greedy Gut, Greedy

Gut. / Eat all the meat up, meat up, meat up." As they diagrammed it, with "clap" standing for the hands coming together, "slap" meaning bringing the cupped hand to the chest, the routine went:

Clap	clap	clap	slap	slap;	clap	slap	slap,	clap	slap	slap
1 &	2 &	3	&	4 &	1	&	2 &	3	&	4&

They continue: "They clap in three distinct pitch ranges: bass, baritone, and tenor . . . the pitch . . . determined by the position in which the hand is held. . . . To clap bass, cup your palms slightly and clap with your palms at right angles to one another . . . only the palms [coming together to produce this effect]. . . . To clap baritone, the left palm is cupped and struck with the fingers, slightly cupped of the right hand. . . . A strong baritone clap on a hard palm can sound like a pistol shot. . . . Tenor is clapped variously, . . . sometimes . . . like the baritone, except that the left palm and right fingers are *not* cupped. To get the highest pitch of all, strike the fingers of both hands together in a flattened-out but relaxed position" (pp. 22–23).

Jones and Hawes illustrate how the hand may be held for each pitch, pointing out that this is "not a casual stunt." For patting is heard as an entire percussion orchestra, and is judged as such, in terms of how vigorous, layered, balanced the effect becomes. "Each person in a group clapping 'music'—that is, accompanying a song—may either duplicate, at his own pitch, a rhythm being taken by another person, or he may perform variations on his own; with experienced clappers, the latter is invariably the case. Essentially the Sea Islanders' clapping patterns seem to cluster around the following framework:

	one	and	two	and	three	and	four	and
Baritone		X				X	X	(X)
Bass	X		X				X	
Tenor		X	(X)	X	(X)	X	(X)	(X)

This should be thought of as the core pattern; each part may be . . . varied extensively . . ." (p. 23).

27. Wyeth, *With Sabre and Scalpel*, pp. 59–60. He explains what "keeping time" really meant, indicating that the patting he learned was to produce a triplet at each beat, by patting on one knee, then the other, and then clapping with the hands. "In patting, the position was usually a half-stoop or forward bend, with a slap of one hand on the left knee followed by the same stroke and noise on the right, and then a loud slap of the two palms together." He adds the further

complication that the pat on the left knee was carried out in double-time to the pat on the right knee: "the left hand made two strokes in half-time to one for the right, something after the double stroke of the left drumstick in beating the kettle drum." As we have seen above in the Jones-Hawes work, the metrical structure of the Sea Islanders' clapping is even more dense and complicated.

28. Jones and Hawes, p. 19: ". . . their handclapping *is* music—in every sense of the word; it is varied and expressive and subtle, completely different from a routine beating out of time."

29. Sidney Lanier, *The Science of English Verse* (New York: Scribners, 1880), pp. 186–87.

30. Lewis Paine, *Six Years in a Southern Prison* (New York: n.p., 1851), pp. 179–80.

31. So, at least, I have observed in recent manifestations of patting called "hambone." In this "hand jive" routine, the song is called out in basic 4/4 meter, and then, as "hamboning" takes over after the verse, a number of different meters and textures are patted by different members of the group, slapping under their arms, against the forearm held in front of the body, and against pant-leg, the last of which may produce different textures depending upon how tightly the cloth is stretched by the patter. See Roger D. Abrahams, *Positively Black* (Englewood Cliffs, N.J.: Prentice-Hall, 1970), pp. 139–40. Jones and Hawes, in *Step It Down*, pp. 34, 220, give a full description of how the practice is played, relating it to Juba.

32. Wyeth, *With Sabre and Scalpel*, p. 60.

33. Tom Fletcher, *The Tom Fletcher Story—100 Years of the Negro in Show Business* (New York: Burdge, 1954), p. 19; quoted in Lynne Fauley Emery, *Black Dance in the United States from 1619 to 1970* (Palo Alto: National Press, 1972), p. 92. "Walk-chalk" comes up in minstrel songs in contexts indicating that it was a part of the conventional stage vocabulary; e.g., see *Nigger Melodies,* p. 34. This dancer, named Tom, was drawn into a contest that resulted in his master betting on his abilities to beat the man from the next plantation. It ended in a series of whirls which resulted in the other man's spilling "just a spoonful of water" so that Tom was declared winner. B. A. Botkin describes this scene in *Lay My Burden Down: A Folk History of Slavery* (Chicago: Univ. of Chicago, Phoenix Books, 1945), pp. 56–57. See also Georgia Writers Project, *Drums and Shadows* (Athens: Univ. of Georgia, 1986; repr. of 1940 ed.), p. 159; Stuckey, *Slave Culture,* p. 65; Fry, *Night Riders,* p. 108. Katrina Hazzard-

Gordon mentions a related practice called "set de flo' ": "a circle was drawn to make an area in which the competing dancers performed. The musician, usually a fiddler, would call out complicated step routines for the dancers to negotiate without stepping on or outside the drawn circle." She goes on to describe the water-on-the-head trick. Katrina Hazzard-Gordon, *Jookin': The Rise of Social Dance Formations in African-American Culture* (Philadelphia: Temple Univ., 1990), p. 20.

34. The naming of the cakewalk is a bit of a puzzle. Emery (p. 91) includes a story from an ex-slave in Virginia in which it was argued that the name came from the cake given as a prize for the couple who danced best. Eileen Southern, in *The Music of Black Americans: A History* (New York: Norton, 1971), p. 273, mentions both the chalk-line dance and the prize cake stories. The latter is the primary definition of "cakewalk" given in the first volume of the *Dictionary of American Regional English,* vol. 1, ed. Fredrick Cassidy (Cambridge, Mass.: Harvard Univ., 1985), p. 507: "A social entertainment, once especially favored by Blacks, in which a cake was the prize awarded for the fanciest steps, or figures executed by those who walked or paraded around it. And in some descriptions, the cake is featured at the center of the room, and is the object around which the dancers parade."

The cakewalk is often described as a kind of signifying dance, making fun of the high manners of the white folks; see Ruby Blesh and Harriet Janis, *They All Played Ragtime* (New York: Oak, 1966), p. 96; and Stearns and Stearns, *Jazz Dance,* p. 22, quoting Shep Edmonds, ninety years old, in the late 1940s: "They did a take-off on the high manners of the white folks in the 'big house,' but their masters, who gathered around to watch the fun, missed the point." From the evidence of such proceedings in the corn shuckings the masters probably did get the point and were amused by it—after all, it confirmed their stereotype of the slaves imitating them, albeit in jest.

The first quotation in the *Dictionary of American Regional English* indicates that the cakewalk was part of a fund-raising activity within the black community. And in many places in the anglophonic West Indies, I have spoken with people who say that the *cakewalk*—their term still—is the custom that when someone gets married a multitiered cake is baked and the best dancers from the community go from yard to yard, with the cake balanced on the head and a plate carried in the hand, getting contributions for the married couple to use in setting up house. This, of course, brings it closer to the water-balancing dance.

35. Levine, *Black Culture and Black Consciousness,* p. 16.

36. Ibid.

37. Aunt Cicely Cawthon, in Rawick, *The American Slave,* suppl. series 1, vol. 3, pt. 1, p. 190.

38. Both usages are given in the *Dictionary of American Regional English,* p. 372.

39. Robert Cantwell, *Bluegrass Breakdown: The Making of an Old Southern Sound* (Urbana: Univ. of Illinois, 1984), p. 124.

40. Barrow, "A Georgia Cornshucking," p. 878. See also Nettie Powell, *History of Marion County, Georgia* (Columbus, Ga.: Historical Publishing Co., 1931), p. 33: "The music was supplied by old time fiddlers with a great deal of beating straws"; and William C. Handy, *Father of the Blues* (New York: Macmillan, 1941), p. 5: "A boy would stand behind the fiddler with a pair of knitting needles in his hands. From this position the youngster would reach around the father's left shoulder and beat on the strings in the manner of a snare drummer."

41. Jones and Hawes, *Step It Down,* p. 58.

42. Ibid., p. 89.

43. Georgia Writers Project, *Drums and Shadows,* pp. 186–87; quoted in Stuckey, *Slave Culture,* pp. 64–65.

44. Roscoe Lewis, *The Negro in Virginia* (New York: Arno, 1943), p. 93, quoted in Stuckey, *Slave Culture,* p. 66.

45. See *Dictionary of American Regional English,* p. 516, *Call* n1, "In a song or rhyme: a solo line or stanza which is followed by a response or refrain. . . . *chiefly among Black speakers.*"

Chapter Five:
Signifying Leadership on the Plantation

1. *Weevils in the Wheat: Interviews with Virginia Ex-Slaves,* ed. Charles L. Perdue, Jr., Thomas Borden, and Robert K. Phillips (Charlottesville: Univ. of Virginia, 1975), p. 278. This story is the sort commonly called "Marster-John" tales. For a number of texts of this type, see Zora Neale Hurston, "High John de Conquer," *American Mercury* 57 (1943), 450–58; J. Mason Brewer, "John Tales," in *Publications of the Texas Folklore Society,* vol. 21, pp. 81–104; Richard M. Dorson, *American Negro Folktales* (New York: Dell, 1958), pp. 124–71; Harry C. Oster, "Negro Humor: John and Old Master," *Journal of the Folklore Institute* 5 (1968), 42–57;

John Q. Anderson, "Old John and the Master," *Southern Folklore Quarterly* 25 (1961), 195–97; and Charles Joyner, *Down by the Riverside: A South Carolina Slave Community* (Urbana: Univ. of Illinois, 1984), pp. 184–89.

2. Nicholas Cresswell, *The Journal of Nicholas Cresswell: 1774–1777* (New York: Dial, 1924), p. 19. Cf. Rhys Isaac, *The Transformation of Virginia, 1740–1790* (Chapel Hill: Univ. of North Carolina, 1982), pp. 84–85.

3. John Pendleton Kennedy, *Swallow Barn, or A Sojourn in the Old Dominion* (New York: Putnam, 1854; rev. of 1832 novel), pp. 100–102. "Long Time Ago" is a song widely reported in the Afro-American worksong literature, especially as a sea chantey. Here, see the survey in Roger D. Abrahams, *Deep the Water, Shallow the Shore* (Austin: Univ. of Texas, 1974), pp. 3–24. Kennedy provides vignettes of other plantation men-of-words, including the old retainer Old Jupiter, depicted as a "native philosopher," given to orations on set topics.

4. This is the spelling used by Henry Louis Gates, Jr., in *The Signifying Monkey: A Theory of African-American Literary Criticism* (New York: Oxford Univ., 1989). Gates employs the term to refer to the system by which language use not only is coded as in-group black talk but provides a way into the culture-specific universe of black figuration or troping. (His thesis statement is given on pp. 51 ff.) Discussion of this usage of the term arises from the materials I collected in South Philadelphia in the late 1950s which were commented upon by a number of scholars, many of whom were Afro-Americans. As I first outlined the idea of "signifying," in *Deep Down in the Jungle: Negro Narrative Folklore from the Streets of Philadelphia* (Chicago: Aldine, rev. ed. 1970), p. 54, it referred to "an ability to talk with great innuendo, to carp, cajole, wheedle and lie . . . in other instances to talk around a subject, . . . making fun of a person or situation." See also my *Talking Black* (Rowley, Mass.: Newbury, 1976), pp. 50–51. This work was commented upon by Claudia Mitchell-Kernan, in *Rappin' and Stylin' Out: Communication in Black Urban America,* ed. Thomas Kochman (Urbana: Univ. of Illinois, 1972); Thomas Kochman, *Black and White Styles in Conflict* (Chicago: Univ. of Chicago Press, 1981), pp. 52–56, 99–100, 137–38; Ulf Hannerz, *Soulside* (New York: Columbia Univ., 1969), pp. 84–85; and Lawrence Levine, *Black Culture and Black Consciousness: Afro-American Folk Thought from Slavery to Freedom* (New York: Oxford Univ., 1977), pp. 344–58. See also William D. Piersen, *Black Yankees: The Develop-*

ment of an Afro-American Subculture in Eighteenth Century New England (Amherst: Univ. of Massachusetts, 1988), pp. 138–39, which surveys a number of reports from New England. For an early overview of the "satiric songs" of the slaves, see Henry Edward Krehbiel, *Afro-American Folksongs: A Study in Racial and National Music* (New York: Columbia Univ., 1914), pp. 140–51.

This kind of verbal play is widely found in the West Indies and other parts of the black New World, under such names as "'busin'," "cursing," "nigger business," "picong," "mamaguy," and again "rhyming." Many of these practices are discussed in my collected essays, in *Talking Black,* and in *The Man-of-Words in the West Indies* (Baltimore: Johns Hopkins, 1983), pp. 55–76, 88–108.

5. For a survey of this argument, see my *Afro-American Folktales* (New York: Pantheon, 1985), pp. 19–23. John Roberts, in *From Trickster to Badman: The Black Folk Hero in Slavery and Freedom* (Philadelphia: Univ. of Pennsylvania, 1989), pp. 31–44, argues that the scarcity of food enters into the generation of such stories in Africa, and that a similar condition in plantation America provides a strategic linkage for the maintenance of these stories in the New World setting. For a complementary view, in which the reaction to scarcity of food is compared in European Märchen and African and Afro-American tales, see my "From the Belly of the Elephant," in *Folklore Annual,* vol. 3, 1989, pp. 10–23.

6. Rev. T. C. Thornton, *An Inquiry into the History of Slavery* (Washington, D.C.: William M. Morrison, 1841), p. 122.

7. John H. McIntosh, *The Official History of Elbert County, 1790–1930* (Atlanta: Cherokee, 1960), p. 106.

8. Joyner, *Down by the Riverside,* p. 189. Joyner had earlier (p. 183) noted the relationship between indirection and "African concepts of eloquence," citing the work of Ethel M. Albert, " 'Rhetoric,' 'Logic,' and 'Poetics' among the Burundi," *American Anthropologist* 66 (1964), 35–54; and John C. Messenger, "The Role of Proverbs in a Nigerian Judicial System," *Southwestern Journal of Anthropology* 15 (1959), 64–73. I drew upon this same bibliographic resource in "Traditions of Eloquence in Afro-American Communities," in *The Man-of-Words in the West Indies,* pp. 21–40, as well as in "The West Indian Tea Meeting: An Essay in Creolization" in *Old Roots in the New World,* ed. Anne M. Pescatello (Westport, Conn.: Greenwood, 1977), pp. 177–209. Agonistic and usually playful usage lies

at the center of the literature on allusive language in Africa and Afro-America, which I discuss in footnote 4, above. This led a number of commentators to relate this ability to the allusive and generally derisive techniques of the so-called joking relationship found in many African groups throughout the subcontinent. See Alan Dundes' useful survey of the literature in *Mother Wit from the Laughing Barrel* (Englewood Cliffs, N.J.: Prentice-Hall, 1963), pp. 296–97, where he notes resources from East as well as West Africa. See also Levine, *Black Culture and Black Consciousness,* pp. 344–58.

9. John Miller Chernoff, *African Rhythm and African Sensibility: Aesthetics and Social Action in African Musical Idioms* (Chicago: Univ. of Chicago, 1981), pp. 70–71. Here he is drawing on the insights of Robert Farris Thompson, "An Aesthetic of the Cool: West African Dance," *African Forum* 2, no. 2 (Fall 1966), 93–94.

10. Chernoff, p. 71. The emphasis on role playing is important here, for the bard himself is not to be held up to the moral standards he establishes for those to whom he directs his song. He is commenting not upon human behavior in general, but upon those who make claims for virtue as leaders of the people.

11. Karin Barber, "Interpreting Oriki as History and as Literature," in *Discourse and Its Disguises: The Interpretation of African Texts,* ed. Karin Barber and P. F. de Moraes Farias (Birmingham, England: Birmingham Univ., African Studies Series no. 1, Centre of West African Studies, 1989), pp. 13–23.

12. Ibid., pp. 15–16.

13. Ibid., p. 16. For a study of contestive poetry in a tradition which is cognate to the Yoruba, see Kofi Awoonor's amazing little work, *Guardians of the Sacred Word: Ewe Poetry* (New York: Nok, 1974).

14. Barber, "Interpreting Oriki," p. 22.

15. Ibid., p. 19.

16. Thompson, "An Aesthetic of the Cool," p. 98.

17. John Cabell Chenault, *Old Cane Springs: A Story of the War Between the States in Madison County, Kentucky,* rev. and suppl. Jonathan Truman Dorris (Louisville: The Standard Printing Co., 1937), p. 47. This song is exceptionally interesting, insofar as it is a version of the sea chantey "Reuben Ranzo," which tells of the doings of a sea captain gone amok (see Stan Hugill, *Shanties from the Seven Seas: Shipboard Work-Songs and Songs Used as Work-Songs from the Great Days of Sail* [New York: Dutton, 1961], pp. 239–51, and the refer-

ences given there). Jewell Robbins is reported to have sung a similar corn-shucking song, printed in the *Frank C. Brown Collection of North Carolina Folklore,* vol. 3 (Folksong), 238, called "The Old Turkey Hen":

> *Seven years a-boiling*
> *Ho-ma-hala-way*
> *Seven years a-baking*
> *Ho-ma-hala-way*
>
> *They blowed the horn for dinner*
> *Ho-ma-hala-way*
> *The people could not eat her*
> *Ho-ma-hala-way*
>
> *They carried her to the old field*
> *Ho-ma-hala-way*
> *The buzzards could not eat her*
> *Ho-ma-hala-way*

The refrain resembles numerous chanteys in which "haul away" is mentioned.

There are a number of songs in the Ranzo group of chanteys that mention the "Wild Goose Nation." Hugill provides a number of folk explanations of the term, none of which refers directly to the story of the wild goose shot down by Old Master given here. As this song seems to refer to a recognizable Marster-John story, in which Marster tries to kill John only to find that he is too tough and wily to be killed, it is plausible that the very term "wild goose" may have referred to an unkillable slave, and that the sea chanteys are versions which recode the meaning of the song into a sea setting. For the Marster-John tale in which Old Marster gets so mad at his slave that he attempts to kill him in any way he can, but John keeps outwitting him, see Charles Joyner's discussion in *Down by the Riverside,* pp. 184–85, 317. This also may explain, in some part, the origin of the song "The Gray Goose," sung by Huddie Ledbetter, printed in John A. Lomax and Alan Lomax, *Negro Folk Songs as Sung by Lead Belly* (New York: Macmillan, 1936), p. 108. See also the version of "Go Tell Aunt Nancy" in *A Singer and Her Songs: Almeda Riddle's Book of Ballads,* ed. Roger D. Abrahams (Baton Rouge: Louisiana State Univ., 1970), pp. 117–20. This text suggests that the Marster-John story might at one point have been a cante-fable, and from this emerged a work song, which took form as a sea chantey in one area, as "Reuben Ranzo," and a convict labor song in another. It should be noted that almost all of the corn songs reported here are also widely found as sea chanteys. The work-song repertoire, on land and sea, thus appears much more circumscribed than one would expect of a tradition of improvised songs.

For a West Indian cognate form of "singing the master," see Clement Caines, *The History of the General Council and the General Assembly of the Leeward Islands* (Basseterre, St. Christopher: R. Cable, 1804), vol. 1, pp. 110–11, noted in Dena P. Epstein, *Sinful Tunes and Spirituals: Black Folk Music to the Civil War* (Urbana: Univ. of Illinois, 1977), p. 187.

18. [James Kirke Paulding], *Letters from the South* (New York: Eastburn, 1817), p. 127.

19. [George Tucker], *The Valley of the Shenandoah; or, Memoirs of the Graysons* (New York: C. Wiley, 1824, [1796?]), vol. 2, pp. 116–18; repr. in Epstein, *Sinful Tunes and Spirituals,* pp. 172–76. Tucker's depictions are especially interesting as his ironies indicate a deep suspicion of stereotypical thinking about slaves even as he presents in his fictions some of the stock figures of plantation life.

20. Gladys-Marie Fry, *Night Riders in Black Folk History* (Knoxville: Univ. of Tennessee Press, 1975), esp. pp. 93–109.

21. Quoted in Sam Dennison, *Scandalize My Name: Black Imagery in American Popular Music* (New York: Garland, 1982), pp. 137–38. "M.P." refers to mounted patrols.

22. John Wyeth, *With Sabre and Scalpel* (New York: Harper, 1914), pp. 63–64. Wyeth describes the details of one slave-entertainer's routine: "Billy would pause, lay the banjo across his knees, and speak about this style, preluding his remark with one of those long-drawn-out grunts or weirdly intonated expressions of great surprise which only the Africans seems to enjoy.: 'Golly! folks; I went to see Miss Sal last Sat'day night. Sal's a handsome gal, too, no 'ceptions to dat. I ain't more'n had time to 'spress myself on de occasion when Sal say, "Looky dar, Peet!" "Looky whar, Sal?" "Lood at dat patter-roller peeping' frew de crack!" Then a second long grunt or ejaculation of surprise. . . . Golly! chillun; dis yer nigger riz as quick as a nigger could convenient; jumped frew de winder, fell ober de wood-pile, knocked de wood into short sticks, an' took down de road fas' as my laigs could go, an' de white man he tuk airter me, an' ebery jump I make de white man say (then he would sing): "Run, nigger, run. . . ." ' "

23. *God Struck Me Dead: Religious Conversion Experiences and Au-*

tobiographies of Negro Ex-Slaves, ed. A. P. Wilson, Paul Radin, and Charles S. Johnson (Nashville, Tenn.: Fisk Univ., 1945), p. 216, (repr. as vol. 19 in *The American Slave: A Composite Autobiography,* ed. George P. Rawick (Westport, Conn.: Greenwood, 1972). The song has many versions, of which only the first line is constant. The rest of the stanzas tend to report comic scenes that emerge as part of the need to escape. See, for instance, Millie Williams, in Rawick, *The American Slave,* supp. ser. 12 (Texas), p. 4114:

> *Run nigger run, padder-roller catch you,*
> *Run nigger run, Dey give you thirty nine,*
> *Dat nigger run, dat nigger flew,*
> *Dat nigger lost his Sunday shoe.*

See also Levine, *Black Culture and Black Consciousness,* p. 125. But see Eugene Genovese, *Roll, Jordan, Roll: The World the Slaves Made* (New York: Pantheon, 1974), p. 618.

24. [George Tucker], *The Valley of the Shenandoah,* p. 116–18.

25. *The Family Magazine* (1836), 42.

26. He is discussing the phenomenon as it emerged in "Patting Juba" discussed in the last chapter. Beverly Tucker to Edgar Allan Poe, in Edgar Allan Poe, *Complete Works,* ed. James A. Harrison (New York: Sproul, 1902), vol. 17, p. 22; repr. in Epstein, *Sinful Tunes and Spirituals,* p. 142.

27. *The Family Magazine* (1836), 42. (Written by "A Gentleman who travelled through Virginia some years since.")

28. Houston A. Baker, Jr., *Blues, Ideology and Afro-American Literature: A Vernacular Theory* (Chicago: Univ. of Chicago Press, 1984), p. 5.

29. James Battle Avirett, *The Old Plantation* (New York: F. T. Neely, 1901), p. 146.

30. James Hungerford, *The Old Plantation and What I Gathered There in an Autumn Month* (New York: Harper and Bros., 1859), p. 191.

31. E. C. Perrow, *Journal of American Folklore* 28 (1913), 139.

32. "Negro Minstrelsy—Ancient and Modern," *Putnam's Magzine* (Jan. 1855), 77.

33. Rev. I. M. Lowery, *Life on the Old Plantation in Ante-Bellum Days* (Columbia. S.C.: The State Company, 1911), p. 97.

34. Garnett Andrews, *Reminiscences of an Old Georgia Lawyer* (Atlanta: J. J. Toon, 1870), p. 11.

35. Election Day provided the model for activities of this sort. This national holiday called for the mustering of the troops by the whites of the neighborhood. According to the journal keeper Emily Burke, the musicians in the muster in the South were all slaves: ". . . the appearance and . . . the manner in which military parades are conducted all over the South. In the first place all their musicians are colored men, for the white gentlemen would consider it quite beneath their dignity to perform such a piece of drudgery as to play for a company while doing their military duty. These colored musicians are dressed in the full uniform of the company to which they belong, and, on the morning of the day in which the several companies are to be called out, each band in uniform, one at a time, marches through all the streets to summon all the soldiers to the parade ground. This performance also calls out all the servants that can obtain permission to attend the training, and it is not a few of them that not only follow but go before the companies wherever they march. They are excessively fond of such scenes, and crowds of men, women and children never fail of being present on all such occasions, some carrying their masters' young children on their heads and shoulders, while many are seen with large trays on their heads, loaded with fruit, sweetmeats and various kinds of drinks to sell. . . . In Savannah there are five of that kind of companies that exist in all the states and are called by all names, composed of all such persons as only perform military duties because they are obliged. In Savannah they are called ragamuffins, and I never heard a name more appropriately applied. Scarcely any two were dressed alike or took the same step, and, whenever I saw them approaching, some with shoes on one foot and a boot on the other, some with their guns wrong end up and others with them on their shoulders, wearing their knapsacks bottom up and wrong side out . . ." See Emily Burke, *Pleasure and Pain: Reminiscences of Georgia in the 1840's* (Savannah: Beehive Press, n.d.), pp. 26–27.

Miss Burke, in fact, may have been witnessing an active countermuster, which was a common feature of popular culture during this period in American history. Descriptions of the muster, both as a time of high ceremony and mockery, are found in many works of recent social history. The muster, which was regarded as a civic obligation for the men in the new republic, involved a parade which was subject to a considerable amount of good-hearted joking, because the troops *were* so often a ragtag bunch. One of the most common scenes of holiday fun featured a mocking of the mustered troops, with the jokers

wearing motley costumes, carrying sticks or other such found objects
as guns, and performing the marching maneuvers with less than orderly
drills. See Susan G. Davis's account of the event, formal and otherwise,
in *Parades and Power: Street Theater in Nineteenth-Century Philadelphia* (Philadelphia: Temple Univ., 1986), esp. pp. 41–111 *passim;*
and William Piersen, *Black Yankees: The Development of an Afro-
American Subculture in Eighteenth Century New England* (Amherst:
Univ. of Massachusetts, 1988), pp. 121–22. William Cullen Bryant,
in *Letters of a Traveller* (New York: Putnam, 1850), p. 87, describes
a scene at a corn-shucking dance in which this motive came to the
fore: "From the dances a transition was made to a mock military
parade, a sort of burlesque of our militia trainings, in which the words
of command and the evolutions were extremely ludicrous." The scene
ends with a round of speechifying.

36. Mary Ross Banks, *Bright Days on the Old Plantation* (Boston:
Lee and Shepherd, 1882), pp. 122–23. For descriptions of similar
techniques for elevating power figures under harvest ritual occasions
in West Africa, see A. A. Opoku, *Festivals of Ghana* (Ghana Publishing
Corporation, 1970), esp. pp. 14–32.

37. For example, David C. Barrow, "A Georgia Cornshucking," *Cen-
tury Magazine* 24 (1882), 874; *New York Sun* (November 11, 1895):
"They choose up sides just as the captains in spellin'-matches do";
Avirett, *The Old Plantation,* pp. 142–43; and Daniel Drake, M.D.,
Pioneer Life in Kentucky (Cincinnati: Robert Clarke, 1870), p. 55.

38. William L. Van Deburg, *The Slave Drivers: Black Agricultural
Supervisors in the Antebellum South* (New York: Oxford Univ., 1979),
pp. 24–25. It is worth pointing out here, though perhaps tangential
to the major argument, that there is increasing evidence among historians that the slaves had a number of ways not only of developing
their leaders but of celebrating their elevation to positions of honor.
The most widely reported Afro-American election festivities were
Pinkster Day in Albany, New York, and the election of black governors
in Narragansett, Rhode Island, and elsewhere. Sterling Stuckey, in
*Slave Culture: Nationalist Theory and the Foundations of Black Amer-
ica* (New York: Oxford Univ., 1987), pp. 76–77, notes: "Blacks selected 'their best and ablest men' as governors."

For the studies of Pinkster Day and other such elections, see James
Eights, "Pinkster Festivities in Albany Sixty Years Ago," *Collections
of the History of Albany* (Albany, 1867), repr. in *After Africa,* ed.
John Szwed and Roger D. Abrahams (New Haven: Yale Univ., 1983),

pp. 378–81; E.A.A., "Sassafras and Swinglingtow, or Pinkster was a Holiday," *American Notes and Queries* 6 (1946), 35–40; A. J. Williams-Myers, "Pinkster Carnival: Africanism in the Hudson River Valley," *Afro-Americans in New York Life and History* 9 (1985), 7–17; Shane White, "Pinkster: Afro-Dutch Syncretization in New York City and the Hudson Valley," *Journal of American Folklore* 102 (1989), 68–75; and Shane White, "Pinkster in Albany, 1803: A Contemporary Description," *New York History* (April 1989), 191–99.

On the phenomenon of black governors and their Election Day, see Frances M. Caulkins, *History of Norwich, Connecticut* (Hartford: n.p., 1866), pp. 330–31; Nathaniel B. Shurtleff, "Remarks on Negro Election Day," *Proceedings of the Massachusetts Historical Society* 13 (1873–75), p. 7; Jane Shelton, "The New England Negro: A Remnant," *Harpers New Monthly* 88 (1894), 535–38; Orville H. Platt, "Negro Governors," *Papers of the New Haven Colony Historical Society* 6 (1900), 319; Hubert H. S. Aimes, "African Institutions in America," *Journal of American Folklore* 18 (1905), 15; Lorenzo Greene, *The Negro in Colonial New England* (New York: Atheneum, pp. 249–55; Telfer H. Mook, "Training Day in New England," *New England Quarterly* 11 (1938), 675–97; and Melvin Wade's survey article, "Shining in Borrowed Plumage: Affirmation of Community in the Black Coronation Festivals of New England, ca. 1750–1850," *Western Folklore* 40 (1981), 211–31. See also Piersen's overview in *Black Yankees,* pp. 117–40, drawn from a wide number of newspaper and journal accounts. Samuel Kinser, in *Carnival American Style: Mardi Gras at New Orleans and Mobile* (Chicago: Univ. of Chicago, 1990), pp. 41–48, provides an overview of these elections throughout trans-Caribbean Afro-America, relating the practices to festive events.

39. Masters of eloquence or invective are "men-of-words," talkers to be approached with caution and respect. The strong appeal of word power is common among African Americans throughout the New World; it is traceable to the great eloquence traditions of Africa, and was strongly reinforced by the slaveholders' own high valuation of speech making. See the articles collected in my *Man-of-Words in the West Indies,* especially "Traditions of Eloquence in Afro-American Communities," pp. 21–40; and also my "West Indian Tea Meeting: An Essay in Creolization," in Pescatello, *Old Roots in the New World,* pp. 177–209. The term "men-of-words" misleads a bit, for though most of those who avail themselves of the role are male, there are many female wordsmiths who enter into high-serious speech making.

In this connection, and still to be investigated, is the role of the market woman, the person entrusted both in the American South and in the West Indies with selling the products of the dwellers of the quarters (and later the village). These higglers were and are widely admired and feared for their verbal abilities to bargain and to curse. For a useful survey of white Southern attitudes and practices in speech making, see Waldo W. Braden, *The Oral Tradition in the South* (Baton Rouge: Louisiana State Univ., 1983), pp. 22–45.

40. Wyeth, *With Sabre and Scalpel*, p. 58.

41. John F. Szwed and Morton Marks, "The Afro-American Transformation of European Set Dances and Dance Suites," *Dance Research Journal* 20, no. 1 (Summer 1988), 33.

42. Ibid., p. 32.

43. Barrow, "A Georgia Cornshucking," p. 78.

44. The caller was sometimes a fiddler, as is indicated by one report from Montgomery, Alabama (Jane M. and Marion Turnbull, *American Photographs*, vol. 2, p. 72, quoted in Epstein, *Sinful Tunes and Spirituals*, p. 154). The writer observed "about sixty negroes, all dancing . . . to the music of two violins and a banjo . . . a negro was standing on a chair calling out what figures were to be performed. . . ."

While he was not referring only to the harvest dance, George Washington Cable (in *The Cavalier* [New York: Charles Scribner, 1901], pp. 213–18) described a black fiddler calling a dance during the Civil War. Indeed, he even gave a tune that the caller used, and noted that part of the technique involved the fiddler's learning the names of everyone present so that he could build on their names as he gave out his instructions. And a reporter from Tennessee, John Curwood Moore (in *Ol' Mistis and other Songs and Stories from Tennessee* [Philadelphia: John C. Winston, 1897, p. 213] noticed a similar scene from an African American dance:

The fiddler, inspired by the music of his fiddle and the muse of inspiration, has rhymed his calls to music, and keeping time with his feet to the flying bow, sings out his peculiar chant:

> Great big fat man down in the corner
> Dance to de gal wid de blue dress on her;
> You little bit er feller widout eny vest
> Dance to de gal in de caliker dress.
> Git up, Jake, an' turn your partner,
> Shake dem feet as you kno' you 'orter;

> *You little red nigger wid de busted back*
> *Git up an' gib us de "chicken rack."*
> *All hands round—O, step lite, ladies,*
> *Don't fling yer feet so fur in de shadies;*
> *Come, you one-eyed nigger, fling*
> *Dem feet an' gib us de "pigeon wing."*

See also James P. Johnson, in Tom Davin, "Conversations with James P. Johnson," *The Jazz Review* 2, no. 5 (July 1959), 15–16: "One of the men would call the figures and they'd dance their own style of square dances. They were . . . 'Join hands' . . . 'Sashay' . . . 'Turn around' . . . 'Ladies right and gentlemen left' . . . 'Grab your partner' . . . 'Break away' . . . 'Make a strut' . . . 'Cows to the front, bulls to the back.' " Just how much this was affected by the Afro-American aesthetic becomes clear when Johnson notes that at some point each dancer "did their personal dances."

Szwed and Marks argue that the relationship between Afro-American musicians and the development of reels, quadrilles, and the cotillion is immensely complicated. They survey the literature on set dancing throughout Afro-America in "The Afro-American Transformation of European Set Dances and Dance Suites," pp. 29–36.

45. Solomon Northup, *Twelve Years a Slave* (Auburn, N.Y.: Derby and Miller, 1853), pp. 216–17.

46. Leslie Howard Owens, *This Species of Property: Slave Life and Culture in the Old South* (New York: Oxford Univ., 1976), p. 165. Owens describes discovering a letter detailing a case in which the slave Robin organized a group of slave entertainers which then was hired out by his master (pp. 168–69). See also Joseph E. Marks III, *America Learns to Dance: A Historical Study of Dance Education in America before 1900* (New York: Exposition, 1957), p. 41, where he notes that there were slave dancing masters as well; and Paul A. Cimbala, "Fortunate Bondsmen: Black 'Musicianers' and their role as an Antebellum Southern Plantation Elite," *Southern Studies* 18 (1979), 291–303.

47. Epstein, *Sinful Tunes and Spirituals,* pp. 147–48. Additional support for this position is amply provided by Eileen Southern, *The Music of Black America: A History* (New York: Norton, 1971), pp. 44–45, 65, 68, 120, 144, 167–68, 170–71.

48. The uniqueness of American fiddling style arises from the im-

position of the same kinds of sprung rhythms onto the basic four-square composition of the reel, the jig, and the quadrille that gave American fiddle tunes their syncopated effects. See Robert Cantwell, *Bluegrass Breakdown: The Making of an Old Southern Sound* (Urbana: Univ. of Illinois, 1984), pp. 71–72. Alan Jabbour, in an unpublished manuscript, "Fiddle Tunes of the Old Frontier: In Search of a Fresh Intercultural Model," concludes: "American syncopation first arose in fiddling, with the prominent participation of blacks, in the Upper South during the revolutionary period of the late 18th and early 19th centuries."

The American style of square dance arose as part of the same stylistic configuration, through the development of breakdown music and dance involving fiddler-callers who described the dance steps in rhyme even as they directed and encouraged the dancers. Says Harold Courlander on the subject: "Negro set callers, many of them professionals, brought to the square dances an element of spontaneity and improvisation characteristic of Negro secular music in general, along with imagery and idiom that made the calls unique." See Courlander, *Negro Folk Music U.S.A.* (New York: Columbia Univ., 1963), p. 203. See also Willis James's "The Romance of the Negro Folk Cry in America," *Phylon* 16 (1955), p. 18: "There were scores of Negroes throughout the South who achieved lasting reputations as 'set callers.' In fact, their popularity rose to such heights that they were in many cases professionals, being paid a fee to bring color and entertainment to the dance. They invented an entirely new system of 'callin' sets. As they would call the figures, frequently they would dance very original solo steps and give out their calls in a musical phrase pattern."

Chapter Six
Powerful Imitations

1. The unique "sound" is produced not only by the combination of string and percussion instruments of both African (banjo) and European (fiddle) derivation, originally played as musical accompaniment for dancing, even on the stage. For a detailing of the development of the bluegrass organization from its minstrel roots, see Robert Cantwell, *Bluegrass Breakdown: The Making of an Old Southern Sound* (Urbana: Univ. of Illinois, 1984), pp. 74, 254–74.

2. Robert C. Toll, *Blacking Up: The Minstrel Show in the Nineteenth*

Century (New York: Oxford Univ., 1974); George F. Rehin, "The Darker Image: American Negro Minstrelsy through the Historian's Lens," *American Studies* 9 (1968), 365–73; William F. Stowe and David Grimsted, "White-Black Humor," *Journal of Ethnic Studies* 3 (1976), pp. 78–96; Eric Lott, " 'The Seeming Counterfeit': Racial Politics and Early Blackface Minstrelsy," *American Quarterly* 43 (1991), 223–53. The place of minstrelsy at the center of American popular culture was first pointed out by Constance Rourke, *American Humor: A Study of National Character* (New York: Doubleday, 1931).

3. The literature on touring American theatricals is large and diffuse. Three recent books are helpful in recognizing the tremendous variety of theatricals throughout the century: Lawrence Levine's, *Highbrow Lowbrow: The Emergence of Cultural Hierarchy in America* (Cambridge, Mass.: Harvard Univ., 1988); Robert C. Allen's *Horrible Prettiness: Burlesque and American Culture* (Chapel Hill: Univ. of North Carolina, 1991); and Robert Bogdan's *Freak Show: Presenting Human Oddities for Amusement and Profit* (Chicago: Univ. of Chicago, 1988). Though monographic and biographic, Neil Harris's life of P. T. Barnum, *Humbug* (Chicago: Univ. of Chicago, 1973), remains the best single source for an understanding of public theatrical life of that era. See also Joe McKennon's *Pictorial History of the American Carnival* (Sarasota, Fla.: Carnival Publishers, 1972).

4. Horace Greeley, "The Black Opera," *New York Tribune* (June 30, 1855), quoted in Lott, "Early Blackface Minstrelsy," p. 224.

5. [J. K. Kinnard, Jr.], "Who are Our National Poets?" *Knickerbocker Magazine* (Oct. 1845), 332.

6. A number of social historians have attempted to account for the development of blackface minstrelsy in sociopolitical terms without looking at its formation in actual plantation scenes. See Alexander Saxton, "Blackface Minstrelsy and Jacksonian Ideology," *American Quarterly* 27 (1975), 3–28; Sylvia Wynter, "Sambos and Minstrels," *Social Text* 1 (1979), 149–56; Joseph Boskin, *Sambo: The Rise and Demise of an American Jester* (New York: Oxford Univ., 1986), pp. 65–95; and Lott, "Early Blackface Minstrelsy."

7. Toll, *Blacking Up*, p. v. He is quoting from *Charley Fox's Minstrel Companion* (Philadelphia: 1863), p. 5; *Democratic Review* 17 (1845), 218–19; and [Kinnard] "Who Are Our National Poets?" p. 333.

8. Mark Twain, *The Autobiography of Mark Twain*, ed. Charles Neider (New York: Harper and Row, 1966), pp. 64–65.

9. Mary Boykin Chesnut, *A Diary from Dixie*, ed. Ben Ames Williams (Boston: Houghton Mifflin, 1949), p. 275.

10. Nicholas Cresswell, *The Journal of Nicholas Cresswell: 1774–1777* (New York: Dial, 1924), pp. 52–53. See also Rhys Isaac, "Ethnographic Method in History: An Action Approach," *Historical Methods* 13 (1980), 58.

11. Andrew Burnaby, *A Concise Historical Account of All the British Colonies in North America* (Dublin: Printed for C. James, 1776), p. 213; cited in Dena J. Epstein, *Sinful Tunes and Spirituals: Black Folk Music to the Civil War* (Urbana: Univ. of Illinois, 1977), p. 121. Epstein gives further examples of white imitations of slave dances.

12. Quoted in Marshall Stearns and Jean Stearns, *Jazz Dance: The Story of American Vernacular Dance* (New York: Macmillan, 1963), p. 22.

13. The term is used in an early report from the *South Carolina Gazette* (September 17, 1772), quoted in Peter H. Wood, *Black Majority: Negroes in Colonial South Carolina from 1670 to the Stono Rebellion* (New York: Knopf, 1974), p. 342.

14. The account was given in n.a., "The Origin of Jim Crow" in the *Boston Transcript* of May 27, 1841, and has been followed by commentators since. See Rourke, *American Humor*, p. 72; Hans Nathan, *Dan Emmett and the Rise of Early Negro Minstrelsy* (Norman: Univ. of Oklahoma, 1962), p. 52; Toll, *Blacking Up*, p. 28.

15. Edward Le Roy Rice, *Monarchs of Minstrelsy from "Daddy Rice" to Date* (New York: Kenny Publishers, 1911), pp. 9–10. My thanks to Bob Cantwell for bringing this passage to my attention.

16. Indeed, the story is a commonplace in the history of American popular music and dance, told by many white country performers, such as Jimmy Rodgers, Merle Travis, Ike Everly, and Bill Monroe. For Monroe, see Cantwell, *Bluegrass Breakdown*, pp. 30–32.

17. Rourke, *American Humor*, p. 72.

18. Toll, *Blacking Up*, pp. 43–48. For an overview of the topic of interactions between country performers in the twentieth century, see Tony Russell, *Blacks, Whites and Blues* (New York: Stein and Day, 1970).

19. "Inteview with Ben Cotton," *New York Mirror* (1897), quoted in Toll, *Blacking Up*, p. 46.

20. Quoted in Russell, *Blacks, Whites and Blues*, pp. 11–12.

21. Joel Chandler Harris, *Uncle Remus: His Songs and His Sayings* (New York: Appleton, 1880), pp. xix–xx.

22. Mark Twain, *Autobiography*, p. 15.

23. Mark Twain to Rev. J. H. Twichell, Lucerne, Aug. 22, 1897, in *Mark Twain's Letters*, Vol. II, arr. with comment. by Albert Bigelow Paine (Harper Bros., 1917), p. 645.

24. Kinnard, "Who Are Our National Poets?," p. 333. Another writer, Y. S. Nathanson, in "Negro Minstrelsy Ancient and Modern," originally published in *Putnam's Monthly* (January 1855), p. 73, draws upon the discussion of national literature and balladry from Great Britain, paralleling the authentic plantation productions with border balladry: "They are no senseless and ridiculous imitations forged in the dull brain of some northern self-styled minstrel, but the veritable tunes and words which have lightened the labor of some weary negro in the cotton fields, amused his moonlight hours as he fished, or waked the spirits of the woods as he followed in the track of the wary raccoon. It is impossible to counterfeit, or successfully imitate, one of these songs as it would be for a modern poet to produce a border ballad like Chevy Chase."

25. Isaac D. Williams, *Sunshine and Shadow of Slave Life, Reminiscences* as told by Isaac D. Williams to "Tege" (East Saginaw, Mich: Evening News Printing, 1885), pp. 60–61. In the postbellum period, the continuing play of the plantation scene was a great embarrassment among black educators and professionals. They were especially annoyed at the cooptation of the spirituals, for they felt that the minstrel stage profaned them and produced singing in an inappropriate style. Touring singing groups from Hampton, Fisk, and a number of other predominantly Negro institutions were formed in response to this discomfiture, and served as a means of raising funds. At the formation of the Hampton Folklore Society, a branch of the American Folklore Society, in 1895, a statement was made to this point by the important Afro-American scholar-educator R. R. Moton. See Donald J. Waters, *Strange Ways and Sweet Dreams: Afro-American Folklore from the Hampton Institute* (Boston: G. K. Hall, 1983), pp. 44–46. Moton recorded his ever-changing feelings in his *Finding a Way Out: An Autobiography* (New York: Doubleday, Page, 1920), pp. 29–30.

26. Charles Dickens, *American Notes*, 1842 (London: OxfordUniv., 1957), pp. 91–92. See also Marian Hannah Winter, "Juba and American Minstrelsy," in *Chronicles of the American Dance*, ed. Paul Magriel (New York: Holt, 1948), p. 42; also quoted in Stearns and Stearns, *Jazz Dance*, p. 45.

27. Winter, "Juba and American Minstrelsy," p. 44.

28. Toll, *Blacking Up,* p. 30.

29. Winter, "Juba and American Minstrelsy," p. 42; Stearns and Stearns, *Jazz Dance,* p. 46. Just when Mr. Interlocutor was introduced is unclear, but it happened sometime in the early 1840s as well. The claim that the form was then fully invented has some validity. Through the introduction of more than one performer on the stage, and through the enactment of mock battles and other competitive activities, the spirit of the corn shucking and other such slave holidays was reflected.

Something of this sense of competition was already present in the theatrical presentations of these dances, as can be seen in the career of Juba. He made his greatest claim for himself through having defeated all of the greatest blackface dancers of his time in dancing competitions. The advertisements for his 1848 New England tour billed him as "The Wonder of the World . . . Acknowledged to be the Greatest Dancer in the World, Having danced with John Diamond at the Chatham Theatre for $500, and at the Bowery Theatre for the same amount" (Winter, p. 41). With the development of the minstrel show format, the contest became a regular part of the proceedings.

30. Program of Virginia Serenaders, Worcester, Mass., quoted in Toll, *Blacking Up,* p. 72.

31. See Robert Rydell, *All the World's a Fair* (Chicago: Univ. of Chicago, 1984), pp. 72–89.

Coda: Freedom Mighty Sweet

1. James Lane Allen, "Mrs. Stowe's Uncle Tom's at Home," *Century Magazine* 34 (1887), 866.

APPENDIX I

The Corn-Shucking Accounts

The following are all the reports of the corn-shucking ceremony in the American South that I have been able to locate. Records are included of the event as it was practiced by whites as well as by blacks, and occasional joint shuckings also. The accounts are arranged chronologically according to the year of the performance, if that can be discovered; otherwise, according to the date published. The ex-slave accounts from the Work Projects Administration and related files are given separately in Appendix II.

[George Tucker], *The Valley of the Shenandoah; or, Memoirs of the Graysons,* New York: C. Wiley, 1824, (1796?) vol. 2, pp. 116–18; repr. in Dena Epstein, "Slave Songs in the United States before 1860," *Music Library Association Notes,* 1963, pp. 210–11; and her *Sinful Tunes and Spirituals: Black Folk Music to the Civil War,* Urbana: Univ. of Illinois, 1977, pp. 172–76.

The corn songs of these humble creatures would please you . . . for some of them have a small smack of poetry, and are natural at expressions of kind and amiable feelings—such as, praise of their master, gratitude for his kindness, thanks for his goodness, praise of one another, and, now and then, a little humorous satire. The air of these songs has not so much variety or melody, and requires not more flexibility of voice than they all possess, as they all join in the chorus. Some one . . . strikes up, and singly gives a few rude stanzas, sometimes in rhyme, and sometimes in short expressive sentences, while the rest unite in chorus, and this he continues, until some other improvisatore relieves him. [This was] one of the favorite occasions, on which their talent for "shocking" out the Indian corn—at which time, all the negroes of the plantation, and sometimes many from the neighborhood, are assembled, and sit up nearly the whole night. This is a practice prevailing more or less throughout this state [Virginia], and I believe, the other slave states; but it prevails most in the lower country, where the negroes are in the greatest numbers, and the plantations the largest; and yet, there are thousands among us, who never attended a corn-shocking, or even heard a corn-song— separated are the two classes of black and white, and so little curiosity does that excite, which is and always has been near us. . . . No wonder, then, the rude ditties of our hewers of wood and drawers of water, should not provoke curiosity or human interest.

Rev. T. C. Thornton, *An Inquiry Into the History of Slavery,* Washington, D.C.: William M. Morrison, 1841 (1816?), p. 122.

. . . the negroes at the corn huskings or picking matches, when they are singing one of their wild songs, often made as they go along. The leader sings his part, and all hands join in the chorus, so that they can sometimes of a calm day or evening, be heard at least three miles. . . . We give the reader a part of one of their wild songs. . . .

LEADER—*I loves old Virginny*	CHORUS—*So ho! boys! So ho!*
L. *I love to shuck corn.*	C. *So ho, &c.*
L. *Now's picking cotton time.*	C. *So ho, &c.*
L. *We'll make the money, boys.*	C. *So ho, &c.*
L. *My master is a gentleman.*	C. *So ho, &c.*

L. *He came from Old Dominion.*   C. *So ho, &c.*

L. *And mistress is a lady.*   C. *So ho, &c.*

L. *Right from the land of Washington.*   C. *So ho, &c.*

L. *We all live in Mississippi.*   C. *So ho, &c.*

L. *The land for making cotton.*   C. *So ho, &c.*

L. *They used to tell of cotton seed.*   C. *So ho, &c.*

L. *As dinner for the negro man.*   C. *So ho, &c.*

L. *But boys and gals it's all a lie.*   C. *So ho, &c.*

L. *We live in a fat land.*   C. *So ho, &c.*

L. *Hog meat and hominy.*   C. *So ho, &c.*

L. *Good bread and Indian dumplings.*   C. *So ho, &c.*

L. *Music roots and rich molasses.*   C. *So ho, &c.*

L. *The negro up to picking cotton.*   C. *So ho, &c.*

L. *The old ox broke his neck.*   C. *So ho, &c.*

L. *He belong to old Joe R——*   C. *So ho, &c.*

L. *He cut him up for negro meat.*   C. *So ho, &c.*

L. *My master say he be a rascal.*   C. *So ho, &c.*

L. *His negroes shall not shuck the corn.*   C. *So ho, &c.*

L. *No negro will pick the cotton.*   C. *So ho, &c.*

L. *Old Joe hire Indian.*   C. *So ho, &c.*

L. *I gwine home to Africa.*   C. *So ho, &c.*

L. *My overseer says so.*   C. *So ho, &c.*

L. *He scold only bad ne-*
groes.

C. *So ho, &c.*

L. *Here goes the corn*
boys.

C. *So ho, &c.*

The first leader having sung out his song, all at once a second leader
will break out with his, and begins unceremoniously perhaps
with—

L. *General Washington*
was a gentleman.

C. *Here goes the corn.*

L. *I don't love the ped-*
lars.

C. *Here goes the corn.*

L. *They cheat me in my*
rabbit skins.

C. *Here goes the corn.*

L. *When I bought their*
tin ware.

C. *Here goes the corn.*

[The author then tells of a minister who made his slaves work
on Sunday.—R.D.A.]

The negroes put him into their corn songs; and said this excellent
gentleman, "Sir, I assure you that it is now twenty-five years since
that happened, and they are not yet done singing their song about
the old parson." Let us then also give the reader a part of it.

L. *The parson says his*
prayers in church.

C. *It rain, boys, it rain.*

L. *Then deliver a fine ser-*
mon.

C. *It rain, boys, it rain.*

L. *He cut the matter*
short, my friends,

C. *It rain, boys, it rain.*

L. *He say the blessed*
Lord send it.

C. *It rain, boys, it rain.*

L. *Now's the time for*
planting bacco.

C. *It rain, boys, it rain.*

L. *Come, my negroes, get*
you home.

C. *It rain, boys, it rain.*

L. *Jim, Jack, and Joe and*
Tom.

C. *It rain, boys, it rain.*

L. *Go draw you plants*
and sell them out.

C. *It rain, boys, it rain.*

L. *Don't you stop a mo-ment, boys.*	C. *It rain, boys, it rain.*
L. *'Twas on a blessed Sabbath day.*	C. *It rain, boys, it rain.*
L. *Here's a pretty preacher for you.*	C. *It rain, boys, it rain.*

Poor fellow; we are told that he was actually sung out of the neighborhood.

William Faux, *Memorable Days in America,* London: W. Simpkin and R. Marshall, 1823, p. 211.

My host had a large party of distant neighbours assembled to effect a corn shucking, something like an English hawkey, or harvest home. All, gentle and simple, here work hard till eleven at night. Corn shucking means plucking the ears of Indian corn from the stalk, and then housing it in cribs, purposely made to keep it in, for winter use. The stalk is left in the field; the leaves, while half green, are stripped off, and tied up in bundles, as hay for horses and cattle, and good food it is, much resembling in form the flags in English marshes. . . . The hawkey supper commenced; all seemed fun, created by omnipotent whiskey. . . .

Henry Watson (to Theodore Watson), Nov. 7, 1834, Henry Watson Papers, Duke Univ., quoted in Leslie Owens, *This Species of Property: Slave Life and Culture in the Old South,* New York: Oxford Univ., 1976, pp. 173–74.

A noted spectacle during the harvest was "the husking and the gathering into barns of the yellow maize or corn." Here was a signal for general celebration. Slaves came from nearby plantations to husk and socialize, to sing into the early morning hours. "The tunes they sing are always slow," . . . "the down-trodden; slaves . . . They make a great deal of noise. . . . They then keep time with their song & do not feel their fatigue, & in fact are not fatigued as they otherwise would be. The[y] work more cheerfully. As all keep time, the lazy ones keep it without being sensible of their exertion, besides they might otherwise, and often do, fall asleep at their work."

Elmore Symmes, "Aunt Eliza and Her Slaves," *New England Magazine,* 15 (1896), 537 (Kentucky, 1820s).

The custom of having corn husked on a moonlight night by all the darkies in the neighborhood . . . has passed way with slavery.

Henry Chivers, letter to Edgar Allan Poe, quoted in Jay B. Hubbell, *The South in American Literature,* Durham: Duke Univ. Press, 1954, pp. 554–55 (from a letter of March 12, 1853, referring to a performance before 1828).

If you could only hear it sung, as I have, in the middle hour of the night, by a great Chorus of three hundred of the best bass voices that ever thundered lofty peals of passionate joy, in that omnipresence of the immaculate Silence filling the canopy of Heaven with the Bachanal unsilence of the Refrain—you would be more than delighted.

> *Jinny had de black eye—*
> *Jinny was de gal!*
> *Oh! Jinny had de black eye—*
> *Jinny was de gal!*
> *Jinny was my darling!*
> *Jinny was de gal!*
> *Oh, Jinny was my darling—*
> *Jinny was de gal!*
> *Git away de Cawn, Boys!*
> *Git away de Cawn!*
> *Jinny took to sighing—*
> *Jinny was de gal!*
> *Oh! Jinny took to sighing—*
> *Jinny was de gal!*
> *Jinny had de heart ache—*
> *Jinny was de gal!*
> *Oh! Jinny had de heart ache—*
> *Jinny was de gal!*
> *Git away de Cawn, Boys!*
> *Git away de Cawn!*
> *Jinny lem me kiss her—*
> *Jinny was de gal!*
> *Oh! Jinny lem me kiss her—*
> *Jinny was de gal!*
> *Jinny said she lubbed me—*
> *Jinny was de gal!*

> *Oh! Jinny said she lubbed me—*
> *Jinny was de gal!*
> *Git away de Cawn, Boys!*
> *Git away de Cawn!*
> *Jinny! what de matter?*
> *Jinny was de gal!*
> *Oh! Jinny what de matter?*
> *Jinny was de gal!*
> *Jinny! I am dying!*
> *Jinny was de gal!*
> *Oh! Jinny! I am dying!*
> *Jinny, ain't you gal?*
> *Oh! Jinny! I am dying!*
> *Jinny! kiss me gal!*
> *Git away de Cawn, Boys!*
> *Git away de Cawn!*
> *Git away de Cawn, Boys!*
> *Shuffle out de Cawn.*

The Family Magazine, 1836, p. 42 (written by "A Gentleman who travelled through Virginia some years since").

About eighty or a hundred men were seated around a huge heap of corn, tearing off the husk, and throwing away the denuded ears into spots where they were at once separate from the corn-pile, called *par excellence*, and convenient to the operators. On the summit of the pile, sat a person, selected for his skill in improvisation, who gave out a line in a sort of rapid chant, at the end of which the whole party joined in a chorus. The poet seemed to have no fixed object in view, but to sing. He passed from one subject to another without regard to connexion. I have retained in memory the following lines, which may serve to give some idea of their style of composition. They seldom use the sign of the possessive case:—

> *Oh, Jenny, gone to New-town*
> CHORUS *Oh, Jenny gone*
> > *away!*
> *She went because she wouldn't stay,*
> *Oh, Jenny gone away!*
> *She run'd away, an' I know why,*
> *Oh, Jenny gone away!*

For she went a'ter Jones's Bob,
   Oh, Jenny gone away!
Mr. Norton, good ole man,
   Oh, Jenny gone away!
Treats his niggers mighty well,
   Oh, Jenny gone away!

Young Tim Barnet no great thing,
   Oh! &c
Never say, come take a dram.
   Oh! &c
Master gi's us plenty meat,
   Oh! &c
Might apt to fo'git de drink.
   Oh! &c

After running on in this way for ten or fifteen minutes, any one of the company who may be so disposed, strikes in at the top of his voice with a new tune. The hint is not lost on the leader, who immediately adopts as well as he can, his words to the air, if such may be called, and moves on with perfect readiness in the same rambling style, contemning both rhyme and metre. By the by, it is curious to see how they get over any difficulty about adapting their unequal lines to the tune. The latter is a bed of Procrustes. If the verse is too short, some word is dwelt upon until the measure of time is filled—if there be more than enough, the redundant syllables, sometimes to the number of three or four, are run rapidly through upon one note.

An old negro regulated the movements of the bottle, but the vigilance of "Uncle Abraham" could not entirely prevent excess, as was manifested by an occasional burst of wild shrieks from one of the party.

The shucking continued until about eleven o'clock at which time they all retired to a very plentiful supper; and I could not perceive next morning that their exertions either in singing or drinking had done much damage.

James S. Lamar, *Recollections of Pioneer Days in Georgia*, n.p., 1928, pp. 21–28 (reports from 1837–38).

Another of the enjoyable occurrences during my early boyhood was the annual *cornshucking.* Northern people and others who know no better call this *husking!* But the external integuments of the ears of corn are known among *civilized* folks as *shucks,* hence our "corn shuckings." We had one of these every fall, as did each of our neighbors. They were always at night. The corn was hauled in from the fields and piled high in the lot near the corn house. When the season had been favorable the heap was very large, and was made in the form of a crescent, thus making room for a large number of shuckers to stand or sit around the outer curve and throw the corn as shucked, into a pile between the horns of the crescent. When all was ready, invitations were sent out, somtimes a day or two in advance, asking the neighbors to come to a corn-shucking on such a night. These frolics were always particularly enjoyed by the boys, and they always came in full force, together with the young men and many of the married men from the neighborhood. At the house a bountiful feast was prepared, and several young ladies and some matrons were on hand to assist in that "function."

During the *early* years of this country's history the "shuckers" were all white people and the corn-shuckings were comparatively tame. The parties would gather about dark, take their places at the corn pile, and, while the work went steadily on, would chat and joke, and chew tobacco, and tell anecdotes. There was one man named Lewis Skinner, who seemed to have an inexhaustible stock of anecdotes. He had a quiet manner. He was dry and deliberate. He never seemed to crack a smile himself, but he kept all who were in hearing of him in a state of pleased expectancy, knowing that he would be sure to get there; and when he did, there was always a roar of laughter. This would "remind" somebody, and by the time he got through, Skinner would be ready again. And so it went on for an hour or two. Some one would wake up to the fact that, owing to the attention given to the anecdotes, the work of the evening was lagging. Then there would be a spurt. Then some young men would try their powers on some song which they had heard, and for a while the shucked corn would rain down upon the piles, and by this time the shucks had vastly accumulated behind the men, a state not to be resisted by any small boy. We turned "summersets" in them. We buried each other beneath them. We ran races through them, pushing each other down, rejoicing in the hurtless falls, and shouting and screaming with delighted glee and merriment.—Talk about your town boys' birthday and other parties. If you would know the meaning of a sure-enough and not a make-believe good time, imagine a parcel of country boys at an old-time corn-shucking, turned loose in a big pile of shucks. The fun is spontaneous, rollicking, boisterous, but it is *fun*.

At length the man placed about the center of the crescent, put there because he is known to be a fast shucker, shucks through the pile at that point, and cuts it in two. And now come the race of the two ends which party can finish first—and there is hurrahing and stimulation and bragging and jeering and guying and all the excitement of intense rivalry. The shucks pile up behind faster than the boys can move them out of the way. The cleaned corn in front has grown into a great heap. The end of the work is in sight. The home stretch has come. Some of the shuckers can no longer find room to work at the diminished corn heap. These stand back and hurrah. Presently they raise the stirring corn song "Look for the last ear," with its refrain "Jolly, jolly." The leader of the song pats and stamps and throws up his hands, and shouts out all manner of extemporized "poetry," such as "Last ear, red ear." "Last ear blue ear." "Where is the last ear?" "Who'll find the last ear?" while every voice roars the refrain, "Jolly, jolly!" And so this final spurt winds up, first at one end followed by crowing and taunting, and presently at the other, and the work is done. Then they all set to and take up the shucks, putting them into open pens, made commonly of rails, expressly prepared for them. Before this is ended the owner of the corn has been slipping and dodging about a good deal, trying to get out of sight. But sharp eyes keep him in view, and when the last armful of shucks has been put in place, he is *caught,* and, in spite of a mighty struggle and a show of resistance, he is hoisted upon the shoulders of some powerful man, the rest falling to line, and is borne to the house while the welkin rings again with an appropriate corn song. They carry him once or twice around the house, and finally indoors to the feast, where he is seated at the head of the table, looking and feeling very much ashamed—the more so because the women are present and laughing at him. Having placed him in his seat, amid laughter and all sorts of free and easy remarks and comments, they step back, and in an instant all is changed. The frolic with its unrestrained hilarity is over, the gentleman of the house rises from the chair and takes the role of host as if nothing extraordinary had gone before, invites them to be seated at the table, and disperses the generous and thoughtful hospitality characteristic of the times. The feast is abundant and the very best that can be prepared. It is disposed of by going straight through from end to end without much formality or many pauses. Fresh meats, chicken-pie, ham, cold turkey, fried chicken, hot coffee, and several kinds of plate pies, were leading items of the usual menus. All would be over and the guests safe at home by midnight. They could retire with the reflection that they had rendered an important neighborly service, had eaten an excellent supper, and had enjoyed friendly and pleasant social intercourse.

Old-Time Negro Corn-Shuckings.

When I was about eight or nine years old there was introduced into our neighborhood the negro cornshuckings. They were common else-where in the South, but were practically unknown in the new country where we lived. I wish I was able to give an adequate idea of them, as they have entirely passed away never to return. But this is not easy—the main feature being the *singing* of the negroes, which can-not be represented, either in prose or in poetry, and which they themselves cannot now reproduce. The emancipation of the race, while it has brought them prospective benefits of the highest value, which I sincerely hope they may ultimately reach, has also entailed upon them a weight of responsibility and care too great for their present strength. It has largely pressed out of them, especially those in the country, the light-hearted joviality and child-like frolicsome-ness, which were once regarded as social characteristics. I would not if I could reproduce what is in my mind because of any value that I attach to it, for it has none; but only to perpetuate in some degree the memory of one of the joyous outflowings of their life of servitude which is destined, at not distant day, to be forgotten. I might also in this way express my sense of kindliness to a humble person who in my boyhood contributed much to my pleasure.

It was I think about the year 1837 or '38. Father had made and gathered a very large corn crop, and as usual there was a corn-shucking. The neighbors were on hand and shucking was steadily but leisurely going on. About half past eight or a little later we heard, coming from the top of a long high hill two miles to the east, the sound of the negroes singing, and it soon developed that some one in going to mill has casually mentioned to some darkey over on the creek several miles away, that there was to be a corn-shucking at our house, telling him at what time. The chance was too good to be lost. He hustles around and sends word to one and another, and so gets up a company of twenty or thirty who of their own violition [sic—R.D.A.] came to the corn-shucking. The sound drew nearer and nearer, and swelled out louder and louder. The corn-shuckers stopped, listened and waited. In due time the negroes arrived singing at the very top of their voices, marched right into the lot, surrounded the corn pile, signaled the white men away and took their places.

They have in the Northeast little patent contrivances called corn huskers, an arrangement of small grappling hook (sic) fitted to leather gloves, by means of which it is said, the very disagreeable work of husking is facilitated; but for a really perfect contrivance give me a cornfield darkey's pair of hands, plated as they were with horn almost from wrist to finger tips. Of course, he can sit in a corn house of a rainy day and mumble and fumble over the job turning out ears at a rate of almost one ear every two minutes. But see him at a corn-shucking, aroused, alert, determined, stimulated by song, and with the prospect of a dram immediately behind him, and my opinion is he can beat any patent contrivance ever yet invented. The shucks seem to fall off the ears as if by some magic touch. He hardly gets the ear in his hands before the shuck is behind him and the corn cast before him. And when about thirty stout, active fellows are working at that rate, a large pile of corn begins very soon to grow beautifully less.

All the time the singing goes on. They have a leader or foreman who is responsible for the "composition." This he sings one or two lines at a time, in some cases as loud as he can bawl, in others in a subdued crooning sort of way. Some of his tunes are rapid and snappy, some slower and half serious, some seem to be mournful echoes of a life far away, and many are of a sort of love ditties of current time and present surroundings; but the very spirit of the song, whatever it may be, seems to enter into the shuckers and regulate their movements. The main thing attained, and apparently the main objective sought, is the bringing out of the choral refrain which in itself is absolutely without sense and without significant connection with the words of the leader's song. But it is noise in measured time and infallibility of movement. It is pleasing to the ear, and wonderful in its effect upon the feelings. I do not pretend to any accuracy in my recollection of the following songs. It is the *tunes* that come back to me as I return in thought to that far-off time—the tunes not the words; and of course, the tunes I am unable to give, either on paper or with the voice. The words I record, are at least in the spirit of the original, and in some cases nearly in exact reproduction of it.

The first song . . . I cannot give at all. The chorus I remember was "Jolly, jolly ho," sung on a high key and the "ho" brought out with tremendous power. It could have been heard for miles. The leader was on top of the cornpile, marching slowly to right and left in front of his chorus, and giving out, with many gesticulations and powerful voice, the lines of his song, each one so contrived and sung only by the chorus.

The leader, so it seemed to me, had had some trouble with Dinah. She had changed from smiles to frowns. She had gone back on her word. She had trampled upon his affections. He was sick at heart, and was going away to leave her. But he seemed undecided, so I judged, whether he would go to Alabama or Old Virginny. Meanwhile the chorus stood bravely by him. At every deepening of woe, he was still encouraged to be *Jolly—jolly ho!*—It was sort of Africanized Greek tragedy, in which the chorus is always on hand to support the hero, and get him safely through an emergency. I do not pretend that familiarity with an old-time Georgia corn-shucking will perfectly illuminate Euripides or Aeschelus—but it will help a little.

"Possum up a Gum Tree" was less classical in conception, and not as roaring in execution, but it was sung with great heartiness, notwithstanding. It was about as follows:

LEADER   *Possum up a gum tree,*
CHORUS   *I yi, my pretty boy,*
          Raccoon in de holler,
             I yi, my pretty boy,
          Towser on de possum track,
             I yi, my pretty boy,
          Towser tree de possum,
             I yi, my pretty boy,
          Nigger come to gum tree,
             I yi, my pretty boy,
          Nigger shake the gum tree,
             I yi, my pretty boy,
          Possum drap from gum tree,

I yi, my pretty boy,
Sh wa-wa, shwa, shwa, shwa,
I yi, my pretty boy, . . .

Of course in the rendition every line with its chorus was repeated, so as to hold the mind in suspense and postpone the *denouement*. The last line, which I have indicated rather than expressed, was a wonderful representation, in perfect time and tune, of the sounds made by the dog and possum when the capture was effected.

After a while they began to think it was time to have a dram. I may say that on occasions of this sort it was then the universal custom to furnish whiskey. Church people and all did it. The moral question as to the right or wrong of the practice, had not yet come to the surface. The jug was at intervals passed around with an empty glass, which was handed to each man in turn. He held it out for liquor to be poured into it until he said it was enough. They took very little— many of them none at all. And I must say that I never saw a drunken man on any of these occasions. But now to the song. It began with a sort of crooning recitative:

LEADER   *How's ye feeling brudders?*
                  Seem to me
                  de wedder's gittin
                  to be powerful dry
                  *ober here in dis neighbor*hood!

CHORUS   O dear, I'm so dry!
                  I'm a chokin'
                      O dear, I'm so dry!
                  Stop dat coughin',
                      O dear, I'm so dry!
                  Who dat sneezin',
                      O dear, I'm so dry!
                  Oh my brudders, wake up an' tell me
                  if any of yer 'member what de jug used
                  to say, long time ago.
                      Ho google, my google guggle—
                      ho google, my google google.
                  O dat's de talk! but now she's sick and
                  lying out da in the fence corner, and it
                  'pears like never will say—
                      Ho google my google guggle.

> *Wonder what's de matter.*
> > Ho google my google guggle.
> *She's down wid comsum'tion.*
> > Ho google my google guggle.
> *Ho! I look out da and see her comin'*
> *dis way,*
> > google guggle,
> *Walkin' fast,*
> > google guggle,
> *Mos' here,*
> > google guggle,
> *Now all togedder,*
> > google guggle,
> *Make yer bow,*
> > google guggle,
> *Den one by one,*

CHORUS
> > Google guggle,
> > *Mind what yer 'bout da,*
> > Google guggle,
> > 'Touch her light boys,*
> > Google.

ALL
> > Hoh-h-goo-google-gug-gug-gug-guggle,
> > *my time come at last!*

Certainly, all this is less than nothing to *read* it. But let thirty good voices, with their various shades of difference, mingle harmoniously in *singing* it, and the effect will be altogether different. The words were nothing—it was the music. And we may still compare our darkies with classical men, for even Mendelssohn has composed *Songs* without words! I shall not attempt, ever to represent *Songs,* when I can give neither words nor music. There was a very effective one, considered as a stimulus to rapid shucking, which began with the chorus:

> *Pull de co'n.*

and which rapidly moved through such phrases as—

> *Pull down,*
> *Pull de co'n.*
> *Every body,*
> *Pull de co'n.*

> *Pull fas' an,*
> *Pull de co'n.*
> *Wake up, Sambo,*
> *Pull de co'n.*
> *Roosters crowin',*
> *Pull de co'n.*
> *Day's a-breakin,*
> *Pull de co'n.*

And so on and on, indefinitely.

There was also a stirring domestic song beginning:

> *What 'bout da, Nancy Jane?*
> *Ho, Nancy Jane, ho, Nancy Jane.*

And it went on to picture Nancy Jane as sitting up for her lord and master at home in the little cabin nodding over the fire—the pickaninny in the cradle—"de Spider on de coals an' de hoecake in the Spider"—and at length she is called to wake up and—

> *Rock de cradle, Nancy Jane,*
> *Ho, Nancy Jane, ho, Nancy Jane.*

There were also love songs, referring mostly to "Dinah." But it was noteworthy that in all the more powerful choruses, the word *jolly* evidently predominated. It came in as "Jolly, jolly", or as "Ho, jolly, jolly", or as "Jolly, jolly ho."

When the shucking was over, and the shucks put away, the negroes insisted upon giving my father the usual ride to the table; and then they respectfully retired, and after the whites had finished, they got as good a supper as anybody.

Daniel Drake, M.D., *Pioneer Life in Kentucky,* Cincinnati: Robert Clarke, 1870, pp. 48–56 (1840s).

In the new soil, corn, with moderate cultivation, yielded from sixty to eighty bushels to the acre. Every domestic animal fed and flourished on it—the horse, the cow, the sheep, the hog, and the dog, who, as wheat-bread came into use, would not eat it. The blades of corn up to the ears were "pulled," as the latter began to harden and when partly dry were tied, with blades, into bundles; the tops above the ears were cut off and "shocked." After the corn was pulled, the tops were hauled in, and covered the long fodder house, in which the blades and husks were stowed away, while the corn was measured and thrown into a crib of long round poles. Here, then, were provender and provision for the coming winter. Neither wheat, nor rye, nor barley, nor the far-famed potato, could have been substituted for the admirable maize. Several things in its cultivation can be done by small boys, and from my eighth year I participated in them. When the field was "cross-furrowed," the furrows being about four feet apart, dropping the corn was a simple task, and father, following with the hoe, would cover it. When I was a little older and the furrows ran in one direction only, much greater skill was requisite; for the rows must be kept straight and parallel, that cross-plowing might be practiced. The method then was, as it still is, to cross the furrows at right angles, in lines four feet apart, by the aid of stakes or sharpened poles, generally of hickory or pawpaw, with the bark peeled off, so as to be white and easily seen. . . .

By the month of August the corn is in silk, and the air becomes redolent with the peculiar odor of the tassels. The young and milky grains then begin to form. . . . Now approached the daily feast of green corn—the era of "roasting ears," which began as soon as the grains were half-grown, and continued until no more milk would flow out on piercing the integument with the thumb nail. . . . My first business in the morning was to pull, and husk and silk enough for breakfast; and, eaten with new milk, what breakfast could be more delicious? In the latter part of summer and early autumn, after the corn was "laid by," various rank weeds . . . would spring up among it, rendering the "pulling" and hauling-in a most uncomfortable work. . . . We now come to the "husking;" . . .

. . . the corn-husking was always at night. . . . When the crop was drawn in, the ears were heaped into a long pile or rick, a night fixed on, and the neighbors notified rather than invited, for it was an affair of mutual assistance. As they assembled at night-fall the green glass quart whisky bottle, stopped with a cob, was handed to every one, man and boy, as they arrived, to take a drink. A sufficient number to constitute a sort of quorum having arrived, two men, or more commonly two boys, constituted themselves, or were by acclamation declared captains. They paced the rick and estimated its contractions and expansions with the eye, till they were able to fix on the spot on which the end of the dividing rail should be. The choice depended on the tossing of a chip, one side of which had been spit upon; the first choice of men was decided in the same manner, and in a few minutes the rick was charged upon by the rival forces. As others arrived, as soon as the owner had given each the bottle, he fell in, according to the end that he belonged to. The captains planted themselves on each side of the rail, sustained by their most active operatives. There at the beginning was the great contest, for it was lawful to cause the rail to slide or fall toward your own end, shortening it and lengthening the other. Before I was twelve years old I had stood many times near the rail, either as captain or private, and although fifty years have rolled away, I have never seen a more anxious rivalry, nor a fiercer struggle. It was there that I first learned that competition is the mother of cheating, falsehood, and broils. Corn might be thrown over unhusked, the rail might be pulled toward you by the hand dexterously applied underneath, your feet might push corn to the other side of the rail, your husked corn might be thrown so short a distance as to bury up the projecting base of the pile on the other side:—if charged with any of these tricks, you of course denied it, and there the matter sometimes rested; at other times the charge was affirmed, then rebutted with "you're a liar," and then a fight, at the moment or at the end, settled the question of veracity. The heap cut in two, the parties turned their backs upon each other, and making their hands keep time with a peculiar sort of time, the chorus of voices on a still night might be heard a mile. The oft-replenished whisky bottle meanwhile circulated freely, and at the close the victorious captain, mounted on the shoulders of some of the stoutest men, with the bottle in one hand and his hat in the other, was carried in triumph around the vanquished part amidst shouts of victory which rent the air. Then came the supper, on which the women had been busily employed, and which always included a "pot-pie."

Eugene A. Vail, *De la littérature et des hommes de lettres des Etats Unis d'Amérique,* Paris: Charles Gosselin, 1841, pp. 325–27; repr. in trans. in Elizabeth Langhorne, "Black Music and Tales from Jefferson's Monticello," *Journal of the Virginia Folklore Society,* 1 (1979), 60–67.

A CORN SHELLING SONG*

> *I bought me a fine horse in Baltimore County,*
> > *Oh! Nancy, Oh!*
> *And then a house with seven chimneys,*
> > *Oh! Nancy, Oh!*
> *I bought me a chair to sit next to my Nancy,*
> > *Oh! Nancy, Oh!*
> *And boots of leather to walk with my Nancy,*
> > *Oh! Nancy, Oh!*
> *Oh Miss Nancy is proud and haughty,*
> > *Oh! Nancy, Oh!*
> *Oh Nancy dear, Nancy my dear, why don't*
> > *you marry me?*
> > *Oh! Nancy, Oh!*

Lewis N. Paine, *Six Years in a Southern Prison,* New York: n.p., 1851, pp. 180–83 (Upson County, Ga., 1841).

. . . the shucking frolic is considered . . . a . . . jubilee. A farmer will haul up from his field a pile of corn from ten to twenty rods long, from ten to twenty feet high. This pile consists of nothing but ears. They always break the ears from the stalk, and never cut it at the ground, as the Northern farmers do. It is so arranged that this can be on a moonlight evening. The farmer then gives a general "invite" to all the young ladies and gentlemen in the neighborhood, to come and bring their slaves; for it takes no small number to shuck such a pile of corn.

The guests begin to arrive about dark, and in a short time, they can be heard in all directions, singing the plantation songs, as they come to the scene of action. When they have all arrived, the Host makes the following proposition to his company. "You can shuck the pile, or work till eleven o'clock, or divide the pile and the hands, and try a race."

The last offer is generally accepted. Each party selects two of the shrewdest and best singers among the slaves, to mount the pile and sing, while all join in the chorus. The singers also act the part of

---

*Translated into French and then back into English by Elizabeth Langhorne.

sentinels, to watch the opposite party—for it is part of the game for each party to throw corn on the other's pile.

As soon as all things are ready, the word is given, and they fall to work in good earnest. They sing awhile, then tell stories, and joke and laugh awhile. At last they get to making all the different noises the human voice is capable of, all at the same time—each one of each party doing his best to win the victory. One unacquainted with such scenes would think that Bedlam *had* broken loose, and all its in-mates were doing their best to thunder forth their uproarious joy.

This is continued till the task is finished. They have plenty of liquor to keep up the excitement.

The victorious party peal forth their shouts and jests in a deafening volley, and the negroes seem fairly beside themselves. They jump, roll, and tumble about, as though "kingdom come" was already in their possession. As soon as the pile is finished, the slaves keep a sharp eye on the Host, lest he should slip out of their sight, and get to the house; for it is a rule with them cornshuckings always to tote [him] on their heads; and the moment he gives the word to proceed to the house, he expects his doom—and by dodging and running he tries to escape it. But a dozen stalwart negroes pounce upon him, and it is always understood that he is not to hurt them, or prevent them, if he can, by wrestling and running; but when the negroes get their iron gripe [sic—RDA] on him, it is useless to struggle. If he should get angry, it will make no difference; the masters of the slaves will run to their rescue, and order them to seize him; and nothing suits them better than this. They lay hold of him, and down he comes, and on to their heads he goes, in just no time at all; and they bear him off in triumph to the house; where he receives the jokes and gibes of the young ladies, and of his family.

On arriving at the house they find that the young ladies have not been idle; for the long tables smoke and groan with the loads of poultry, pig, and all kinds of eatables, which would make a Lord Mayor and all his Aldermen smile with a peculiar emphasis. They sit down to the table with the appetites of alligators; for they have been sharpened by active exercise, and by the play of good humor and jokes, that have circulated freely all the while. After each one has had no inconsiderable portion of what was before him, they rise from the table with the roundness of a drum, and the tightness of one of its heads.

. . . As soon as the table is cleared the girls give a wink; and in a trice the room is stripped of everything. . . . The negro fiddler then walks in; and the dance commences. After they have enjoyed their sport sufficiently, they give way to the negroes, who have already supplied themselves with torchlights, and swept the yard. The fiddler walks out, and strikes up a tune; and at it they go in a regular tear-down dance; for here they are at home. The sound of a fiddle makes them crazy; and I do believe that if they were in the height of an insurrection, and any one should go among them, and play on the violin, they would all be dancing in five minutes.

William Cullen Bryant, *Letters of a Traveller,* New York: G. P. Putnam, 1850, pp. 84–87 (Barnwell District, S.C.).

But you must hear of the corn-shucking. The one at which I was present was given on purpose that I might witness the humors of the Carolina negroes. A huge fire of *light-wood* was made near the corn-house. Light-wood is the wood of the long-leaved pine, and is so called, not because it is light, for it is almost the heaviest wood in the world, but because it gives more light than any other fuel. In clearing land, the pines are girdled and suffered to stand; the outer portion of the wood decays and falls off; the inner part, which is saturated with turpentine, remains upright for years, and constitutes the planter's provision of fuel. When a supply is wanted, one of these dead trunks is felled by the axe. The abundance of the light-wood is one of the boasts of South Carolina. Wherever you are, if you happen to be chilly, you may have a fire extempore; a bit of light-wood and a coal give you a bright glaze and a strong heat in an instant. The negroes make fires of it in the field where they work; and, when the mornings are wet and chilly, in the pens where they are milking the cows. At a plantation, where I passed a frosty night, I saw fires in a small inclosure, and was told by the lady of the house that she had ordered them to be made to warm the cattle.

The light-wood fire was made, and the negroes dropped in from the neighboring plantations. The driver of the plantation, a colored man, brought out baskets of corn in the husk, and piled it in a heap; and the negroes began to strip the husks from the ears, singing with great glee as they worked, keeping time to the music, and now and then throwing in a joke in an extravagant burst of laughter. The songs were generally of a comic character; but one of them was set to a singularly wild and plaintive air. . . . These are the words:

Johnny come down de hollow.
  Oh hollow!
Johnny come down de hollow.
  Oh hollow!
De nigger-trader got me.
  Oh hollow!
De speculator bought me.
  Oh hollow!
I'm sold for silver dollars.
  Oh hollow!
Boys, go catch de pony.
  Oh hollow!
Bring him around the corner.
  Oh hollow!
I'm goin' away to Georgia.
  Oh hollow!
Boys, good-by forever!
  Oh hollow!

The song of "Jenny gone away," was also given, and another, called the monkey-song, probably of African origin, in which the principal singer personated a monkey, with all sorts of odd gesticulations, and other negroes bore part in the chorus, "Dan, dan, who's de dandy." One of the songs, commonly sung on these occasions, represents the various animals of the woods as belonging to some profession or trade. For example—

De cooter is de boatman—

The cooter is the terrapin, and a very expert boatman he is.

De cooter is de boatman,
  John, John Crow.
De red-bird de soger.
  John, John Crow.
De mocking-bird de lawyer.
  John, John Crow.
De alligator sawyer.
  John, John Crow.

The alligator's back is furnished with a toothed ridge, like the edge of a saw, which explains the last line. When the work of the evening was over the negroes adjourned to a spacious kitchen. One of them took his place as musician, whistling, and beating time with two sticks on the floor. Several of the men came forward and executed various dances, capering, prancing, and drumming with heel and toe upon the floor, with astonishing agility and perseverance, though all of them had performed their daily tasks and had worked all the evening, and some had walked from four to seven miles to attend the corn-shucking. It became necessary for the commander to make a speech, and confessing his incapacity for public speaking, he called upon a huge black man named Toby to address the company in his stead. Toby, a man of powerful frame, six feet high, his face ornamented with a beard of fashionable cut, had hitherto stood leaning against the wall, looking upon the frolic with an air of superiority. He consented, came forward, demanded a piece of paper to hold in his hand, and harangued the soldiery. It was evident that Toby had listened to stump-speeches in his day. He spoke of "de majority of Sous Carolina," "de interests of de state," "de honor of ole Ba'nwell district," and these phrases he connected by various expletives, and sounds of which we could make nothing. A (sic) length he began to falter, when the captain with admirable presence of mind came to his relief, and interrupted and closed the harangue with an hurrah from the company. . . .

[A] light-wood fire was made, and the negroes dropped in from the neighboring plantations, singing as they came . . . various dances, capering, prancing and drumming with "heel and toe upon the floor" that came after the feast.

Charles Lanman, *Haw-He-Noo: Or Records of a Tourist,* Philadelphia, 1850, pp. 141–44; repr. as *Adventures in the Wilds of the United States and British American Provinces,* Philadelphia: John W. Moore, 1856, pp. 276–79.

The rural custom denominated *corn husking* or *corn shucking* is peculiar to the Southern States. It occurs at night, in the autumn of the year, is participated in by negroes alone, and has for its main object the husking and the gathering into barns of the yellow maize or corn.

Intelligence having previously been circulated throughout the district, that a husking is to occur on a certain night, at a certain plantation, the first step is, to prepare for the contemplated meeting. The corn yielded by the present harvest is hauled in from the surrounding fields, and deposited in huge heaps, immediately around the crib or barn into which it is eventually to be deposited. The roof of the crib having been built so as to be easily removed, and for the purpose of allowing the corn to be thrown into the building from a considerable distance, it is accordingly transferred to some out-of-the-way place, there to remain until re-appropriated to its legitimate use after the husking is ended. The next step is to bring together at convenient points around the barn and the stacks of corn, huge quantities of light wood, which is to be employed for the several purposes of tempering the night air, affording necessary light, and rendering the approaching scene as cheerful as possible. And while all these preparations are being made by the men, others of quite as much importance are occupying the attention of the women belonging to the plantation, whose business it is to prepare the feast which necessarily follows the actual business of husking; while the children are probably spending their time in clearing away the rubbish from a level spot of ground in the vicinity of the bonfires, where it is more than probable we may yet have the pleasure of witnessing a negro dance.

Night has settled upon the world, and the whole space enclosed by the planter's mansion and his almost innumerable outhouses, is filled with a hum of talking and laughing voices—the loud talking and the hoarse laughing of perhaps two hundred negroes, exclusive of woman [sic—R.D.A.] and children. The torch is now applied to the piles of dry wood, and by the brilliant light of the several fires the *huskers* move to their alloted places around the corn house and seat themselves upon the ground. They are divided into what might be termed four divisions (occupying or flanking the several sides of the house,) each one of which is *"headed"* by one of the smartest men in the company, whose province it is not only to superintend his division, and with the assistance of several boys to throw the corn, as it is husked into the crib, but to take the lead in singing which among the blacks, always accompanies the business of husking the corn. All things being ready, a signal is given, and the whole party fall to work as if their very lives depended upon their handling a specified quantity of the white and yellow grain. At the same instant commences a mingled sound of shouting and singing voices, which presently swell into a loud and truly harmonious chorus, and the husking scene is in its prime. The very fires seem elated with the singular but interesting prospect which they illumine, and shoot their broad sheets of flame high into the air. Song follows song, in quick succession, and in every direction piles of beautiful corn seem to spring out of the earth as if by magic, and with the quickness of magic are transferred into the great receptacle, which is itself rapidly becoming filled. Rude indeed are the songs they sing, the words are improvised and the ideas are simple, but there is a pathos and harmony in the chorus which fails not to delight the ear. Amusing stories are occasionally told, and then resoundeth far over the quiet fields seeping moonlight, boisterous peals of laughter. One, two, three, and perhaps four hours have elapsed, and now it is midnight, when the announcement is made by some patriarch of the company that the corn is all husked, and the crib is nearly full. One more song is called for, during the singing of which the roof is replaced upon the corn house, and after congregating around the fires, partly with a view of comparing notes as to the amount of labor performed, but more especially for the purpose of drying the sweat from their sable faces, the entire party of huskers move to the spacious kitchen attached to the planter's mansion.

And here an entirely new scene presents itself to our view. Board tables have been spread in every available corner, and even in the more sheltered portions of the adjoining yard, and everywhere is displayed a most sumptuous entertainment, consisting not only of the substantials of life, strangely served up in the form of a thick soup, but abounding even in luxuries. Good whisky and perhaps peach brandy is supplied in reasonable quantities, and the women, having finished their allotted duties, now mingle with the men, and the feasting company presents as merry and happy a picture of rural life as can well be imagined. Each negro devotes himself to his particular mess, and somewhat after the manner of the aborigines. Jokes of questionable elegance and delicacy are uttered to a considerable extent, and many compliments paid to the *"lib'ral and magnan'mous massa ob dis plantation."* On such occasions, as might not be supposed, acts of decided impropriety but seldom occur, and it is not often that a sufficient quantity of spirit is imbibed, either materially to injure the health or produce intoxication. In this particular, even the *down-trodden* slaves, as they are called, may often set a worthy example for the imitation of those who occupy a more elevated rank in society.

We now come to describe the concluding scene of the corn-husking entertainment, which consists of a dance upon the spot cleared away by the boys in the vicinity of the late fires, which are replenished for further use. The scraping of fiddles and the thumping of banjos having been heard above the clatter of *spoons, soup-plates,* and *gourds,* at the various supper tables, a new *stampede* takes place, and the musicians are hurried off to the dancing ground, as if this were deemed the climax of earthly happiness. "On with the dance, let joy be unconfined." But there seemeth no need for the poet's advice on the present occasion, for the sable congregation now assembled, seem animated with an almost frantic excitement. The dance is the famous *"Virginia Reel,"* and at least a hundred individuals have formed themselves in the proper places. No sooner do the instruments attain the necessary pitch, than the head couples dash into the arena, now slowly and disdainfully, now swiftly and ferociously, and now performing the *double shuffle* or the *pigeon-wing.* Anon they come to a stand, while others follow, and go through the same fantastic performances, with the addition perhaps of an occasional leap or whirl. The excitement is becoming more intense than ever, and it is evident that those whose business it is to stand still, are actually dancing in their shoes. Louder than ever wails the music—order is followed by confusion—and in the madness of the dance there is no method. The brilliant watch-fires cast a ruddy glow upon the faces of the dancers, and when, as it sometimes happens, an individual chances to wander without the circle, his leaping and uncouth figure pictured against the sky, resembles more the form of a lost spirit than a human being. Music, dancing, shouting, leaping, and laughing, with other indescribable antics, are mingled together in a most unique manner, constituting a spectacle only equalled by the midnight dances of painted savages. For hours does this frolic continue, and perhaps is brought to an end by the crowing of a cock, or the first glimpse over the eastern hills, of coming day. And then comes the breaking up of the assembly, so that by the usual breakfast hour, the negroes have reached the several plantations to which they belong, and after spending rather an idle day, are ready for any other *husking* to which they may be invited, and which their masters will permit them to attend.

Mrs. R. H. Marshall, "A Negro Corn-shucking," ed. David J. Winslow, *Journal of American Folklore,* 86 (1973), 61–62 (Laurens, S.C., 1852).

Would you not like to be here next fall at their corn shuckings? It would be fine sport for you. I believe I promised a description of one in this letter. When the overseer has a quantity of corn to husk, he allows his Negroes to invite those on the neighboring plantations to come and help them in the evening. When all things are ready, they light the torches of pitch pine (their [sic—R.D.A.] being an abundance of it about here) and march while singing one of their corn songs to the spot. Then the captain mounts the heap of corn, and all sing a *call song* for the others to come, which is immediately answered from the other plantations in a song that "they are coming." You can hear them distinctly for more than a mile. They sing as they march all the way, and when they arrive at the spot, they all join in one *grand chorous*—and make the forest ring with their music. Then they appoint captains to succeed each other from different companies—who mount the heap in turn and play their *monkey pranks*—while they take the lead in singing as those around them shuck and toss their corn into the crib—seemingly the happiest beings that live. I was never more amused than while watching their movements and listening to their songs. Some of them have very fine voices. We waited until twelve o'clock and left them to enjoy their supper, prepared for them by their overseer.

Robert Criswell, *Uncle Tom's Cabin Contrasted with Buckingham Hall, the Planters House,* New York: 1852.

That evening the "corn-shucking" or husking came off. The corn was piled in large heaps before the row of cabins. and although it was a bright night, being the full of the moon, each little window of the slaves' habitations was illuminated by a couple of tallow candles, so that every object was distinctly visible.

Around the large corn heaps were seated over two hundred men and women, (many of whom were from the neighboring plantations,) tearing off the husks and throwing the ears into separate piles; and in the midst of their employment all were chattering, laughing, singing and telling stories, much to the amusement of themselves and the young gentlemen, who were seated a little apart, observing the proceedings.

On the top of one of the heaps was mounted Uncle Cato, one of the principle slaves and a great favorite. . . . He was noted for his talent of improvision. He would sing one or more lines of a song and the chorus would be repeated by all the others. Some of the women had excellent voices, especially the coquet, Miss Polly, a pretty mulatto, who had Caroline's Jake beside her, and who wore the identical scarlet handkerchief on her head in the form of a turban, smiling now and then on Jeff, who took no notice, but sat at a distance scowling defiance at his rival.

One of the songs ran thus:

> *The lubly Moon it shine so bright,*
> *We doesn't want no oder light,*
> >   CHORUS: *sing, darkeys, sing!*
> *De man up dere, he look at us,*
> *He think we make a great, big fuss,*
> >   CHORUS: *sing, darkeys, sing!*
> *Possum-dog he cotch a coon,*
> *Nigger skin him pretty soon,*
> >   CHORUS: *sing, darkey, sing!*
> *Sold de skin and got de chink,*
> *Berry sorry dat I drink.*
> >   CHORUS: *sing, darkey, sing!*

After this the whiskey was handed about by the overseers and the slaves became very merry, began to caper and sing more than before.

> *Massa Eugene hab good whiskey,*
> *Makes de niggers bery friskey,*
> >   CHORUS: *shucking ob de corn.*
> *O, ho! de niggers jolly!*
> *See dah, de pretty Polly!*
> >   CHORUS: *shucking ob de corn.*
> *Dat ar Jake, he sits beside her,*
> *Will she hab dat big black spider?*
> >   CHORUS: *shucking ob de corn.*
> *Jeff's so mad, he look like tunder—*
> *O-o-o-o! who dat hit me wid dat corn dah?*
> >   CHORUS: *Jeff, he trew dat corn.*

By this time the husking was finished. It being quite late, and as the song was concluded they all jumped up and had a regular break-down, exhibiting such ridiculous antics that Melville and Eugene laughed till they could laugh no longer from sheer exhaustion.

Then Buckingham ordered them to disperse and retire to their cabins; and the friends returning to the house, soon after sought their beds.

Frederika Bremer, *Homes of the New World*, New York: Harper, 1853, p. 370.

These songs have been made on the road; during the journeyings of the slaves; upon the rivers, as they paddled their canoes along or steered the raft down the stream; and in particular, at the corn-huskings, which are to the negroes what the harvest-home is to our peasants, and at which they sing impromptu whatever is uppermost in their heart or in their brain. Yes, all these songs are peculiarly improvisations, which have taken root in the minds of the people, and are listened to and sung to the whites, who, possessed of a knowledge of music, have caught and noted them down.

"Negro Minstrelsy—Ancient and Modern," *Putnam's Magazine*, Jan. 1855, p. 77.

The annual cornshucking season has its own peculiar class of songs, never heard but on that festival; their rhythmical structure or caesural pauses not being adapted to the measured cadence of the ears. Standing at a little distance from the corn heap, on some dark and quiet night, watching the sable forms of the gang, illuminated at intervals by the flashes of the lightwood knot, and listening to the wild notes of their harvest songs, it is easy to imagine ourselves unseen spectators of some secret aboriginal rite or savage festival. Snatches of one or two songs which on such occasions I have heard, recur to me. Could I in the following specimen give you any idea of the wild grandeur and stirring music of this refrain, I should need no apology for presenting it to my readers.

> De ladies in de parlor,
> > Hey, come a rollin' down—
> A drinking tea and coffee;
> > Good morning ladies all.

> De gemmen in de kitchen,
> > Hey, come a rollin' down—
> A drinking brandy toddy;
> > Good morning, ladies all.

I put the above in a class to which I have given the name of descriptive songs. By this I do not mean to be understood as hinting that it is an accurate description of a "whitefolks" party. On the contrary, it probably originated in the tipsy brain of its dusky author; or, perhaps, in a moment of discontent may have been composed as an exaggerated satire. The allusion to the kitchen, as the place where the gentlemen are engaged in the pleasing and congenial occupation, goes to show that the minstrel had in his view a colored party, which I am inclined to think was in fact the case. But at this stage of our critical knowledge on the subject of negro literature, such speculations are alike tedious and unprofitable.

The comic ballads of the South, form a large and highly interesting class of songs, more especially as they are of a sort most readily transplanted, and most grateful to the public taste. Apart from their fun, however, they lack the merit which distinguishes many other kinds of African composition. The negro is humorous rather than witty, and his comic songs consist of ludicrous images, instead of witty conceits. I do not remember, in the whole course of my investigations, to have met with anything like a pun in a genuine plantation melody. The following shucking song has nothing to recommend it to public attention, save the questionable rhyme to "supper." The lovers of "Ole Dan Tucker" will be pleased and interested with a coincidence in which there cannot be the slightest ground for a suspicion of plagiarism.

> Cow bog [sic—R.D.A.] on middle e' island—
>   Ho! meleety, ho!
> Cow boy on middle e' island—
>   Ho! meleety, ho!
>
> Misses eat de green persimmon,
>   Ho! meleety, ho! [Repeat]
>
> Mouf all drawd up in a pucker,
>   Ho! meleety, ho! [Repeat]
>
> Staid so till she went to supper,
>   Ho! meleety, ho! [Repeat]

[Hardin E. Taliaferro], "Skitt," *Fisher's River North Carolina Scenes and Sketches,* New York: Harper and Bros., 1859, pp. 218–19.

Their gatherings were frequent.... One neighbor would help another harvest his grain, taking it in turn till they were all through. Corn-shuckings were conducted in the same way.... They "swopped work."

James Battle Avirett, *The Old Plantation,* New York: F. T. Neely, 1901, pp. 140–46 (Orange County, North Carolina, 1850s).

... the three great high feasts on the plantation are "Crismus, hog killin', and corn shuckin' "—the first an immovable one, while the last two are movable feasts in the African almanac. Pending any one of these notable events in plantation life, everybody is more or less excited and thoroughly occupied. What are Uncle Philip and Uncle Jim doing now? With a tape line they are making an honest, fair division of that immense corn pile, as nearly equal in bulk and barrels as these well-trained eyes and hands can make it. They have now agreed upon the dividing line, and look how carefully they fasten it with a long pole laid across the corn pile, held firmly in its place by strong stakes driven firmly into the ground. Old Master is called and he says that the division is just and fair, and that settles it. The estimate is that there are about seven hundred and fifty barrels of corn in that immense pile, which lies there like a big boulder of food which a wave of God's loving providence has swept across the pathway of these sunny-hearted sons of toil. Busy, very busy, are several of the servants in preparing the supper which always follows. Beef, mutton and pork are in that happy process of plantation cookery known as barbecue, and are in great abundance. Some quantities of bread, wheat and corn, with bushels of sweet potatoes and great baskets of pies and cakes as to require a full staff of these natural born cooks. The carpenters are erecting the simple and substantial tables, and Aunt Daphne is unrolling yard after yard of homemade white cloth to serve as table covers. Well, all the necessary preparations are going on under the eye of "old Mistuss," whose judgment with these people is oracular: for this is the fortieth harvest which she has celebrated in her married life. She has learned from the old planter that some two hundred and fifty servants, not counting the women and the children, must be fed, and this without stint. As the day grows older and the preparations continue, you observe that the servants are beginning to arrive from the orchards and the lake. Some are busy making their "shucking pegs" of seasoned hickory, while the more fortunate have hunted up the iron or steel ones which they used last year, and maybe for ten years. The shucking peg is a sharpened spike about five inches in length, fastened at the center to the forefinger on the right hand, thus saving their fingernails and facilitating the shucking process to a remarkable degree. The dexterity and rapidity with which they strip off the shuck, to one who never witnessed it, are simply incredible. About sunset the assembly bell rings and the servants assemble in front of Ben's house in the barn yard. Here they come, swinging along with the easy motion of body so expressly indicative of good health. No rheumatism here this evening; no stiffness of joints, no aches, no pains. Even old Handy walks along like a boy, while Buck and George are larking around, determined to have all the fun that is possible. Here they come! Here they come! And the cry is till they come! "My sakes! Whey'd all dese niggers come' f'om enyway! Dey fa'ly darkens de yerth! dey shu'ly duz!" said Uncle Amos as he came up, taking off his hat. "Ole Marster, der's plenty of 'visions fo de hole country to eat." What are these men doing there? They are drawing up two or three of the wagons in position so that from them, as from a stage, "all de white fokeses can jes' hab dere fun at de co'n shucking," says old Peter, who is attending to this feature of the preparations.

While this is going on, you see some forty or fifty women, boys and girls, some with baskets and others with rakes, getting ready to rake back the shucks from the feet of the men and carry them to those tall rail pens where they will be carefully packed away for the winter feed of the cattle. After half an hour or more has passed, waiting for the latest arrival of the reinforcements, whose deep, rich voices you can hear now coming in several directions from the plantations around, every note of which is full of that peculiar joy so well known to the African ear, and which can come from none other than the plantation darkies throat—well, here they are at last, and before anything else is done, they must pass in review before old master, because there are some servants on the adjoining estates that he will not allow to attend pleasure makings of any character on his plantation. They are the disreputable darkies of that portion of the county and are regarded as unfit associates for his servants. He takes his position on the steps . . . and with hats off the procession files by. Presently Uncle Philip announces that Isaac and Arnold are the two chosen captains; whereupon there is a great yell of approbation. These two young men then begin the division of hands, after a most novel plan to you, dear reader, who have never attended a corn shucking. By this time, a dozen or more half grown boys come forward, their pine torches flaming with bright light, and the scene becomes weird and very animated. Here stand the two captains and splendid specimens of youthful vigor they are. Here comes Uncle Jim, and as he walks up he takes a knife out of his pocket, saying to the captains: "Dis is fur de furst ch'ice ob de shuckers," and with that he throws the knife in the air calling out, "Cross or pile?" to which Isaac must make an answer. If he says "cross," and the knife on the ground shows a metal bar on the uppermost side of the handle, Isaac wins on that throw and *vice versa*. Then Uncle Jim addresses Arnold on the same conditions as he applied to Isaac. The captain who wins the best two out of three or who first guesses twice right has the first choice of hands, and you may be sure they guard their rights almost religiously. Then the choice goes on, each captain choosing his followers until they have gone through the whole number of two hundred and fifty hands or more, each man, as his name is called ranging himself behind his captain. Then the captains resort to the arbitrament [sic—R.D.A.] of the cross and pile, as before seen, in the choice of the two halves of the corn pile. The victorious captain, with two or three of his most trusted followers, will then carefully walk over the whole pile of corn, closely inspecting it, so as to hit upon that half which, in his judgment, has the less number of barrels to be shucked, thus making way for victory. After he had decided, he keeps his counsel until they have had a word or two from the old master, in the way of caution against bad temper or any tricks which may serve to irritate or make their adversaries angry. Then, with as much solemnity as any old Greek would employ in consulting the Delphic oracle, the two captains come out to the dividing line of the corn, shaking hands in perfect silence, everybody around them as silent as the grave, make a cross on the ground and spit on it for luck. Then, as if shot from as many Parthian bows, the two captains call their respective followers to them and the corn shucking is on in all its glory. Such noise, such confusion, such bantering, such boasting, until the two captains settled themselves down at the base of the dividing line, marked by the long cypress pole, along which they must shuck through the pile in such a way as not to cause the pole to fall over on either side. The scene which now follows beggars description. Dear old Sir Walter Scott, who has delighted the Anglo-Saxon reader of Waverley in his matchless description of the Tournament of Ashby de la Souche, would fail in its portrayal. The gifted author of Ben Hur succeeding in his chariot race would not attempt it. The author has seen hundreds of men wild with excitement at big fires in large cities—as a young lawyer, when politics ran high in the joint discussion of the old Southern campaigns, he has witnessed how far excitement would sweep men away in wild fury—but these were white men and less emotional than all these three hundred Africans ranged around this pile of corn. While the corn shucking is going on and these men are warming up fully to their work, let us look into those wagons over there. The young people from a number of the adjoining estates have come over to enjoy the fun . . . they begin to wager, here a pair of kid gloves, there a handsome driving whip or a silver dog whistle, or this and that and the other, on the corn shucking. My sakes! what a chorus of magnificent voices is that we hear as the air is rent with the songs of these corn shuckers. Hear them for a moment as they sing away, the ears of corn flying towards the corn house as thick as snowflakes in a storm, while the shucks are raked away in the opposite direction. Each company seems to have its own leader while the others will join in the chorus. In all your life did you ever hear such fine voices—some as clear and strong as Kent bugles and others as soft as a German flute. Mark you, the women and the boys and girls are all joining in the chorus. Hear them as the leader, in a clear strong voice, calls out:

Massa is in de grate [sic—R.D.A.] house countin' out his money,
    CHORUS: *Oh, shuck dat co'n an' trow't in de ba'n,*
Mistis in de parler eatin' bread an' honey.
    CHORUS: *Oh, shuck dat co'n an' trow't in de ba'n,*
Sheep shell co'n by de rattle of his ho'n,
    CHORUS: *Oh, shuck dat co'n an' trow't in de ba'n,*
Send to de mill by de whipperwill.
    CHORUS: *Oh, shuck dat co'n an' trow't in de ba'n.*

And then a hundred voices would ring out half a dozen times or more, repeating the chorus until the leader would again call out:

    Ole Dan Tucker he got drunk,
        CHORUS: *Fell in de fiah an' kick'd*
      up a chunk.
    A red-hot coal get in his shoe,

> *An' oh, lawd me, how de ashes flew.*
> *Marster an' Mistus lookin' mighty fine—*
> *Gwine to take a journey; gwine whar dey*
>   *gwine;*
> *Crab grass a-dyin', red sun in de west—*
> *Saturday's comin', nigger gwine to rest.*

And then the full chorus half a dozen times over. The truth is, the scene in all its varied features simply beggars description, and while this is in no wise descriptive of it, it may serve to give the reader some idea of what a full round of melody we would have, when, as was often the case, three hundred voices would swell out in the chorus. Meantime the work went on, and the deeper they went into the great pile of corn the higher would rise their excitement, and the deeper and richer their voices in simple-hearted song. Some of these were descriptive, others simply recitative, in the conduct of which some of the leaders were quite gifted—making up the song as they went along. Frequently it was that plantation incidents, events in the community or the personal peculiarity of some servant would be brought out by the leader in giving a cue to the chorus which was to follow. No pile of corn, no body of men could stand up long under such telling work. And yet it went on for two hours or more until the faster shuckers had gone through the pile and were now about-facing, when the excitement as they neared the close of the race deepened every moment. Stop your talking in the wagon for a moment or two! Listen to those short, quick, nervous cries as they call out, in quivering energy, "Oh, shuck dat co'n and trow't in de ba'n." They show clearly that the race is about to close. Presently as the victorious side winds up the race, you would think a cyclone had broken loose, for the way that a cloud of shucks were thrown up in the air, in token of their victory. Two or three of the strongest of the company then caught up the victorious captain on their shoulders and bore him away in triumph to the old planter to be crowned as the victor, amidst such shouts and cries of joy as you, dear reader, have never heard unless at an old-fashioned plantation corn shucking. Corn shucking, not corn husking. White people husk corn, negroes shuck it—wonderful difference between the two processes is there—quite as much as between the white man playing on his violin and the negro playing on his fiddle. What a proud negro captain . . . as his "ole marster" crowns him with a new hat, shakes his hand, drops a five dollar gold piece into it and tells him to take the other captain by the hand and invite him and everybody else up to supper. This he does, and such a crowd and such a supper—plenty and to spare for every man, woman and child there, with Uncle Philip as a master of ceremonies, directing Handy, Cain, George and Buck to "wate on dem comp'ny niggers fus', after dey dun gib de two captains plenty ob supper an' lots ob good coffee."

In the earlier part of his life the old planter's custom had been to give them plenty of whiskey, but far too many fights and far too much blood were the outcome of the whiskey. He substituted, in the latter days of his life, the best coffee for whiskey. After everybody had fully enjoyed their well deserved meal, and, in fact, every feature of the corn shucking, there followed some fine singing of the good old plantation songs, among which were "Old Dog Tray," "Marster's in de Cold, Cold Groun'," "Carry me Bac' to Ole Berginny," and a half a dozen or more of those old-fashioned songs, when all would go to their homes, not for "de nite," because it's "mos' de broke ob day."

James Lee Love, "Recollections," in James Lee Love Papers, 1860–1864, Univ. of North Carolina Library, vol. 14, Apr. 1863, pp. 29–30 (compares white and black practices).

For a "corn shucking" the farmer would have his entire crop in the husks or "shucks" as we called it (we never used the word "husks") hauled into the barnyard near his corn crib, and piled into a long pyramidal heap. The neighbors and their wives would be invited in on a certain autumn moonlight night.

The men would attack the corn pile and "shuck" the heap; sitting on a log or box or upturned vessel of any kind that would furnish a seat. Usually the pile was nearly surrounded by the shuckers. Each shucker wore on his right hand a wooden pin about five inches long. A leather strap attached to it made a ring into which one or more fingers were inserted to hold the pin firmly in position. The pin was held in the palm of the right hand, and its end projected about an inch beyond the index finger. This projecting end was carved by whittling so as to make a fairly sharp but substantial tip just opposing the thumb of the right hand. It was made of hard wood—oak or hickory. The ear of corn was picked up and held in the left hand, the "silk" end of the ear upwards; then the pin was inserted in the shuck near the silk end, the shuck torn open by the pin and the thumb, the front of the shuck stropped down to the butt of the ear, the left hand grasped the other or back half of the shuck and stripping it to the butt, then, grasping the whole inverted shuck in one hand, usually the left, and the clean ear of corn in the other hand, the ear was broken off, the shuck thrown behind the shucker and the ear of corn thrown behind the shucker and the ear or corn thrown into the corn pile.

The fun there was in racing against your nearby mates to see who could get his ear of corn out quickest; also in the search for an ear of red corn. Practically white corn alone was raised—very little yellow corn—and a few red ears would be among them. The finder of a red ear announced the fact vociferously, and there was hearty rivalry in finding red ears.

When the corn was all shucked the supper would be ready. The latter was served out of doors, usually, for the kitchens were too small, in the moonlight. Indeed the big chicken pot pie with its wealth of dumplings had to be cooked out of doors in the "wash kettle"—no ordinary kitchen utensil was big enough. There were no stoves then, and all the cooking had to be done over open wood fires. The women, therefore, had as hard a task, and a more disagreeable one in preparing the feast, as the men who shucked the corn. . . . But the big feast was a joy; a neighborly good deed had been done in shucking the corn, and thus the country life was made happier by such mutual cooperation.

Francis Fedric, *Slave Life in Virginia and Kentucky*, London: Wertheim, McIntosh and Hunt, 1863, pp. 47–51.

In harvest time, thirty or forty years ago, it was customary to give the slaves a good deal of grog, the masters thinking that the slaves could not do the hard work without the spirits. A great change has taken place now in this respect; many of the planters during harvest give their slaves sixpence a day instead of the whiskey. The consequence is that there is not a fifth of the sickness there was some years ago. The country is intensely hot in the harvest time, and those who drank grog would then want water; and, having got water, they would want grog again; consequently, they soon either were sick or drunk. All round where I dwelt the sixpence was generally substituted for the spirits; the slaves are looking better, and there are fewer outbreaks in the fields. In the autumn, about the 1st of November, the slaves commence gathering the Indian-corn, pulling it off the stalk and throwing it into heaps. Then it is carted home, and thrown into heaps sixty or seventy yards long, seven or eight feet wide. Some of the masters make their slaves shuck the corn. All the slaves stand on one side of the heap, and throw the ears over, which are then cribbed. This is the time when the whole country far and wide resounds with corn-songs. When they commence shucking the corn, the master will say, "Ain't you going to sing any tonight?" The slaves say, "Yers, sir." One slave will begin:—

> *Fare you well, Miss Lucy,*
> ALL *John come down de hollow.*

The next song will be:—

> *Fare you well, fare you well*
> ALL *Weel ho. Weell ho.*
> CAPTAIN *Fare you well, young ladies all.*
> ALL *Weel ho. Weell ho.*
> CAPTAIN *Fare you well, I'm going away.*
> ALL *Weel ho. Weell ho.*
> CAPTAIN *I'm going away to Canada.*
> ALL *Weel ho. Weell ho.*

One night Mr. Taylor, a large planter, had a corn shucking, a Bee it is called. The corn pile was 180 yards long. He sent his slaves on horseback with letters to the other planters to ask them to allow their slaves to come and help. On a Thursday night, about 8 o'clock, the slaves were heard coming, the corn-songs ringing through the plantations. "Oh, they are coming, they are coming!" exclaimed Mr. Taylor, who had been listening some time for the songs. The slaves marched up in companies, headed by captains, who had in the crowns of their hats a short stick, with feathers tied to it, like a cockade. I myself was in one of the companies. Mr. Taylor shook hands with each captain as the companies arrived, and said the men were to have some brandy if they wished, a large jug of which was ready for them. Mr. Taylor ordered the corn-pile to be divided into two by a large pole laid across. Two men were chosen as captains; and the men, to the number of 300 or 400, were told off to each captain. One of the captains got Mr. Taylor on his side, who said he should not like his party to be beaten. "Don't throw the corn too far. Let some of it drop just over, and we'll shingle some, and get done first. I can make my slaves shuck what we shingle tomorrow," said Mr. Taylor, "for I hate to be beaten."

The corn-songs now rang out merrily; all working willingly and gaily. Just before they had finished the heaps, Mr. Taylor went away into the house; then the slaves, on Mr. Taylor's side, by shingling, beat the other side; and his Captain, and all his men, rallied around the others, and took their hats in their hands, and cried out, "Oh, oh! fie! for shame!"

It was two o'clock in the morning now, and they marched to Mr. Taylor's house; the Captain hollowing out, "Oh, where's Mr. Taylor? Oh, where's Mr. Taylor?" all the men answering "Oh, oh, oh!"

Mr. Taylor walked, with all his family on the verandah; and the Captain sang:

	"I've just come to let you know.
MEN	*Oh, oh, oh!*
CAPTAIN	*The upper end has beat.*
MEN	*Oh, oh, oh!*
CAPTAIN	*But isn't they sorry fellows?*
MEN	*Oh, oh, oh!*
CAPTAIN	*But I'm going back again,*
MEN	*Oh, oh, oh!*
CAPTAIN	*But I'm going back again.*
MEN	*Oh, oh, oh!*
CAPTAIN	*And where's Mr. Taylor?*
MEN	*Oh, oh, oh!*
CAPTAIN	*And where's Mr. Taylor?*
MEN	*Oh, oh, oh!*
CAPTAIN	*And where's Mrs. Taylor?*
MEN	*Oh, oh, oh!*
CAPTAIN	*I'll bid you fare you well,*
MEN	*Oh, oh, oh!*
CAPTAIN	*For I'm going back again.*
MEN	*Oh, oh, oh!*
CAPTAIN	*I'll bid you, fare you well* *And a long fair you well.*
MEN	*Oh, oh, oh!*

They marched back again and finished the pile. All then went to enjoy a good supper, provided by Mr. Taylor; it being customary to kill an ox, on such an occasion; Mr., Mrs. and the Misses Taylor, waiting upon the slaves at supper. What I have written cannot convey a tenth part of the spirit, humour, and mirth of the company; all joyous—singing, coming and going. But within one short fortnight, at least thirty of this happy band were sold, many of them down South. . . .

Henry A. Woods, "A Southern Corn-Shucking," *Appleton's Journal,* Nov. 12, 1870, p. 571.

Some few years ago, while travelling in the South, an opportunity was presented of gratifying one of my most earnest wishes, viz. to attend a *bona fide* corn-husking. This important jubilee was to take place on an adjoining plantation, some two miles distant from the house at which I was stopping; and on the appointed evening arriving, I set forth for the scene of busy festivity, about dusk, the most delightful portion of a Southern day in early autumn. The sun's hot breath had been cooled to a delightful temperature by the evening breeze, and the nostrils were saluted by the agreeable and healthful aroma arising from the dense forests of pine, while the ear was intoxicated with the liquid melodious outpourings of our American nightingale; in fact, almost the entire paraphernalia of Southern loveliness greeted my every sense, as I strolled leisurely along through the intervening woodlands, until night, which in that latitude rapidly follows sunset, overtook me, and quickening my footsteps, I arrived. Some fifteen or twenty or more had congregated from the neighboring plantations, and reinforcements of twos and threes were constantly arriving. . . . In about half an hour the huge corn-pile was surrounded by a hundred or more of the stalwart negroes, and an exciting contest began, as to who should "walk the pile," the competition being each possessed of powerful and melodious voices, and a ready gift of improvisation. Frequently two divisions of the corn are made, and the parties separate, gathering around their respective piles, each striving to outdo the other.

The contest being decided, the favored one, highly elated, mounted the corn, and walking forward and backward, began to sing, while the others swelled the chorus with their deep, sonorous voices, easily distinguishable for miles around.

Some scraps of these songs will linger in my memory, sufficient to impart an idea of their peculiar character:

SOLO	CHORUS
Here's your corn pile,	*Shuck it, shuck it;*
Here's your corn pile,	*Shuck it, shuck it;*
Yaller river horses,	*Feed 'em, feed 'em;*
A little more whiskey,	*Marse Jim, Marse Jim;*
O, the debil,	*Catch him, catch him;*
Give this nigger,	*Corn-bread, corn-bread;*
Give this nigger,	*Corn-bread, corn-bread;*
Coon in the hollow,	*Tree him, tree him;*
'Possum in the simmon tree,	*See him, see him,*
Susan in the cow pen,	*Milking, milking;*
Make the corn fly, etc.	*Faster, faster; etc.*

This song, though utterly devoid of sense, was even rendered attractive by the melodious voices of the negroes, and as they sang it the huge pile seemed to melt beneath their nimble fingers. Resting a few moments, the leader proceeded with another song, if possible, more grotesque than the first.

Fortunately, I remember its burden *in toto,* as I deem it worthy of preservation:

SOLO	*Obadiah,*
CHORUS	*Jumped in the fire;*
SOLO	*Fire too hot,*
CHORUS	*Jumped in the pot;*
SOLO	*Pot too black,*
CHORUS	*Jumped in the crack;*
SOLO	*Crack too high,*
CHORUS	*Jumped in the sky;*
SOLO	*Sky too blue,*
CHORUS	*Jumped in a canoe;*
SOLO	*Pond too deep,*
CHORUS	*Jumped in the creek;*
SOLO	*Creek too shallow,*
CHORUS	*Jumped in the tallow;*

SOLO	*Tallow too soft,*
CHORUS	*Jumped in the loft;*
SOLO	*Loft too rotten,*
CHORUS	*Jumped in the cotton;*
SOLO	*Cotton so white,*
CHORUS	*Stayed all night.*

Various other songs of a similar nature succeeded, until the corn-pile totally disappeared, while the ample crib overflowed with the golden grain, plainly testifying to the expertness of the corn-huskers.

Long, temporary tables, lighted by blazing torches, fastened at irregular intervals to the trees, were loaded with huge platters of beef, mutton, corn-bread, and that indispensable article of Southern diet, "sweet 'taters," and around this plentiful, though homely feast, the negroes eagerly gathered, their appetites being considerably sharpened by their previous exercise. Having feasted to their hearts' content, the men were joined by the colored matrons and maids, neatly attired in colored homespun, the reigning belles rejoicing in numerous odds and ends of ribbon floating from their sable braids; and we left them executing those unique, fantastic dances so peculiar to their race—keeping perfect time to the enlivening music of violin, banjo, and bones.

James Lane Allen, "Mrs. Stowe's 'Uncle Tom' at Home in Kentucky," *Century Magazine,* 34 (1870), 863.

Garnett Andrews, *Reminiscences of an Old Georgia Lawyer,* Atlanta: J. J. Toon, 1870, pp. 10–12.

I have often sat at my father's stile, during the nights of November and December, and listened to the corn-songs floating on the frosty night-air from some neighbor's corn pile—for the voices of the negroes were generally musical, and strong as a steam whistle.

When starting for the festivity—for the shuckings were so considered—a solitary refrain might be heard a mile or so away, then another would join, and as they approached, more and more, until they arrived, singing, at the corn-pile in a company of fifteen or twenty; sometimes two or three of such companies would approach at the same time, making the night resonant with melody—I say melody, for I know of no music so melodious to my ear at a short distance, as an old time corn-song. Arriving at the corn-pile, some leader—by common tacit consent—assumed the office of "General," which was to "give out." "Giving out" was a recitative which he remembered or made up—according to the inspiration of the moment—when the great ring around the corn-pile answered in the chorus of "Ha, Hi, Ho." I remember one ran thus:

> *Did you ever hear the cow laugh?*
> *Ha, Hi, Ho,*
> *And how you think the cow laugh?*
> *Ha, Hi, Ho,*
> *The cow say moo, moo, moo,*
> *Ha, Hi, Ho,*
> *And what you think the cow want?*
> *Ha, Hi, Ho,*
> *The cow want corn and that what the cow want.*
> *Ha, Hi, Ho.*

The "General" would continue to express the same solicitude for such of the corn-eating animals, as he might sympathize with, until satisfied.

Most of the planters having come from Virginia and made money, first by growing tobacco and then cotton, would go back to that state and Maryland and buy slaves; hence many of their songs referred to old "Virginny," Richmond and Baltimore.

The "General," sticking a corn-shuck in his hat, by way of distinction, would mount the corn-pile and frequently, in his recitative, address the ring as his children, his soldiers or his army. Sometimes he would, in the enthusiasm of the occasion, fall on his knees and clap his hands above his head, then rise, holding them, clasping an ear of corn, in the same attitude, then with legs of the form of the letter V inverted, and his left arm akimbo—all the time "giving out"—as he would wave his right, in his rhapsody, gracefully—as if monarch of all he surveyed; then, with a stage strut, he would move to another part of the pile to encourage his soldiers there, and picking up another ear and holding it with out-stretched arm, high above his head, would lean back, as if gazing at the stars behind him, and go through such other extravagant attitudes as the genius of the actor and fervor of the moment might inspire.

During the shucking, his son or overseer would visit, occasionally, the ring, with the bottle, when the shucking would become "fast and furious," and if not taken round often enough the "General would put a petition or remonstrance into his recitative."

At the end of the shucking, came the chairing of the planter, his son, or overseer, around the "big house," accompanied by an appropriate corn-song. And finally came the supper in the kitchen when the enjoyment was at the highest.

Since "freedom came about," the old corn-song seems to have died out with slavery. Its sound now would seem like a voice from the grave of the buried feudal power and wealth of the old slave holders.

William Wells Brown, M.D., *My Southern Home, or the South and Its People,* Boston, A. G. Brown and Co., 1880.

An old-fashioned corn-shucking took place once a year on "Poplar Farm," which afforded pleasant amusement for the out-door negroes for miles around. On these occasions, the servants, on all plantations, were allowed to attend by mere invitation of the blacks where the corn was to be shucked.

As the grain was brought in from the field, it was left in a pile near the corn-cribs. The night appointed, and invitations sent out, slaves from plantations five or six miles away, would assemble and join on the road, and in large bodies march along, singing their melodious plantation songs.

To hear three or four of these gangs coming from different directions, their leaders giving out the words, and the whole company joining in the chorus, would indeed surpass anything ever produced by "Haverly's Minstrels," and many of their jokes and witticisms were never equalled by Sam Lucas or Billy Kersands.

A supper was always supplied by the planter on whose farm the shucking was to take place. Often when approaching the place, the singers would speculate on what they would have for supper. The following was frequently sung:—

> *All dem puty gals will be dar,*
> > *Shuck dat corn before you eat.*
> *Dey will fix it fer us rare,*
> > *Shuck dat corn before you eat.*
> *I know dat supper will be big,*
> > *Shuck dat corn before you eat.*

> *I think I smell a fine roast pig,*
>> *Shuck dat corn before you eat.*
> *A supper is provided, so dey said,*
>> *Shuck dat corn before you eat.*
> *I hope dey'll have some nice wheat bread,*
>> *Shuck dat corn before you eat.*
> *I hope dey'll have some coffee dar*
>> *Shuck dat corn before you eat.*
> *I hope dey'll have some whisky dar,*
>> *Shuck dat corn before you eat.*
> *I think I'll fill my pockets full,*
>> *Shuck dat corn before you eat.*
> *Stuff dat coon an' bake him down,*
>> *Shuck dat corn before you eat.*
> *I speck some niggers dar from town,*
>> *Shuck dat corn before you eat.*
> *Please cook dat turkey nice an' brown.*
>> *Shuck dat corn before you eat.*
> *By de side of dat turkey I'll be foun,*
>> *Shuck dat corn before you eat.*
> *I smell de supper, dat I do,*
>> *Shuck dat corn before you eat.*
> *On de table will be a stew,*
>> *Shuck dat corn, etc.*

Burning pine knots, held by some of the boys, usually furnished light for the occasion. Two hours is generally sufficient time to finish up a large shucking; where five hundred bushels of corn is thrown into the cribs as the shuck is taken off. The work is made comparatively light by the singing, which never ceases till they go to the supper table. Something like the following is sung during the evening:

> *De possum meat am good to eat,*
>> *Carve him to de heart;*
> *You'll always find him good and sweet,*
>> *Carve him to de heart;*
> *My dog did bark, and I went to see,*
>> *Carve him to de heart;*
> *And dar was a possum up dat tree,*
>> *Carve him to de heart.*

CHORUS   *Carve dat possum, carve dat possum children,*
                Carve dat possum, carve him to de heart;
         Oh, carve dat possum, carve dat possum
            children,
         Carve dat possum, carve him to de heart.

         I reached up for to pull him in,
             Carve him to de heart;
         De possum he began to grin,
             Carve him to de heart;
         I carried him home and dressed him off,
             Carve him to de heart;
         I hung him dat night in de frost,
             Carve him to de heart.

CHORUS   *Carve dat possum, etc.*

         De way to cook de possum sound,
             Carve him to de heart;
         Fust par-bile him, den bake him brown,
             Carve him to de heart;
         Lay sweet potatoes in de pan,
             Carve him to de heart;
         De sweetest eatin' in de lan','
             Carve him to de heart.

CHORUS   *Carve dat possum, etc.*

Should a poor supper be furnished, on such an occasion, you would hear remarks from all parts of the table,— "Take dat rose pig 'way from dis table." "What rose pig? you see any rose pig here?" "Ha, ha, ha! Dis ain't de place to see rose pig." "Pass up some dat turkey wid clam sauce." "Don't talk about dat turkey; he was gone afore we come." "Dis de las' time I shucks corn at dis farm." "Dis is a cheap farm, cheap owner, an' a cheap supper." "He's talkin' it, ain't he?" "Dis is de tuffest meat dat I is been called upon to eat fer many a day; you's got to have teeth sharp as a saw to eat dis meat." "Spose you ain't got no teef, den what you gwine to do?" "Why, ef you ain't got no teef you muss *gum it!* "Ha, ha, ha!" from the whole company was heard.

On leaving the corn-shucking farm, each gang of men, headed by their leader, would sing during the entire journey home. Some few, however, having their dogs with them, would start on the trail of a coon, possum, or some other game, which might keep them out till nearly morning.

> *Johnny come down de hollow.*
> *Oh hollow!*
> *Johnny come down de hollow.*
> *Oh hollow!*
> *De nigger-trader got me.*
> *Oh hollow!*
> *De speculator bought me.*
> *Oh hollow!*
> *I'm sold for silver dollars.*
> *Oh hollow!*
> *Boys, go catch de pony.*
> *Oh hollow!*
> *Bring him around the corner.*
> *Oh hollow!*
> *I'm goin' away to Georgia.*
> *Oh hollow!*
> *Boys, good-by forever!*
> *Oh hollow!*

Jethro Rumple, *A History of Rowan County, North Carolina,* Salisbury, N.C., 1881, p. 172.

Later in the fall was the time for pulling and shocking the corn. A huge long heap, or straight or crescent-shaped, contains thirty, fifty, or a hundred loads of corn in the shucks, was piled up in the barnyard. On a given day a boy was sent out to ask hands to come in to the shucking on a night appointed. Fifty hands perhaps might come just at dark. A rack would be placed in the middle, and hands divided by two captains who threw up "cross and pile" for first choice of hands. Then came the race, the shouting, the hurrahing, and the singing of corn songs if any negroes were present. And generally a bottle of brandy was circulated several times and was sampled by most of those present. Quite a number would sometimes get excited by the liquor, but it was considered disgraceful to get drunk. Sometimes a fight would occur, especially if the race was a close one. The winning side would carry their captain around the pile in triumph, but a well directed ear, sent by some spirited hand on the beaten side, would strike a member of the triumphal procession and thereby bad blood would be excited, and a promiscuous fight occur.

There was also singing and jokes and a general feeling of jollity; for the "women folks" were all in the kitchen—neighborhood wives all—preparing a great feast of chicken pies, cakes, and other good things—pork and turkey—though there wasn't much turkey. Chicken and chicken dumplings were the chief parts of the feast. I suppose at some farms there may have been, and no doubt was, some "liquor" passed around at the corn pile, but not at our house.

After the corn was shucked, and the shucks put into a pen, came the shucking supper—loaf, biscuits, ham, pork, chicken pie, pumpkin custard, sweet cakes, apple pie, grape pie, coffee, sweet milk, buttermilk, preserves, in short a rich feast of everything yielded by the farm. It required a good digestion to manage such a feast at ten or eleven o'clock at night, but the hardy sons of toil had a good digestion. Or if anything were wanting, a tramp of four or five miles, on an opossum or coon hunt, lasting till one or two o'clock in the morning would be sufficient to settle the heartiest shucking supper that ever was spread on the farmers' tables in bountiful Old Rowan County.

David C. Barrow, Jr., "A Georgia Corn Shucking," *Century Magazine* 24 (1882), pp. 873–78.

The first work toward gathering the corn crop in Georgia is to strip the stalks of their blades, i.e., "pull the fodder," which is done in August or September. This work is done by hand, the laborer stripping the blades from stalk after stalk until he gets his hands full, and then tying them together with a few blades of the same; and this constitutes a "hand." These hands are hung on the stalks of corn a day or two until they are "cured," after which they are tied up, three or four together, in bundles, and these bundles are stacked in the fields, or hauled up to the stables and thrown into the fodder-loft. The corn is thus left on the naked stalk until some time in October or November, by which time it will have become hard and dry. If Georgians, like the Western farmers, had nothing to gather in the fall but the corn, we might spend the whole fall gathering it; but, on any farm where cotton is cultivated to any considerable extent, most of this season of the year must be devoted to gathering and preparing it for market. King Cotton is a great tyrant, and unless you are a willing and ready subject, he will make you suffer.

It will appear, then, that the corn must be disposed of in the quickest possible manner. Now, if the corn were thrown in the crib with the shuck on it, it would probably be eaten by vermin; and, besides, the farmer would be deprived of the use of his shucks, which form the chief item of food for his cattle during the winter. If we had large barns, we might throw the corn in them and shuck it at our leisure; but we have no barns—at least, very few—in Georgia.

Out of these conditions has sprung the corn-shucking; and it has grown into importance, even more as a social than as an economic feature among our farming people. It is peculiarly suited to negro genius. Among no other people could it flourish and reach the perfection which it here attains.

The farmer who proposes to give a corn-shucking selects a level spot in his lot, conveniently near the crib, rakes away all trash, and sweeps the place clean with a brush broom. The corn is then pulled off the stalks, thrown into wagons, hauled to the lot, and thrown out on the spot selected, all in one pile. If it has been previously "norated" through the neighborhood that there is to be plenty to eat and drink at the corn-shucking, and if the night is auspicious, there will certainly be a crowd. Soon after dark the negroes begin to come in, and before long the place will be alive with them—men, women, and children. After the crowd has gathered and been moderately warmed up, two "gin'r'ls" are chosen from among the most famous corn-shuckers on the ground, and these proceed to divide the shuckers into two parties, later comers reporting alternately to one side or the other, so as to keep the forces equally divided. The next step, which is one of great importance, is to divide the corn-pile. This is done by laying a fence-rail across the top of the corn-pile, so that the vertical plane, passing through the rail, will divide the pile into two equal portions. Laying the rail is of great importance, since upon this depends the accuracy of the division; it is accompanied with much argument, not to say wrangling. The position of the rail being determined, the two generals mount the corn-pile, and the work begins. The necessity for the "gin'r'ls" to occupy the most conspicuous position accessible, from which to cheer their followers, is one reason why they get up on top of the corn; but there is another, equally important, which is to keep the rail from being moved, it being no uncommon thing for one side to change the position of the rail, and thus throw an undue portion of the work upon their adversaries. The position of "gin'r'l" in a corn-shucker differs from that of the soldier in that the former is in greater danger than any of his followers; for the chances are that, should his side seem to be gaining, one of their opponents will knock the leader off the cornpile, and thus cause a momentary panic, which is eagerly taken advantage of. This proceeding, however, is considered fair only in extreme cases, and not unfrequently leads to a general row. If it is possible, imagine a negro man standing up on a pile of corn, holding in his hand an ear of corn and shouting the words on the next page, and you have pictured the "corn gin'r'l." It is a prime requisite that he should be ready in his improvisations and have a good voice, so that he may lead in the corn-song. The corn-song is almost always a song with a chorus, or, to use the language of the corn-shuckers, the "gin'r'ls give out," and the shuckers "drone." These songs are kept up continuously during the entire time the work is going on, and though extremely simple, yet, when sung by fifty pairs of lusty lungs, there are few things more stirring.

The most common form is for the generals to improvise words, which they half sing, half recite, all joining in the chorus. As a specimen of this style of corn-song, the following will answer:

FIRST GEN.	*Here is yer corn-shucker.*
ALL HANDS	*Oh ho ho ho ho.*
SECOND GEN.	*Here is yer nigger ruler.*
ALL HANDS	*Oh ho ho hoho.*
BOTH GENS.	*Oh ho ho ho ho.*
ALL HANDS	*Oh ho ho ho ho.*
FIRST GEN.	*Don't yer hyer me holler?*
ALL HANDS	*Oh ho ho ho ho.*
SECOND GEN.	*Don't yer hyer me lumber?*
ALL HANDS	*Oh ho ho ho ho, etc.*

In this the generals frequently recount their adventures, travels and experiences. The writer knew of a negro who went down to the seacoast, and when he returned, carried by storm a corn-shucking of which he was general, with the words: "I've bin ter de ilund."

Of course, "Brer Rabbit" must come in for his share of the honor, as he does in the following song, which is illustrative of the negro's appreciation of rabbit cunning. It is sung just as the other was, the generals and shuckers alternating:

GEN. *Rabbit in de gyordin.*
CHO. *Rabbit hi oh.*
GEN. *Dog can't ketch um.*
CHO. *Rabbit hi oh.*
GEN. *Gun can't shoot um.*
CHO. *Rabbit hi oh.*
GEN. *Mon can't skin um.*
CHO. *Rabbit hi oh.*
GEN. *Cook can't cook um.*
CHO. *Rabbit hi oh.*
GEN. *Folks can't eat um.*
CHO. *Rabbit hi oh, etc.*

Any reader who has followed so far, may by courtesy be called a corn general, and is therefore at liberty to add indefinitely to the verses, or repeat them as he pleases. Any words at all may be taken and twisted into a chorus, as illustrated in the following:

GEN. *Slip shuck corn little while.*
CHO. *Little while, little while.*
GEN. *Slip shuck corn little while.*
CHO. *Little while, I say.*
GEN. *I'm gwine home in little while, etc.*

The finest corn-song of them all is one in which the chorus is, Ho mer Riley ho." The words here given were some of them picked up in South-west Georgia, and some in other portions of the State. Competent judges say there is really music in this song, and for this reason, as well as to give readers who have never heard the corn-song an idea of the tunes to which they are sung, the notes of this song are given below. No full knowledge of the way in which the song is rendered can be conveyed by notes, but it is believed that the tune is properly reported.

Little Billy Woodcock lived o'er de mountin,
Ho mer Riley ho: in er mighty buildin'
lived Billy Woodcock, Ho mer Riley, ho!

Little Billy Woodcock got er mighty long bill.
Ho mer Riley ho.

He stuck it through de mountin and clinch it on tother side.
    Ho mer Riley ho.
Possum up de gum stump, Raccoon in de holler.
    Ho mer Riley ho.
Rabbit in de ole feel fat ez he kin waller.
    Ho mer Riley ho.
Nigger in de wood-pile cant count seb'n.
    Ho mer Riley ho.
Put him in de fedder bed he thought he waz in Heb'n.
    Ho mer Riley ho.
Did yer ever see er gin sling made outer bramdy?
    Ho mer Riley ho.
Did yer ever see er yaller gal lick 'lasses candy?
    Ho mer Riley ho.

There is one more very short song which is sung by all hands. The work of finishing the shucking of the last few ears is called "rounding up" the corn-pile, and is almost invariably in the following words:

> *Round up, dubble up, round up corn;*
> *Round up, nubbins up, round up corn.*

These words are repeated, over and over, until the last of the corn is shucked, and the work finished.

An amount of work which would astonish the shuckers themselves, and which, if demanded of them in the day-time would be declared impossible, is accomplished under the excitement of the corn-song. They shuck the corn by hand, sometimes using a sharp stick to split open the shuck, but most commonly tearing them open with the fingers. As the feeling of rivalry grows more and more intense, they work faster and faster, stripping the shuck from the ears so fast that they seem to fly almost constantly from their hands.

A staid New England farmer and his friends, gathered in a comfortable, well-lighted barn, quietly doing the laborious part of his "husking-bee," would think they had been transferred to pandemonium if they could be conveyed to a Georgia corn-shucking and see how our colored farmers do the same work; and I imagine the social gathering which follows the husking-bee, and the frolic which is the after-piece of the corn-shucking, resemble each other as little as do their methods of work.

It is no rare occurrence for a corn-shucking to terminate in a row instead of a frolic. If one side is badly beaten, there is almost sure to be some charge of fraud; either that the rail has been moved, or part of the corn of the successful party thrown over on the other side "unbeknownst" to them, or some such charge. These offenses are common occurrences, and are aided by the dimness of the light. If any of these charges can be proved, a first-class row ensues, in which ears of corn fly thick and fast, and sometimes more dangerous weapons are used. The owner of the premises can always stop them, and does do so. Negroes have great respect for proprietorship, and yield whenever it is asserted. It is most often the case, however, that the race has been about an equal one, and that good humor prevails amid the great excitement.

The first thing in order is to express thanks for the entertainment, which is done by taking the host, putting him on the shoulders of two strong men, and then marching around, while all hands split their throats to a tune, the chorus of which is "Walk away, walk away!" This honor, though of questionable comfort, or rather most unquestionable discomfort, must be undergone, for a refusal is considered most churlish, and a retreat gives too much license to the guests. The general feeling that most handsome behavior has been shown toward the host, raises the opinion that guests entertain for themselves, and they are prepared to begin in earnest the sports of the occasion. The fun usually begins by some one who is a famous wrestler (pronounced "rasler") offering to throw down anybody on the ground, accompanying the boast by throwing aside his coat and swaggering round, sometimes making a ring and inviting "eny gemman ez warnts ter git his picter tuk on de groun'," to come in. The challenge is promptly accepted, and the spectators gather around, forming a ring, so that they may be in a position to watch, and, at the same time, encourage and advise their friends. They keep up a continual stream of talk during the whole time and not unfrequently come to blows over the merits of the wrestlers.

The "rasler's" account of his performance is as much unlike his real conduct as can well be imagined. The fellow who swaggers around boastfully at the shucking will make himself out the most modest person in the world, in recounting his adventures next day. There is a famous corn-shucker and wrestler who is a tenant of the writer, named Nathan Mitchell, more commonly known in the neighborhood as "An' Fran's Nath." He loves to go over his adventures generally in about these words: "Mars Dave, yer know dis hyer Ike Jones whar live down Mr. Brittels'? Well, sir, I went down ter Miss Marfy Moore's night erfore las'. Dey had er little corn-shuckin' down dar, en arter we got done wid de shickin', Ike he kerminced cuttin' up his shines, 'lowed he cud fling down enything ter his inches on de ground, en ef dey didn't b'lieve it, all dey had ter do wuz ter toe de mark. De boys dey all wanted me fer ter try 'im, but I wudnt do it, dase I knowed p'intedly ef I tuk holt er dat nigger he wuz bound ter git hurt. When he seed me sorter hol'in back, he got wusser en wusser, twell finerly I sed: 'Beenst how yer so manish, I'll take one fall wid yer, jest ter give yer sattifacshun.' Wal, sir, I flung dat nigger so hard I got oneasy 'bout him; I wuz nattally feared I had kilt him, and I aint here ef he didn't git up en swor it wuz erdogfall. Gemini! den I got mer blood up. I sed, I did: 'Jest buckle round me.' En no soomer en he tuk his holt, en gin de work ter cut mer patchin, den I tuk him up wid de ole h'ist, en flung him clean over mer shoulder, right squar on top of his hed. De wust uv it wus, arter dat he wanted ter go fite An' Kalline's little Jim, kase he sed 'Dat jarred de gemman.' I tole him ef he toch dat chile, I gim de wust whippin' ever he toted. I don't like dat nigger, nohow."

I happened to hear this same man telling one of his companions about some corn-"gin'r'l," who got up on de corn-pile en kep' singin' en gwine on twell I got tired, en took him berhine de year wid er year er corn en axed him down"; from which I inferred he had been guilty of the misconduct of throwing at the generals, which has already been mentioned, and which he was sufficiently ashamed of to try and hide from me.

A corn-shucking which is to be considered in the light of a finished performance should end with a dance. Of late years, colored farmers who are "members" frequently give corn-shuckings where no dancing is allowed, but it is common for the party to have a dance before they disperse. These dances take place either in one of the houses, or else out of doors on the ground. The dance of late years is a modification of the cotillion, the old-time jig having given place to this, just as in the cities the German and the others have ousted the old-time dances. There is a great deal of jig-dancing in these cotillions, and the man who cannot "cut the pigeon wing" is considered a sorry dancer indeed; but still it purports to be a cotillion. Endurance is a strong point in the list of accomplishments of the dancer, and, other things being equal, that dancer who can hold out the longest is considered the best. The music is commonly made by a fiddler and a straw-beater, the fiddle being far more common than the banjo, in spite of tradition to the contrary. The fiddler is the man of most importance on the ground. He always comes late, must have an extra share of whisky, is the best-dressed man in the crowd, and unless every honor is shown him he will not play. He will play you a dozen different pieces, which are carefully distinguished by names, but not by tunes. The most skilled judge of music will be unable to detect any difference between "Run, Nigger, Run," "Arkansaw Traveler," "Forky Deer," and any other tune. He is never offended at a mistake which you may make as to what piece he is playing; he only feels a trifle contemptuous toward you as a person utterly devoid of musical knowledge. The straw-beater is a musician, the description of whose performances the writer has never "read or heard repeated." No preliminary training is necessary in this branch of music; any one can succeed, with proper caution, the first time he tries. The performer provides himself with a pair of straws about eighteen inches in length and stout enough to stand a good smart blow. An experienced straw-beater will be very careful in selecting his straws, which he does from the sedge-broom; this gives him an importance he could not otherwise have, on account of the commonness of his accomplishment. These straws are used after the manner of drum-sticks, that portion of the fiddle-strings between the fiddler's bow and his left hand serving as a drum. One of the first sounds which you hear on approaching the dancing party is the *tum tee tum* of the straws, and after the dance begins, when the shuffling of feet destroys the other sounds of the fiddle, this noise can still be heard.

With the cotillion a new and very important office, that of "caller-out," has become a necessity. The "caller-out," though of less importance than the fiddler, is second to no other. He not only calls out the figures, but explains them at length to the ignorant, sometimes accompanying them through the performance. He is never at a loss, "Gemmen to de right!" being a sufficient refuge in case of embarrassment, since this always calls forth a full display of the dancers' agility, and gives much time.

The corn-shucking is one of the institutions of the old plantations which has flourished and expanded since the negroes were freed. With the larger liberty they enjoy there has come increased social intercourse, and this has tended to encourage social gatherings of all kinds. Then, too, the great number of small farmers who have sprung up in the South since the war necessitates mutual aid in larger undertakings, so that at this time the corn-shucking, as an institution, is most flourishing. No doubt with improved culture its features will be changed, and, in time, destroyed. Indeed, already it is becoming modified, and the great improvement which the negro race is continually manifesting indicates that in time their simple songs and rough sports must yield to higher demands.

Mary Ross Banks, *Bright Days on the Old Plantation,* Boston: Lee and Shepherd, 1882, pp. 114–32.

. . . one bright bright morning in December, while I sit up in bed, rub my sleepy eyes, and am about to resign myself to the warm blankets again till the inspiring words "corn-shuckin' " give a new interest to the day; and I gladly obey Bet's injunction and jump nimbly out of bid. "I heerd my miss tell Mr. Reid ter have all de corn hauled out'n de meetin'-field 'ouse fiel', an' put in er pile down dar fo' de corn-crib do', an' dis nigger ain' no fool—I know what dat means. "What do it mean, honey? It mean me, an' Mammy, an' ol' Aun' Riny, an' all us house gang, iz got ter git over groun' wid er bubble-shuffle,—eat ter-day, an' chaw ter-morrer. It mean Tiny an' Siny iz got ter ketch chickens, an' wring der heads off, an' fur Daddy an' Bud Dick ter kill th'ee hogs an' er couple er goats, an' fur ol' man Smart ter clean out de pit, an' fix ter bobbycue de meat. It mean fur de nigger men in de naborhood ter come here soon ez it's dark, an' fur all er dem an' my miss's men-folks ter let in on dat pile er corn, an' bergin ter shuck it like de worl' wuz comin' ter ere een'. An' git de meal ter make de bread fur Jedgment-day dinner. Dat what it means.

"La, honey! dar'll be chicken-pie, an' back-bone stchew, an' hog-head, an' bobbycued goat, an' gigy-cake, an' apple-dumplin', an' tater-puddin', an' 'simmon beer, here, fur dem niggers ter eat an' drink, twell you'll be sick ev de sight er vittles. You ain' nuver ben here when us had er corn-shuckin', is yer, honey? Not sence you wuz big ernuff ter memorize nuthin' bout it.

"Well, dress fas' now, so you kin see all de fun. Bless yer soul, honey! it's de mos' consequenshus time er de whole year, 'cep' Chris'mus and fofe-er-Jewly. Come 'long now an' eat your breakfas' kas I'z in er hurry: I wan' ter 'gin de prepparashuns fur de 'tainment." . . .

Grandma is in the smoke-house . . . sending out the flour, lard, sugar, apples, potatoes, etc., to be, under Mammy Liza's, Aunt Rina's and Bet's skillful hands, converted into those wonderful dumplings and puddings. Bet has enumerated as taking such a conspicuous part in the night's entertainment.

All day the busy negroes run back and forth, from the house to the kitchen, singing merrily, in anticipation of the time coming. Bet issues orders in a most authoritative manner; as she has travelled more than the others and fancies herself quite a leader throughout the "settlement."

Grandma always takes her maid on any visit she makes among her relatives and friends. And this is why Bet considers her position such an exalted one. . . .

After an hour or two spent hanging on, as the preparations progress in the kitchen, I grow tired of the stirring and mixing, so wander out to the yard, where I soon become greatly interested to know how Daddy Smart will proceed to cook meat in "that grave" he has dug. He has thrown fat lightwood splinters and torches, with great sticks of wood into the pit, and now there is a bed of red hickory coals, from which a stream of hot air arises. He next lays poles across the opening, from each of which he proceeds to suspend, by a strong twine, a side of pork or kid. Near the pit stands a large tin bucket containing a mixture of butter, salt, vinegar, black and red pepper, which, together with the drippings from the browning meats, he constantly applies with a mop, that all may be thoroughly seasoned when ready to serve.

After watching and questioning him until I am pretty well initiated into the mysteries of barbequing, and receiving, in good faith, old daddy's assurance, "Dat's de bes' way ter cook human vittles in de worl', missy." I say good-by to him, and continue my walk to the barnyard, where the gathered corn lies in a great heap before the crib-door.

I easily persuade Nick, the wagoner, to take me with him to the field, as he goes for the next load of corn. I climb in, and soon go jolting along at the risk of a fall every few moments, as there is no regard paid to rocks or ruts in the way. Arriving at the field, the baskets of gathered corn are emptied into the wagon, till the body is filled. Nick turns the six mules with a great amount of gee-ing and hawing, apparently as much excited and anxious as if he had not driven and turned them in the same way, for years past. . . .

The afternoon quickly wears away, and I joyfully hail the approaching darkness.

There have been stands erected in front of, and through the barnyard, upon which there is a thick layer of earth piled, and fat light-wood stumps kindled into a bright blaze upon each one. Around these the negroes group themselves, awaiting the arrival of visitors from the neighboring plantations.

Quite an important conference is being held in this interval; and some strong arguments are being introduced for and against different "leaders" proposed.

Finally they settle upon Talbot, Aunt Ann's driver, a tall, burly black, whose duties it will be to make a speech and conduct the ceremonies generally, though leading the singing is considered one of the most important features of the occasion.

The "hands" begin to arrive, and laughter and merry-making at once set in. Anecdotes are told on each other, to the discomfort of some; while others, bent on fun even at their own expense, join in the laughter, which is long and loud, after each story told. All this time the negroes continued to arrive, till now a goodly company has gathered; and Talbot announces it is time for the "frolic" to commence.

Big Frank and Long Jim conduct him to the place of honor he is to occupy as leader, by making a basket, or "cat-saddle" as they term it, of their four hands joined together in such a ways as to form a square seat. Talbot mounts into his carriage; and after he is trotted around the pile three times, the carriers keeping time to a kind of monotonous dirge sung by the company, they make a slight halt as they reach the head of the heap, on this last round. While seated thus, they give a long swing with their arms, which imparts a considerable impetus to Talbot, as at the same time a spring on his part, lands him safe on his feet near the centre of the pile, mid cheers from the lookers-on.

This settles Talbot's position as hero of the occasion; as had he fallen, or made a false spring, the dignity of leadership would have devolved upon a more active representative. He appreciates the importance of his position, and makes the following speech in acknowledgement of the same:—"My berfluvvid niggers, here iz ter shuck Miss Patse's corn. Let us 'view de pertickerlers uv de sitcherwashun in dese few words. Dis corn wuz planted las' Febbywerry, two munts atter Chrusmus. Some uv you niggers had ploughed de groun'; some uv yer come erlong an' busted out de furrers, fur some de yuthers ter drap de corn in. Den some de balance followerd, an' delivered de little grains, an' so de corn wuz planted. All er dis de niggers an' de mules done, but somebody else had ter do sumpin' too. Ol' Marster way up yander had ter say, 'Corn, swell up an' bust, shot out uv de groun', don' lay dar doin' nuthin'; dem ol' mole'll come long an' eat you up ef yer don' hurry.' So de corn come up, an' growed off peart-like. Den de ploughin' an' de hoein', de sunshine an' de rain, all come 'long, an' made de corn grow, twel by fofe-er-Jewly it wuz laid by. Den you niggers could eat yer big dinners, an' 'joice in der water-million crap wid satisfackshun. An', niggers, tiz er crap ter 'joice in. Now dis corn iz done growed, it's got hard, an' you'z done hauled it up. But dat ain' all yit. De crap iz er good un, it wuz worked by er likely set uv niggers, it berlongs ter er good 'oman, er fine lady. Dar's enuff uv it ter feed all you niggers an annymuls, an' ter fatten de hogs fur de winter's killin'. Now my 'spected frien's, le's turn in an' shuck dis corn, so ez ter have er good appertite fur de bobbycued meat what I smells wid my nosters, an' my stummuck craves." This effort is received with a loud shout of approbation and all fall to work most zealously, laughing and talking to each other, as they are seated upon the ground on either side of the corn pile, large baskets placed behind them, into which they toss the shucked ears over their shoulders, rapidly filling, while they are taken by others not engaged in the shucking, and emptied into the crib. Talbot keeps his position on top the heap, walking back and forth through the center, cheering occasionally with such remarks as,—"Dat's de lick, little Ellick!" "You kin beat yo' daddy, young York." "Gentermen, des look at big Frank!" "Some er you niggers take Kumsy way f'um here!" "Dis pile's er 'ducin' too fas'!" "Somebody's fun'al hatter be preached here ter-morrer, ef Miles's Bill don' quit dat bein' ser reckless." . . .

The excitement becomes intense during the singing; and the pile has grown so small, that in a short time the last basket is emptied, and the horn is blown for supper.

But there is too much excitement still for a quiet assemblage round the open pit, whence the juicy meats send out appetizing odors, or the table where stews, dumplings, puddings, and breads are heaped on great wooden trays, near which stand two immense barrels of beer, with a basket of tin cups beside them, for the thirsty laborers to drink.

The overseer has, so far, been merely a looker-on; but he comes in for a share of attention now. Two of the tallest men . . . now come forward; standing close together, side by side, he is hoisted on their shoulders, and thus seated between them is carried around the yard, while all sing in his praise,—

> Oh! Mr. Reid iz er mighty fine man,—
> Er mighty fine man indeed;
>> He plants all de taters,
>> He plows all de corn,
>> He weighs all de cotton,
>> An' blows de dinner-horn;
> Mr. Reid iz er might fine man.

While this is being sung, they march in procession, all keeping time, and beating a kind of accompaniment by striking the right fist on the open palm of the left hand, prolonging the performance till they reach the barrels of beer, where, doubtless, he is glad to dismount from his sturdy bearers' shoulders.

The cups are then passed around as far as they will go. Daddy Miles stands with a long-handled gourd beside one barrel; while Yellow Alf, Bet's husband, dispenses the contents of the second. When all are supplied, Talbot, still acting as spokesman, say, "God bless Miss Patse. I hope she'll live ez long ez she wants ter, an'll give us er corn-shucking' ev'y year. Boys, dere's good vittle here; don' let Miss Patse think you don' know what ter do wid it."

No danger that any such impression be left upon the minds of any, as their appetites, always to be relied on, are now greatly increased by their work in the crisp night air; and 'tis not until the barrels have been exhausted, and the table's plentious store is cleared away, that the eating and drinking cease.

Then in the most solemn manner, grace is said, thanks are returned by Daddy Hercules, and the feast is ended.

As the negroes pass the torch-stands, where the pine knots still burn brightly, many of the visitors snatch up the brands, and waving them high over their heads, start home as happy and lighthearted, apparently as unfatigued, as when they came into the yard four hours ago. As the last lights glimmer in the darkness, the last faint notes of the returning negroes, singing on their way home, sound in the distance. I fall asleep, having enjoyed the corn-shucking fully as much, if in a more quiet way, as did any of the negroes.

S. C. Cromwell, "Corn-shucking Song," *Harper's*, 69 (1884), 807.

> *Shuck erlong, nigger, shuck dis co'n;*
> > *Dar's menny er bar'l in dis ya pile;*
> *Dar's menny er rashin, sho's yo' bo'n,*
> > *Ter feed all de han'd wid arter 'wile.*
> > *Luk at Susing, dat fat gal!*
> > *Whar she git dat ballymeral?*
> > *Mus' er got hit fam ole Miss Sal.*
> *Shuck erlong, shuck dis co'n.*

CHORUS

> *Shuck a ruck a shuck; shuck a ruck a shuck!*
> > *Pars dat tickler down dis way.*
> *Shuck a ruck a shuck; shuck a ruck a shuck!*
> > *Ain' gwine hom ez long ez I stay.*

> *Hyar dat bo' pig, how he squeal!*
> > *Wishin' fo' de slops termorrer mo'n;*
> *If he hatter got in dere fiel',*
> > *Niggers, we'd neber bin shuckin' dis co'n.*
> > *Luk at Moses, how he grin!*
> > *Ain' nuffin ob him but he wool an' chin;*
> > *Mouf ez big ez dat co'n bin.*
> *Shuck along, shuck dis co'n.*

CHORUS

> *Shuck a ruck a shuck; shuck a ruck a shuck!*
> > *Pars dat tickler down dis way.*
> *Shuck a ruck a shuck; shuck a ruck a shuck!*
> > *Ain' gwine home ez long ez I stay.*

Lydia Wood Baldwin, *A Yankee Schoolteacher in Virginia*, New York: Funk and Wagnalls, 1884, pp. 22–26.

It was a merry scene on the old plantation. All the day the carts had been busy hauling the corn to the granary. At nightfall the workers gathered in twos and threes, singing as they trooped along, anticipating the night's revelry. Indoors, Miss Lucy entertained a few friends. The moon rose early and revealed a picturesque scene, and the work progressed bravely. Peachy led the singing:

> *Eighteen hunner an' anoder makes one,*
> *An' now my journey am jus' begun!*
> *Eighteen hunner an' anoder makes two,*
> *De Lord tole Moses what ter do!*
> *Eighteen hunner an' anoder makes three,*
> *De Lord done set de prisoner free!*
> *Eighteen hunner an' anoder makes four,*
> *De Lord done open heben's do'!*
> *Eighteen hunner an' anoder makes five,*
> *De Lord done turn de dead ter life!*
> *Eighteen hunner an' anoder makes six,*
> *Ole Pharo's army got 'n a fix!*
> *Eighteen hunner an' anoder makes seben,*
> *De Lord done ring de bells ob heben!*
> *Eighteen hunner an' anoder makes eight,*
> *De Lord done open heben's gate!*
> *Eighteen hunner an' anoder makes nine,*
> *De Lord done turn de water ter wine!*
> *Eighteen hunner an' anoder makes ten,*
> *Dan'll got 'n de lion's den!*
> *Eighteen hunner an' anoder makes 'leben,*
> *De Lord say de rachus 'll git t' heben!*

"An' dar's whar we'm boun' f'r to go" declared Goodman Jones. "Dar now, you all done drink de whiskey all up—de hull gallon! what a mouth him hab f'r good whiskey!" All grew loud and boisterous.

After midnight, when the corn was all husked, the banjo was tuned afresh, and the whole group of men and women formed a line, singing as they went many times around the big pile of "shucks" where the banjo-player was enthroned. Then he descended and took the lead to "the house," playing while the singers fairly shouted:

> *Oh, it's down yere on de ole plantation,*
> *A shuckin' ob de corn.*
> *T' make de ash-cake 'long wid bac'n,*

> *A fryin' in de morn!*
> *Of all de breads de corn-bread*
> *Am de sweetes' an' de bes'!*
> *Of all de cakes de ash-cake*
> *F'r certain am de bes'!*

Round the house three times, singing, while the revellers inside come out in merry groups to see them.

And then they gathered on the back veranda, where bread and meat and whiskey were served—too much of the latter—and where Mr. Percy Darnell and a few compatriots partook too freely, alas! of the latter refreshment, and grew hilarious with songs and dancing.

F. D. Srygley, *Seventy Years in Dixie,* Nashville: Gospel Advocate Co., 1891, pp. 149–52 (Tennessee white practices).

The corn-shuckings of those days were occasions of neighborhood gatherings of no ordinary importance. We always shucked every ear of corn before putting it into the crib. We hauled it and threw it in a heap, on the ground beside the crib, and then called the neighbors together for a corn-shucking.

We usually began the shucking in the afternoon, and continued till toward the middle of the night. This was necessary, as a matter of economy in time. At that season of the year, we were always greatly pressed with work, and could ill-afford to spare day-light for such co-operative workings. . . . When the nights were dark, we built scaffolds around the corn-heap, covered them with dirt or a flat rock, and built lights on them, of pine knots. Three or four scaffolds well supplied and frequently replenished with good fat pine knots, would light up the grounds for several rods around the corn-heap, almost as bright as day. A small boy would keep up the blazing fires on the scaffolds, which would furnish all the light the workers needed.

The corn was thrown into the crib as it was shucked, and the shucks were stowed away in rail pens, built for them, by the small boys, to be fed to the cows during the winter.

The crowd was always divided, at a corn-shucking, by two men, who threw for "heads or tails," with a silver coin, for the first choice of shuckers. The corn-heap was also divided into two parts, as nearly equal as could be determined by guess and measurement, and the "captains" of the two squads of shuckers again threw for "heads or tails," for choice of sides. The work then began, and from start to finish the shucks flew in every direction and the clean ears of corn fairly raised into the crib. The rivalry between the two squads of shuckers would grow more interesting and exciting as the divided heap of corn gradually melted away, and sometimes the heated determination of both parties to win in the race, would lead to charges of unfairness, angry recriminations and a general fisticuff. When it came to a general row and a free fight, every fellow stood to his post and fought for his party. Such fights were fierce, but short, and when they ended every man resumed his place at the corn-heap and proceeded with his work, with renewed energy, without any feeling of malice or fear of an enemy in his heart.

Corn-shucking was a dusty work, and the shuckers required much water, as well as a liberal supply of a stronger beverage, to allay their oft-recurring thirst. But we lost no time in drinking.

One man was always appointed to carry the beverage to the men around the corn-heap. He took them in regular order, and handed the drink to each man, as he came to them, in a small tin cup. When the race was close and the excitement was very high, a man would not even stop shucking long enough to swallow the drink, but would gulp down the beverage, without the loss of a second, while the waiter held the cup to his mouth.

Whenever a boy or a young man found a red ear of corn, he put it into his pocket, and when he went to the house, after the shucking was over, he presented it to the girl of his choice, and for this simple act of gallantry he was permitted to kiss her publicly. I took a solemn vow, then, that, if I ever lived to be a man, I would farm for a living, raise nothing but corn, plant only red seed and shuck every ear of it myself! But alas! Times have changed and red corn has lost its charm.

Harry Smith, *Fifty Years of Slavery in the United States of America,* Grand Rapids, Mich.: West Michigan Printing Company, 1891.

At the time of gathering the corn they would break off several hundred bushels and take it under the shed or in the barn, and invite a number to help husk it out. After the corn was husked out they would choose leaders and form in two parties, and then dancing, wrestling and various amusements would be in order. Those who lived on Plum Creek were called Plum Creek Tigers and those on Salt River were called Salt River Tigers. Then dancing, boxing and wrestling. Then supper was called, the older eating first. Harry was a Salt River Tiger, and was looking at one of the opposite boys, thinking how he could whip him; so in order to get up a fuss he stepped up to him and called him a name and wanted to know why he spit in his face. Both sides urged the boys on to see the fun, as they called it. The other men, hearing the fuss, still urged them on, and some of the older ones got to fighting in dead earnest; then the boys quit. Men fought all around on both sides, bunting and biting and running into the kitchen, knocked the stove over, setting fire to an old colored cook's dress who ran screaming with all her might out of doors, up-setting the table, breaking dishes in all shapes.

The darkies tore the fences all down around the cabin, hammered each other with the pickets until the white men came out with guns and threatened to shoot them if they did not stop. After the fight was over the owner came out and ordered them to leave his plantation. After they all left, Harry, who had caused all the fuss, thought he would go back and see the girls, and being seen by the overseer, he seized a club and struck Harry, almost breaking his neck. He went home a little the worse, with a sore head, for having got up such a serious disturbance.

Letitia M. Burwell, *A Girl's Life in Virginia Before the War,* New York: Frederick A. Stokes Co., 1895, pp. 131–32 (at Howard's Neck plantation, near Richmond).

The negroes on these estates appeared lively and happy—that is, if singing and laughing indicate happiness; for they went to their work in the fields singing, and returned in the evening singing, after which they often spent the whole night visiting from one plantation to another, or dancing until day to the music of the banjo or the "fiddle." Although the most perfect timists, their music, with its wild, melancholy cadence, half savage, half civilized, cannot be imitated or described. Many a midnight were we wakened by their wild choruses, sung as they returned from a frolic or "corn-shucking," sounding at first like some hideous, savage yell, but dying away on the air, echoing a cadence melancholy and indescribable, with a particular pathos, and yet without melody or sweetness.

Corn-shuckings were occasions of great hilarity and good eating. The negroes from various plantations assembled at night around a huge pile of corn. Selecting one of their number—usually the most original and amusing, and possessed of the loudest voice—they called him "captain." The captain seated himself on top of the pile—a large lightwood torch burning in front of him, and while he shucked, improvised words and music to a wild "recitative," the chorus of which was caught up by the army of shuckers around. The glare of the torches on the black faces, with the wild music and impromptu words, made a scene curious even to us who were so accustomed to it.

After the corn was shucked they assembled around a table laden with roasted pigs, mutton, beef, hams, cakes, pies, coffee, and other substantials—many participating in the supper who had not in the work. The laughing and merriment continued until one or two o'clock in the morning.

R. R. Moton et al., "Negro Folk-Songs," *Southern Workman,* 24, no. 2 (Feb. 1985), 30–32; repr. in Donald J. Waters, *Strange Ways and Sweet Dreams,* Boston: G. K. Hall, 1981, pp. 209–11.

Corn-songs have, in common with the spirituals, the characteristic of the solo or shout, often extemporized to express the thought of the moment by the leader, and the great chorus which answers with its burst of harmony from many voices. In the work-songs the rhythm sets the time of the work on which all are engaged, and the beating of feet, the swaying of the body or the movement of the arm may be retarded or accelerated at will by the leader. They thus formed a useful auxiliary to the plantation discipline and may be said to have had an economic value in carrying on the productive labor of the South. [Here the quartet gave the following two songs:]

CORN SHUCKING SONG

What in the worl' is de marter here,
Oh—oh, ho,
What in the worl' is de marter here,
Oh—oh, ho,

Fall out here and shuck dis corn,
Oh—oh, ho,
Bigges pile ever see sence I was born,
Oh—oh, ho.

Marster's niggers is fat and slick,
Oh—oh, ho,
Case dey gits enough to eat,
Oh—oh, ho,

> *Joneses niggers is mighty po,*
> *Oh—oh, ho,*
> *Dont know whedder dey gets enough er no,*
> *Oh—oh, ho.*
>
> *I loves ol' marster an' mistis too,*
> *Oh—oh, ho,*
> *Case deys rich an' kin an' true,*
> *Oh—oh, ho.*
>
> *Po white trash I does despise,*
> *Oh—oh, ho,*
> *Case dey's always tellin lies,*
> *Oh—oh, ho.*
>
> *Shuck dis corn dis very night,*
> *Oh—oh, ho,*
> *While de stars is shinin' bright,*
> *Oh—oh, ho.*

RUN, NIGGER, RUN, DE PATTEROLER'LL KETCH YER

> *Run, nigger, run, patteroler'll ketch yer,*
> *Hit yer thirty-nine and sware 'e didn' tech yer.*
> (repeat several times.)
>
> *Poor white out in de night*
> *Huntin' fer niggers wid all deir might.*
> *Dey don' always ketch deir game*
> *D'way we fool um is er shame.*
> *Run, Nigger run—*
>
> *My ole mistis promus me*
> *When she died she'd set me free,*
> *Now d'ole lady's ded an' gone,*
> *Lef dis nigger er shellin corn.*
> *Run, Nigger run—*
>
> *My old master promus me*
> *When he died he'd set me free,*
> *Now he's ded an' gone er way*
> *Neber'll come back tell Judgement day.*
> *Run, Nigger run—*

I seed a patteroler hin' er tree
Tryin to ketch po' little me,
I ups wid my foots an' er way I run,
Dar by spilin dat genterman's fun,
Run, Nigger, run—

New York Sun, Nov. 11, 1895; repr. in William S. Walsh, *Curiosities of Popular Customs*, Philadelphia: J. B. Lippincott, 1907, pp. 277–81.

My father owned about three hundred negroes, and as I was the oldest boy of course I was known as "young marster." The event of the year down in the negro 'quarters' was the corn-shuckin', and when corn-shuckin' time came round they were permitted to invite their friends on the neighboring plantations, and would go miles and miles to attend to one of these frolics. The season is just at hand now. Yes, boys, it's corn-shuckin' time in Dixie and I wish I was there. I can see the woods all crimson and brown and gold, and the blue haze of Indian summer over it all, and I can hear the birds as they stop over on their way to the far South. As soon as a corn-shuckin' was talked about, all the darkies would begin to sing,—

Ha, ha, ha, you and me,
Little brown jug, don't I love thee!

They all knew that the little brown jug would be on hand. When the night of the shuckin' arrived, the darkies poured in from every direction. They travelled paths in those days and took near cuts, and they had signals by which to let each other know that they were on the way. Most plantations had a bugler who owned an old wood bugle five or six feet long. These bugles were made of poplar wood coated with tar and kept under for several days. Soaking it kept the instrument from shrinking, and gave it a resonant sound which could be heard for miles on a clear night. The bugles were carried to the corn-shuckin', and the coming darkies would blow and blow, and be answered by the bugler at the corn-pile, and as he did so he would say, "Dar's the niggers comin' from Beyers's plantation," "Dar dey is from Elliott's." As they drew nearer to the pile of corn the bugle-blowers would stop and give way to the quill- or reed-blowers. A set of from three to seven reeds of different sizes and lengths were always on hand, and those darkies would play any tune they'd ever heard on 'em by shifting 'em across their lips. The roads and the paths would resound with the weird music of the quill or reed-blowers as they came in from many directions. They used these instruments, too, in going to their wives' houses at night. You know, fellows, the darkies had right smart intuitive sense about some things. They preferred to have a wife on some other man's plantation than their marster's, and would only visit her on Wednesday and Saturday nights. You could hear them going and coming, blowing their quills for all they were worth.

The corn was divided into two piles as big as a house, and two captains were appointed. Each chose sides, just as the captains in spellin'-matches do, and then the fun began. There was always whiskey enough to please 'em, and not enough for any drunkenness. A man was entitled to the same jug every time he found a red ear of corn, and also to kiss any dusky damsel that he fancied. It was astonishing how many red ears some of 'em managed to find, and very funny to see how anxious the young wenches were for the red ears to come to light. The young marster was always on hand to see that the drams were given out judiciously, and to see that all got a taste. The side which shucked out their pile first got the prize, and it was usually plug tobacco. While the shuckin' was going on the darkies would sing, walk, talk and dance. A leader would mount on top of one pile of corn and call, and all would join in the chorus. The leader at every corn-shuckin' I ever attended began, "I will start the holler," and the crowd yelled the response "Bugleloo!"

> *I will start the holler!*
> *Bugleloo!*
> *I will start the holler!*
> *Bugleloo!*
> *Oh, don't you hear my holler?*
> *Bugleloo!*
> *Massa's got er bugler,*
> *Bugleloo!*
> *A ten-cent bugle,*
> *Bugleloo!*

There were about fifty stanzas to this song, or else the leader improvised as he went on, and he would call until the crowd grew thoroughly sick and wanted a change. They brought him down by

throwing ears of corn at him. Sometimes a fellow that was very stuck
on his voice would mount to call, and it took devilish, rough treat-
ment to get him down. He would probably "hist" a religious tune,
such as—

> Lord, I can't stay away,
> Lord, I can't stay away,
> Lord, I can't stay away.

And the crowd, with groanings and moanings would half sing, half
chant

> Oh, I must come to jedgment to stan' my trial;
> Oh, I must come to jedgment to stan' my trial;
> I can't stay away.

The leader again called,—

> Lord, I can't stay away;
> Lord, I can't stay away.
> Oh, my God, gwine ter rain down brimstone an' fire,
> I can't stay away.
> Gwine to walk on dat glass all mingled wid fire,
> I can't stay away;
> Lord, I can't stay away!
> Lord, I can't stay away!
> I'm gwine ter jine dat heav'nly choir,
> I can't stay away.
> John says he seed forty an fo' thousan';
> I can't stay away.
> Jesus is comin' wid forty an' fo' thousan';
> I can't stay away.

At the end of each verse the crowd would join in with the chorus,
swaying their bodies and nodding their heads in time to the music.
Their dreadful earnestness in singing of the judgement and brimstone
would only arise from a profound belief in such things. Many of the
girls and women would clear away a space and pat and dance. The
night would wear on as the pile of unshucked ears grew smaller and
smaller the spirits of the darkies would rise. They had work, even
when mixed with fun, and as the corn-pile disappeared the crowd
would yell,—

> *Looking for de las' year,*
> *Bang-a-ma-lango!*
> *Lookin' fur de las' year,*
> *Bang-a-ma-lango!*
> *Roun' up de co'n, boys,*
> *Bang-a-ma-lango!*
> *Roun' up de co'n boyus,*
> *Bang-a-ma-lango!*

They always say 'year' for ear, and as the last one was shucked was a mighty rush and scramble. Three or four strapping bucks would lift the young marster to their shoulders and the crowd would fall in behind. Then they would march three times around the 'big house,' as the marster's house was always called, singing as they marched, coming to a halt at the tables under the trees, where they were sure of finding a feast of good things. A beef and a mutton were always killed for corn-shuckin' supper, and then there was an abundance of bacon and cabbage, sweet and Irish potatoes, stewed pumpkin, fruit pies, and pecks and pecks of ginger-cakes and biscuits, and gallons of molasses. Darkies "jes' naterally love coffee" as they say themselves, and everyone had as much as he or she wanted in corn-shuckin' time. It was served in bowls. They would eat awhile and then rest and then eat again. And while they were resting, some would pat and sing, play the jewsharp or quills, while others pulled ears and danced. Others would wrestle and box, and the old men and women would settle themselves about the numerous fat-pine bonfires and talk about "ole marse and ole missy an' young marster," or sing the old negro melodies they love so well. Ah, they felt as grand and as free as they've ever felt since, boys, and there never will be anything to take its place. The old slaves are dying on the old Confeds that fought to keep them. Already "old marster an' ole missy" and Mammy Liza and Daddy Hannibal have passed away, and it is almost time for young marster and the young darkies to go, too. I want to go back, boys. I want to go back to one more corn-shuckin' in the cotton-growin' section; all made up of darkies. I don't want to go where the crowd is mixed, part black and part white. Do you know, I'd like to feel that I was the young marster once more. You can have all the tickets to hear Melba, Nordica, and Eames, and the De Rezkes and Paderewski, if you'll just let me hear the blowin' of the bugles and quills and the old corn-shuckin' songs;

but what's the matter with us all taking a pull at the little brown jug before we go back to work?

Mary A. Livermore, *The Story of My Life,* Hartford, Conn.: A. D. Worthington, 1897, pp. 332–40.

For three or four years Dick had importuned his father to give the servants a "corn-shucking party." He had never been absolutely refused, but his petition was evaded and decisive answer to the boy's request postponed. He was very much attached to the servants, and they gave him a love that was deeper and stronger than that for their own kith and kin. So, when Uncles Henson and Isham, and Aunts Aggy and Pennie began again to agitate the subject of the "corn-shucking," and to glowingly recount its delights, Dick, realizing that a new day had dawned in his sky, half promised them on the spot the coveted gratification.

"I'll ask Pa about it, Mammy," he said to Aunt Aggy, "an' this time I reckon you'll git it."

And sure enough, when he proferred his request on this occasion, it was granted instanter, without hesitation or debate.

"Yes," said Mr. Henderson, "tell Uncle Henson to go ahead with the 'corn-shucking,' and I'll furnish the supper."

"Who shall they invite?" asked Dick. "They mustn't ask the people on plantations so far off but they can easy git home before mornin'."

"Let them invite Mr. Frere's people, the Ashmore's, Field's, Maury's, and Walker's," said Mr. Henderson. "They are our nearest neighbors, and these, with our own hands, will make a big company."

Dick hurried to Aunt Aggy's with the delectable news.

"It's done!" shouted the happy fellow, as he burst into the cabin, tossing up his hat. "We're gwine to have the biggest corn-shuckin' ever seen in this county. Pa says Oncl' Henson may invite the people on these five plantations round us, an' he'll give the supper; an' I tell you it'll be a boss supper."

Old as he was, Uncle Henson jumped out of his chair and "cut the pigeon wing." Aunt Aggy pulled Dick into her lap, hugged, and kissed, and slapped him all at once, shouting between whiles, "It takes you, Mas'r Dick!"

Peter rolled over, and over, and over, like a cart wheel, until he tumbled into a ditch; and Allen, his brother, flew as with winged feet over the plantation, proclaiming the great news as he ran; and in twenty minutes the whole place was in ferment. Preparations were begun forthwith. The day of the "corn-shucking" was appointed, and messengers were dispatched to the neighboring plantations, bearing passes to go and return, from Mr. Henderson, with invitations from Uncle Henson. Every evening, when the working-hours of the day were over, the servants brought in the unhusked corn from the fields, and heaped it about the corn cribs. Pitch pine knots were gathered in large quantities to illuminate the festive occasion, for there was no moon, not the thinnest crescent of one, to shed its light upon the merry-makers. This was a great piece of negligence and indifference on the part of the powers that be, for a round, full moon was regarded as the veritable *sine qua non* of a "corn-shucking."

"We'll show de moon dat we kin git 'long widout her," said wise Uncle Isham, sagely wagging his head.

The cooking began early in the morning of the eventful day. All the resources of the "niggah kitchen," where the meals of the field hands were prepared, were duly monopolized. All the fire-places, turn-spits, big kettles, boiling-pots, and stew pans on the place were brought into requisition. A mighty log near the "negro quarters" was fired early, that at the right time there might be hot ashes and coals for the baking of sweet potatoes and pones of corn bread. A search had been instituted the day before among the hundreds of swine which were never penned, but ran wild until slaughtering time, and a large number of lean young porkers thought suitable for roasting, had been discovered. Aunt Aggy contributed a dozen of her fat geese for the supper, and Mrs. Henderson added the same number of turkeys Some of the negroes had organized a successful coon hunt to glorify the feast and the savory odor of coon stew, prepared in huge cauldrons under Aunt Aggy's direction was wafted to our olfactories by every breeze that stole into the windows.

A holiday from school duties was announced; neither teaching nor studying were possible on this momentous occasion. The children insisted that Aunt Aggy and Uncle Henson should do the honors as host and hostess during the evening, and be dressed as became their position. The wardrobes of their parents were overhauled in search of such cast-off clothing and second-hand finery as could be utilized and by dint of much shortening and taking in of coat and trousers, and an equal amount of letting out and taking down of one of their mother's dresses, these two valuable head servants were so resplendently arrayed by their costumers, that they were the admiration and envy of all their guests. Aunt Aggy's handsome face and figure were well set off by a somewhat *passé* brown silk, and her towering turban and immaculate neckerchief of sheer white muslin. But when did she ever look otherwise than queenly? The evening sky was full of stars, and the soft, warm air blew lightly upon us as we walked down the avenue on the look-out for our expected guests. Long before we saw their dusky figures, we heard their melodious songs echoing and re-echoing through the woods as they marched toward the Henderson plantation. They came in four companies from as many different directions, across lots, by cart-paths, and through the forest, all entering upon our field of vision at one and the same time, when they saluted and marched together. They carried torches which were waved aloft with joyous shouts, as they met; and when they caught sight of hosts and hostesses assembled around the corn cribs, the whole place brilliant with blazing pine knots, their enthusiasm knew no bounds. Shouts of recognition and welcome thrilled the evening air, and fell upon our listening ears.

The greetings and hand-shakings over, the assembled company, costumed in every variety of nondescript garment, with faces of every shade of black, chocolate, and burnt umber, as diverse in aspect as were their garments in fashion, seated themselves in groups around the mounds of unhusked corn. Their diversity was accentuated by the flaring torches which wrought continual changes of light, shade, and expression, reminding one of the shifting figures and colors of a kalaeidoscope. Flirting and coquetting prevailed among the dusky gallants and belles, and the jokes at each other's expense, and the tricks employed to separate lovers, or to bring the wrong couples into juxtaposition, made half the fun of the evening. All the while they steadily stripped the husks from the magnificent ears of golden corn, tossing them into the cribs with such dexterous fling and accurate aim, that not one fell short of, or exceeded its destination. Some, who were famous huskers, entered into competition with others of like reputation, each side seeking to outdo the other. Then the rivalry became so exciting as to halt the other workers, who watched the contest with shouts and cheers and clapping of hands, until Uncle Henson ordered all to resume work, and declared the contest closed. They sang without cessation while they worked, until the cribs were overflowing, and all the corn was husked and then supper was announced.

SOLO   *Religion's like a bloomin' rose*
CHORUS *We'll shuck dis cawn befo' we go!*
       As none but dem dat feels it knows.
          We'll shuck dis cawn befo' we go!
       I was a sinner jess like you.
          We'll shuck dis cawn befo' we go!
       But sing his praises! Bress de lamb!
          We'll shuck dis cawn befo' we go!
       Fo' I am saved, indeed I am!
          We'll shuck dis cawn befo' we go!
       New stan' up squar' in youah own shoes,
          We'll shuck dis cawn befo' we go!
       An' put no faith in solem' views,
          We'll shuck dis cawn befo' we go!

And so on and on, from one kind of doggerel to another, pious or amative, or rollicking according to the leader.

Never was a supper eaten with more zest; never was one eaten up cleaner; there were only bones and potato skins remaining. I had thought beforehand that the supper would suffice for twice the number that had gathered to eat it. I now believe the guests could easily have disposed of another meal equally abundant. Poor, simple, black men and women! The food to them was "angels' food" indeed, as they phrased it. The compliments passed on the supper were very amusing: "Sist' Aggy, dis yere roas' pig's good 'nuff fo' de angel's table in hebben." "Brother Henson, I reckon dat coon stew might make a dead man come t'life t'eat it." "Dis yere's no cheap lace, Aunt Phenie, an' yo's got no cheap Mas'r; an' we hain't had t'sharpen our feef t'night t'eat dis yere supper."

Then followed the leave-taking. There was endless smirking and giggling, with resounding kisses and pretended frights or displeasure, reiterated "good-nights," and continued "good-byes." The torches were re-lighted, each company formed under its leader, and the departing guests retraced their homeward steps, across lots, over cartpaths, and through the forest. Their torches were borne aloft, and again their melodious voices rang out in song as they marched away.

SOLO   *We're gwine home t' die no mo'!*
CHORUS   *We'll meet ag'in in de mawnin'!*
             Our frien's are on de oder sho'!
                   We'll meet ag'in in de mawnin'!
             I'll lead you safe, so nebber fear,
                   We'll meet ag'in in de mawnin'!
             Oh, brudders, haste! de day is near!
                   We'll meet ag'in in de mawnin'!
             Who comes dis way will pay no fare,
                   We'll meet ag'in in de mawnin'!
             Oh, hear de music in de air!
                   We'll meet ag'in in de mawnin'!
CHORUS   *Oh! dat mawnin! dat mawnin!*
                   We'll meet ag'in in de mawnin'!
             Dar'll be no night, fo' hebben is bright,
                   An we'll meet ag'in in de mawnin'!

George Brewer, "History of Coosa County, Alabama" (ms. in Alabama Department of Archives and History, Montgomery, Ala., pp. 197–200.

Another of these social helpful gatherings was in the fall of the year, when the days were getting short and the nights long and the air crisp. The corn would be hauled in long large heaps around the cribs. If the roof was not on highes so as to be raised, or part of the side on hinges, some logs near the top were slipped out, and the remaining ones secured from falling. The neighbors were notified that the "corn shucking" should be on a certain night. Several negroes that were experts in "corn songs" were asked to come and tell others to come. It was generally understood that a corn shucking was free to any who wished to come, so that if the familiar sound of a number of negroes singing corn songs at one place was heard, any negro man or boy felt he had a right to go, and they generally went, for they expected two things that appealed strongly to the negro, and that was a good dram and a good supper. As the hands arrived they went at once to the corn pile and began shucking, throwing the husked ear into the crib, and the shucks to the rear. They commenced at the outer edge of the pile of corn, and cleaned up the corn to the ground as they went. There were usually two or more recognized leaders in singing the corn songs, and as they would chant or shout their couplet, all the rest would join the chorus. There was no poetry or metre, to these songs, but there was a thrill from the melody welling up with such earnestness from the singers that it was so inspiring that the hands would fly with rapidity in tearing off the shucks, and the feet kick back the shucks with equal vigor. As a sample of the songs and chorus, the leader would shout out with a ringing tune, "Pull off the shucks boys, pull off the shucks" and the crowd shout out in a ringing chorus "Round up the corn boys, Round up the corn." Again he would say, "the night's getting off boys, the night's getting off," and they would respond "Round up the corn boys, Round up the corn." Again he would say, "Give me a dram sir, give me a dram," and they again "Round up the corn boys, round up the corn." This singing could be heard of a still night two miles or more.

When the night would be wearing off and still a good deal to shuck, the pile would be divided by some mark, and the shuckers divided as near equally as could be done hurriedly. A negro song leader would be chosen for each pile, and this leader would mount on his pile, cheer up his men, strike up some stirring song, gesticulate violently and sway his body to the music, push corn down to those shucking, and do whatever would stimulate to active work. The interest that would be aroused, and the rapidity with which the shucks would fly would be astonishing. Whichever side shucked out his pile first, would break into a song of victory, but turn in at once and help finish out the other side.

Most of the songs was impromptu suggested by immediate conditions except the chorus, which was uniform. When the corn was shucked it was also cribed [sic—R.D.A.], being thrown into the opening as the shuck was stripped off. As soon as the pile was finished, the crowd gathered up the shucks in great armfuls, and heaved them into rail pens nearby, that had been built ten or twelve rails high. Some would be in the pens treading down the shucks as they were thrown in, and building the pens higher as needed with rails hauled already near by for the purpose.

When this was done, the leaders would pick up the owner on their shoulders and carry him several times around the house, followed closely by all the others singing some of the most stirring corn songs, and praising him in their songs. After thus carrying him around in triumph, they would enter the hallway with him on their shoulders, and seat him in a chair, and with a shuffling dance, go out in the

yard. A hearty dram was then given them, and then they were seated
to a rich supper around. Negroes and whites enjoyed there (sic)
shucking very much, and while there was no approximation to social
equality, there was the best of feeling mutually among them. The
negro did not dream of being familiar, and yet there was nothing like servile fear, but a genuine respect and kindly feeling to the
whites.

Daniel Webster Davis, "Echoes from a Plantation Party," *Southern
Workman,* 28, 2, (Feb. 1899), 55.

When the corn for the winter had been gathered in, many indulgent
masters would allow the slaves to have a "corn shucking." The
master might kill an old steer, now past the possibility of work, and
prepare a big supper. Spirited races would sometimes take place
between rival shuckers, and happy was the man who would come
out ahead. Again it would be a "husking bee," when the same process
would be gone through, only this time it would be for the purpose
of getting the corn off the husk that it might be carried to the mill
and ground into meal for the slaves.

Mrs. James H. Dooley, *Dem Good Ole Times,* New York: Doubleday, Page, 1906, pp. 61–63.

Corn shuckin wuz mornstrous fun I tell you. A week or mo fo de
time, de news gin to spread round, when it gwy be. Twar no sich
bothersome things in dem days is de tellin-foam; un twar no use fur
um, caze de tellin nigger beat de tellin-foam all holler. Evy night
reglar, twuz de darkies' way to walk bout all over creashum. Dey
hyur evything un dey tell evything dey hyur, un a heap dey did'n.
When de night come fur de shuckin, soonsever it git dark, de neighbors gin to drap in, un fus thing you know, look like dey done riz
up out de groun un kiver de whole face uv de yuth, wuss'n locusis.
Sometimes, pear like dar wuz mo niggers den corn, but we meck um
welcom, ef dey did come mo fur what dey gwy git, den fur what dey
gwy do. We all had de name uv givin de tarin-downis suppers in de
whole country. Marse nuver low nobordy git hade uv him in noth'n.
Is dey git het up to de wuck un pitch dey voice in dat rousin ole
song:

Come to shuck dat corn to-night;
Come to shuck wid all yo might;
Come fur to shuck all in sight;
Come to shuck dat corn to-night.

Come to shuck dat golden grain;
Whar dar's nuff dar ay no pain;
Ef you shuck tis all you gain—
Come to shuck dat golden grain;

pears like it shake de vey tops uv de trees, un set de leaves on de groun to whirlin un dancin un jinin in de frolic. Far out in de woods un on de hills, you hear dat chune a ringin, ontwell it wake up de mockin birds un dey answer back un fill out de chorus. Dey always cum down frum de house fur to hear us, un Marse say is how he done bin all over de worl, un hear de finis music what is, from de frorg-porn up, I think he say, to de bes' High-stallion hopper (Italian opera), but dis beat all. He say it meck he blood run hot un den cole, un den pear to stop runnin altoguther. Music am a mighty sarchin sup'n. It always put me in a trimble, whensomuver I hear Dixie un sunshiny things like dat; but cose it doe play de same tricks wid my blood, it do wid Marster's, caze his'n de true blue.

Joe Clay were a powerful singer, un dey name im de cock uv de corn pile, caze he always stan on top'n it, un crow de loudis. One night he sing so loud tryin to show off fo de white folks, he loss he voice, un twuz mo'n a mont fo he come up wid it agin; he were de bal-headis nigger I uver come crost. Dey all say, he voice were so powerful, dat is he sing de strank went up fru de top'n he hade, un kill de roots uv de hyar, ontwell it all drap out un lef im on top, slick is a ingun. Hyar un grass is much de same; too much strank kill de roots uv bofe. But sho's you born, pride had a heap to do wid dat bizniss. You kin twis un tun it much is you choose, but de Bible always come true, un de preacher say, "Pride does go befo de fall." De pride uv de singin come fus, de fallin uv de hyar arterwards.

Rev. I. M. Lowery, *Life on the Old Plantation in Ante-Bellum Days,* Columbia, S.C.: The State Company, 1911, pp. 93–98.

All who have the good fortune to have been born and reared in the country, can recall with pleasing recollections the joy that welled up in all hearts during the harvest. . . . The corn harvest came in the fall, and the corn-shucking always took place at that season. The fodder was generally pulled or stripped in August or September, and the ears of corn were left on the stock to dry until about the first of November. But now the day has come, and the corn breaking has begun. The hands all go to the field, and they break off the ears and throw them into piles. These piles are made in the middle of the same row about twenty feet apart, and contain the corn of some twelve rows. Two wagons, each drawn by a pair of mules or horses, with bodies the same size, are loaded full of corn. At the barn yard it is thrown into two piles preparatory to the corn-shucking. One load is put on this pile, and the other on that, and so on, until the entire crop is hauled in.

The night is set for the corn-shucking; for it was usually had at night, so that the slaves from the adjacent plantations could come and enjoy the sport. Invitations were sent far and near, and they were readily accepted. Great preparations were made in food and drink. The only drink allowed at the corn-shucking was coffee, but it was customary on some of the plantations to have whiskey at corn-shuckings, but Mr. Frierson never allowed it. It was often the case that from fifty to seventy-five men, beside the women, came to the corn-shucking. All these had to be fed. Great pots of rice, meat, bread and coffee were prepared. It was enough for all who came and took part in the corn-shucking.

When all the invited hands had arrived, the first thing in order was the election of two men to be captains, and these captains selected their companies from the crowd present. It was done alternately, something after the manner of school boys when they make up their sides to play a game of baseball. Captain Number One had the first choice, and then his opponent, and so on, until the two companies were made up. These preliminary matters having been arranged, they set in to shucking corn.

The reader will remember that there are two piles of equal size and now there are two companies of shuckers of equal numbers, each company having a captain. It was considered no little honor to be elected captain of a corn-shucking company. His hat or cap was invariably decorated with the office, and everybody—white and colored—did him honor. In the election of these captains regard was had to their ability to sing: for the captains usually led their company in singing while shucking corn. At a given signal each captain took his seat on the top of his pile of corn, and his shuckers surrounded it. While they shucked corn, they engaged in singing corn-shucking songs. Much of the fun of the occasion depended upon which side would win. It was a race that grew more exciting as the piles of unshocked corn grew less. They shucked, they sang and they shouted. Then they knew that a bountiful supper awaited them just as soon as the work was done. On they went—a jolly good set, singing, joking and laughing. In the midst of it all they could sniff the aroma of hot coffee, and the delicious odor of roasted meats and other nice dishes. This, as well as the hope of victory, was quite an inspiration for the boys. Well, the work is done. The last ear of corn has been shucked, and captain number one, with his company has won. See the boys, as they toss their hats into the air! Hear them shout! The victory is theirs. They are a happy set.

Supper is now ready. Long tables—well laden with good things—have been prepared. Fully two score colored women are there to wait on the table. And they eat, and eat, and drink, to their satisfaction. The supper being over . . . the boys spend some time in wrestling, foot racing and jumping before going home. And in all these games they matched one's agility, strength and manhood against that of his fellow. This is kept up until late in the night, and then they retire to the various plantations whither they belong.

Such was the corn-shucking on the old plantation in ante-bellum days. It was very much enjoyed by both the white folks and the slaves. The incidents and the happenings of a corn-shucking were long talked of on all the plantations represented. Nearly all the plantations had their cornshuckings, and they certainly kept things lively during this season of the year in those days.

John Allen Wyeth, *With Sabre and Scalpel,* New York: Harper, 1914, pp. 58–61.

It was on the occasion of my earlier visits to the plantation of my cousin, Mr. James A. Boyd, in Madison County, that I first witnessed a "corn-shucking." In gathering the corn the ears were pulled from the stalks and piled in pens near the cribs. The negroes on one plantation were privileged to invite those of other places near by to come at dark on Saturday night. A bonfire was built at a safe distance, by the light of which the men and the women ranged themselves around the corn-piles and began to strip the shuck, or husk, from the ear, to the cadences of their African chants and wierdly [sic— R.D.A.] melodious singing. One of the number, by reason of his greater accomplishments, took the part of leader, and from the top of the heap sang out or chanted a line of a verse often improvised. When he ceased, the chorus of from fifty to one hundred voices would take up the refrain and carry it in a strange and varying cadence of sounds without words, which typified joy or sorrow, or an emotion in full sympathy with the sentiment expressed by the leader.

I can recall only a few of these lines, and wish I could transcribe the music. For instance, the leader would sing: "I'm gwine away to leave you," and, as this was suggestive of the sadness of parting, the chorus would begin in a low moan, which, rising and falling, would for a minute or two be carried to the fullest tone, and then die away so gradually one could scarcely say just when it ceased. Then the leader would chant in tones a little less tinged with sadness: "I'm gwine to de happy islands!" And, this suggested the consummation of a dream of rest, the chanting of the chorus was more cheeringly rendered.

On these occasions extraordinary liberties were permissible, and not infrequently, as the whole white people of the premises were listening, the bold leader would by suggestion open the way for a holiday, or a barbeque, or a dance, or extra Christmas vacation, when they visited relatives on other plantations. For example:

> *Marster an' Mistus lookin' mighty fine—*
> *Gwine to take a journey; gwine whar dey gwine;*
> *Crab grass a-dyin', red sun in de west—*
> *Saturday's comin', nigger gwine to rest.*

And much more in this happy vein. Meanwhile everyone was busy stripping corn, throwing the ears into the winter crib and packing the shucks in the rail pens. It took usually about three hours for the many hands to strip all the corn raised in the place, and then there was a supper with all sorts of home-made edibles, especially pumpkin pies, sweet cakes, and persimmon beer, a refreshing, unfermented beverage which the negroes made from this fruit.

. . . The real fun began with the dancing. The banjo and the fiddle made up the orchestra, and there were accompanists who "patted" with the hands, keeping accurate time with the music. In patting, the position was usually a half-stoop or forward bend, with a slap of one hand on the left knee followed by the same stroke and noise on the right, and then a loud slap of the two palms together. I should add that the left hand made two strokes in half-time to one for the right, something after the double-stroke of the left drumstick in beating the kettle-drum. In rare instances I have heard that before the triangle came into vogue the dried and resonant jaw-bone of the ox or horse was used this way, the sides being rhythmically struck with a rib. I have no doubt of this, for I learned from one of their songs, handed down by repetition, probably, from pre-American sires, these lines:

> Oh, de jaw-bone walk,
> And de jaw-bone talk,
> And de jaw-bone eat
> Wid a knife and fork
> I laid my jaw-bone on de fence,
> Ain I hain't seen dat jaw-bone
>   sence.

When on these occasions the crowd was very large, they would divide and go to the cabins in smaller parties, or the big floor of the gin-house may have been selected. Strange to say, they did not relish dancing on the ground, in the manner of the American Indian; I don't think this can be explained by the negroes' instinctive love of rhythm, which the Indian does not seem to possess. The shuffle of the feet, in many instances unshod—for in warm weather they would pull off their shoes to keep their feet cool—could not be heard as distinctly on the ground as on a plank floor or a tight puncheon.* I have often seen them dance on the bottom of a wagon-bed, which made an excellent sounding-board. The dances were primitive and gave opportunity for great activity; and when two danced alone, whether of the same sex or not, the object seemed to be to determine

---

*A puncheon was the flat surface of a split log, smoothed with an ax and pinned to the joists to make the floors of the rude cabins constructed before sawmills were introduced. Sometimes they became loose, and rocked forward and back on this single slab. Hence the common expression, "Hunt your puncheon," when something fixed or solid or sure was desired.

which could outdo the other. As the "steps," or gyrations and contortions not only of the body and the legs, but of the arms and the hands, grew more violent and rapid, the spectators would begin to pat and shout words of approval or kindly criticism, until at last one of the contestants gave up and the victor was hailed as the "best man." At midnight the frolic ended, and the visitors returned to their several homes.

Nettie Powell, *History of Marion County, Georgia,* Columbus, Ga., Historical Publishing, 1931.

Log rollings, house raisings, and quiltings were still popular social gatherings. After the corn was pulled and put in the cribs, the farmers invited their neighbors, and had what was called a "corn shucking." The corn was put into piles, and sides were chosen by the young men present. The side that finished first won the prize. When the task was over, a sumptuous supper was served. Then there was a dance in which old and young joined. The music was supplied by old time fiddlers with a great deal of beating straws.

Major A. D. Reynolds, "Origin of One of the Greatest Tobacco Manufacturing Enterprises in the World," in *History of Patrick and Henry Counties, Virginia,* ed. Virginia G. and Lewis G. Pedigo, Roanoke: Stone Printing and Manufacturing Co., 1933, p. 29.

In times past, in the fall of the year, gathering and shucking the corn, especially the latter, was a real festival. Fodder pulling preceded the gathering of the corn by some weeks, the blades were pulled off of the stalks by hand, tied into bundles, dried and stacked so that the top of the stack formed a cone and the rains would not soak in. Some time in October the corn was gathered, hauled to a place near the corncribs and piled upon the ground. Each family had an evening set apart for the shucking. Neighbors both black and white were called in and soon after supper time the work and fun began, and was kept up until a great pile of gleaming corn was on one side and a mountain of shucks on the other, no matter how late the hour.

Singing corn songs was an indispensable part of the program. The songs were given out, and led by a colored man who could cut more "monkey shines" than anyone else. He stood at the crest of the big pile of corn, waving his arms and urged on the work by the words of the song, while the crowd as they joined in the singing tore the shucks from the ears, which they sent whizzing through the air to growing mound, all to the accompaniment of the songs and the capers of the leader.

The drinks were a great feature of the occasion and jugs and flasks were passed at intervals all through the evening.

The closing ceremony consisted of catching the plantation owner, whether he resisted or not, swinging him to the shoulders of two of the huskiest men and marching around the house three times to the tune of the closing song.

All that is changed now, the corn is pulled from the shuck which is left on the stalk, hauled to the storage place and the stalk cut with fodder and shucks (or husks), stacked and used for winter food for cattle.

Luke E. Tate, *History of Pickens County, Georgia,* Atlanta, 1935, pp. 63–64.

The Corn-Shucking carried far into the night and was a time of great merriment for old and young. Like the log-rolling, it was an occasion of such feasting and conviviality, there being a supply of the refined variety of corn for those who wished it. Of course, there was great rivalry among the huskers, each trying to outdo the other, but among the youngsters the glory went not to the one who accomplished the most work, but to him or her who found the most red ears. Some perhaps were more interested in red lips—and I dare say that many a romance dates back to a corn-shucking, and that many gold-wedding days have been brightened by the memory of the glow of an autumn moon around a pile of newly-husked corn. The fiddler might be there, too, and before the shades of night are driven away by the glimmer of dawn the happy couples have danced to the tunes of the Highland.

John Cabell Chenault, *Old Cane Springs: A Story of the War Between the States in Madison County, Kentucky,* rev. and suppl. Jonathan Truman Dorris, Louisville: The Standard Printing Co., 1937, pp. 42–50.

The second week of school began, but my thoughts were wound up in the anticipation of the corn shucking. It was a new thing to me. I had never heard of one's neighbors coming and doing his work on such a scale. I told my teacher that I could not keep my mind off the shucking and that I was puzzled to know how they expected to shuck at night. He referred me to Uncle Robert for information, saying that there were very few Negroes in Harrison County, where he was born and reared and especially in that part of the county where he had lived. . . .

That evening I asked Uncle Robert to explain the nature of the corn shucking that was to come off the next night at Mr. Norris'. He said there was a number of persons in the neighborhood who had but few hands. They generally raised large crops of corn and could with their limited force do all their work in due season, except the shucking.

"Unless corn is gathered promptly after it is dry enough to crib," he explained, "there is likely to be considerable loss—in fact, the longer the corn remains in the shock the greater the loss. Our negroes are fond of going to corn shuckings. I understand that tomorrow night they will set a night they will shuck out Colby McKinney's crop, and so on until every man who is short on hands will have his corn shucked. Mr. Norris [the host—R.D.A.] will get several gallons of whiskey, which will cost him fifty cents per gallon. He will prepare a good supper for the shuckers and the neighbors who may come. I shall not try to explain to you the pleasure the Negroes will get out of these corn shuckings. You will simply have to go over to-morrow night and see for yourself."

. . . Presently a great volume of song a few hundred yards away caught our attention. Some one spoke: "They are beginning to come."

I ran out into the yard and was soon joined by Mr. Norris, who said, "Those singers are my welcome guests tonight, and I must be out to greet them."

Nearer and nearer the singers approached, and the harmony was beautiful. I had never heard the song before and I could not distinguish the words very well, but the harmony was beautiful. At first I believed that all the negroes in the community had gotten together, for it seemed to me that there were a hundred voices or more; but on the arrival of the singers, I learned that they were only the men from the Cabell Chenault plantation. Mr. Norris met them in his front yard and greeted them with "Howdy, Amos; howdy, William; howdy, Jeff," until Shed, Jerry, Jim, Horace, Scott, Big Joe, George, Cuff, Little Joe, Andy, and all the others had passed on towards the residence.

The night was pleasant and the moon by this time was shining brightly. The negroes began to drop around on the grass and joke one another, first about one thing, and then another, but all in the best of humor.

Presently I caught the sound of voices that appeared to be a half a mile away or so. The Negroes sprang to their feet as if by the order of a commander. There was speculation as to who the Negroes were. Then one of them, straining their ears, exclaimed: "I catch de voice ov one ov 'em. It's Larimore's Pleas."

The voices were so far away that I thought it was impossible to distinguish any particular voice, but they all agreed that Scott was right. At this moment off to the northwest but much closer, other voices were heard. Nearly everybody present recognized the voice of Noland's Allen. Still farther to the northwest, more singers were heard, and someone said "That mus' be Marse Jack Martin's niggers."

Then from farther up the river the sound of other voices came. Pete, a little black Negro, said, "I knows dat crowd; I heahs Chambers' Pud."

The voice came nearer and nearer until less prominent singers were recognized. Presently someone said, "All ov 'em niggers 'll get togedder out yonder at de forks ov de road; den you'll hear some singin' sho' 'nough."

Just at this time, voices to the south of us cause all to turn and listen in that direction. Someone in the crowd said, "That's Deatherage's Henry." Then another exclaimed, "Yeah, there's Giles, and now they're jis toppin' de Muddy Creek hill."

Finally, off to the southeast came another volume of song and we all turned in that direction, with hands, palms forward, placed behind our ears. I could hear a voice very different from any I had heard that night. It sounded in the distance like the clarion notes of wild geese in the migratory flights. All were quiet and listening, but noone named the leading singer, whose voice was a clear, distinct tenor, that leaped and bounded far above any of the other singers. It was simply charming, entrancing. White and black, men and women, stood in silence looking up the Texas road as if bound by some spell in that direction. The silence was broken by Cuff's saying: "I heah Moberly's Otaway in dat crowd, too."

Noone answered and as I could not restrain my anxiety to know the tenor singer, I said to Uncle Amos, who was standing near, "How is it that none of you recognized that tenor voice?"

"Oh, we all knows dat voice. Dat's Oldham's Pike. He's such a good singer dat we all jis stand an' listen w'en we fust heah 'im. Ef anyone had said dat wus Oldham's Pike, all de res' would ov laughed at 'im. His voice can be recognized jis ez fur ez you kin heah hit."

By this time voices in song were heard coming from every direction. The sound was simply fascinating. Melodies echoing and reechoing from hills beyond the river and from the hills across Muddy Creek sounded like the intermingling of voices singing in unison near and far away.

As the Negroes drew nearer they all ceased singing except the Oldham crowd. When they came within an hundred yards of the Norris home, Pike could be plainly heard lining the song; then those already in the yard and others coming along the road took up the melody. No camp meeting I had ever attended had in any way equaled that singing. When the approaching singer heard those in the yard, it seemed to be a signal for all to stop singing. Mr. Norris greeting them with a familiar "howdy," which made the Negroes feel welcome, and then returned to the front portico, rapped for silence and said:

"Men, you have done me the kindness to come here tonight to shuck my corn. I have only three hundred shocks. I am unable to tell how many there are of you, but I imagine you will not have to shuck over three shocks each if you finish my crop." Upon being asked if they would like something to drink first: "Yes, suh; we all's mighty thursty," came from all over the yard.

"After you have finished shucking you can have another drink and your supper. And for fear I may not be able to thank you when you quit work, I thank each one of you now for this volunteer service tonight, for I know that you are not here by order of your masters." "No, suh; no suh. We come 'cause we wanted to he'p you all," came from many voices. . . . "Now here are four jugs of whiskey, as good as Walden can make, and here are plenty of glasses. I will ask you, Amos, to take this jug, and you Harrison, this one, and you, Henry, this one, and you Pleas, this one. Each of you pour for the boys. Now come on, fellows, and when you have drunk, go over there to the cornfield and arrange the manner of shucking to suit yourselves. I will now go and spend the remainder of the evening with my neighbors."

The Negroes were eager to get a drink, but as soon as they were served, they filed off to the field. When they were in the field, someone suggested that Colonel Noland's Harrison and Mr. Chenault's Amos be general bosses to see that all the men worked orderly and missed no shocks. This suggestion was promptly agreed to. It was arranged that the shucking was to be by pairs, or two men to a stack. Harrison and Amos were to pair them off, so as to equalize the pairs. The best two shuckers, according to the decision of Amos and Harrison, were to receive special mention at the supper as the best workers. The pairs were shortly arranged. Generally where two expressed a desire to be together, they were thus assigned. In a very short time the teams were at their shocks. Oldham's Pike was to give the signal to begin by singing a song.

All these arrangements were very interesting to me. I doubted, however, that so many men would ever be kept successfully at work. Pike and his partner were given the first shock nearest the county road, and Amos and Harrison went with the other men until all were properly placed, and then returned to Pike at the first row and said, "Start your song." At the command he began:

> *Old marster shot a wild goose*

A hundred voices answered from all parts of the field and each man grabbed a stalk for shucking.

> *Ju-ran-zie, hio ho.*
> *It wuz seben years fallin'*

The multitude of voices cried out as at first—

> *Ju-ran-zie, hio ho.*
>
> *It was seben years cookin'.*
> *Ju-ran-zie, hio ho.*
>
> *A knife couldn't cut it.*
> *Ju-ran-zie, hio ho.*
>
> *A fork couldn't stick it.*
> *Ju-ran-zie, hio ho.*

There was great harmony and perfect concord, although the men were scattered. The Norris farm was not far from the Kentucky River but it was higher than the surrounding land. Consequently the great volume of sound rolled off across the river and echoed and re-echoed in the Estill County hills beyond; and strangely enough these reverberations rolled away across Muddy Creek and echoed and re-echoed in the cedar hills. Such singing this generation will never hear, for I am writing this account many years after it occurred, and only those who have heard something of this kind will believe that echoes from a hundred vigorous voices can cause one to feel that he is listening to thousands of singers scattered over a large area. But it is true, as many yet living will bear me witness—or at least it was true in Old Cane Springs.

I attended many other huskings and I always thrilled while listening to what seemed like thousands of singers in one melodious symphony. Not only were the common Negro melodies of the ante-bellum period sung, but such Foster songs as *Old Black Joe, Massa's in the Cold, Cold Ground,* and *My Old Kentucky Home* rang out on the cool night air. And when Pike's clarion tenor voice led in these songs, especially in *Swing Low, Sweet Chariot* and *Nelly Was a Lady,* followed by a score of deep bass voices, the melody thrilled beyond one's description.

My reverie was finally broken by a call from Uncle Robert to come to supper, and I reluctantly went to the house. A splendid supper was prepared for the white guests. . . .

. . . About nine o'clock I heard an unusual noise out in the field and was about to run out to learn the cause of the commotion when someone near me remarked: "The field is finished, and they will be here in a few minutes." Like a great black cloud the men began filing into the yard, merry and cheerful as when they started to work.

Mr. Norris went to the front of his portico and said: "Boys. I must thank you again for helping me out as you have. My wife and her neighbors have prepared, I think, a good supper for you. I wish I had a table of sufficient length and chairs so that you could each sit and enjoy your supper more, but as that is impossible, you will have to eat as they do at the Baptist Association."

"Good 'nough;' good 'nough," was heard from all sides of the yard, which was full of Negroes by this time.

"Would you prefer to have your drink before or after supper?" Mr. Norris asked. "There is enough left for each of you have another drink, . . ." . . . the Negroes exclaimed, "Stimulant furst, stimulant furst."

They were all promptly served, and then Mr. Norris announced, "Boys, you will find plenty of chicken, turkey, shoat, and mutton, with other good things for the first course, and a washing tub of custard with enough pound cake for each of you to get a slice to eat with it; so file around to the rear of the house where you can be helped."

It was certainly a sight to see those Negroes eat. Mrs. Norris and three other women stood by a table on which there were large bread trays and pans full of chicken, mutton, turkey, and shoat. Then there was another table with a great quantity of bread, and beyond that there were Negro women, who spooned steaming vegetables on the men's bread. There was enough to eat for all, but the food vanished like dew before the sunshine. For dessert everyone was given a cup of custard and a large slice of cake.

While this last course was being served, Uncle Harrison stepped forward and said it was the custom in the midst of an enjoyable meal after a corn shucking to announce who the judges thought were the best shuckers. He stated that he and Amos had watched closely, and while it had been very hard to decide, they had finally concluded that Cabell Chenault's Scott and Amos Deatherage's Giles had shown the most skill in removing the shucks and shocking the fodder; but all had done well and no complaint was filed against anyone for not doing good work. Three cheers rang out for Scott and Giles.

Soon the Negroes began to say, "good nigh, Marse Norris," and "Thank you, Miss Norris, fur de good supper. Call on us 'gin w'en yo' all got mo' corn to shuck"; and all they went towards their homes singing as merrily as when they came. Thus ended my first corn shucking.

Hugh Johnson, "Old Times in the South Contest," ms in the Clarence Poe Papers, North Carolina State Archives, Raleigh, N.C. (sent in the 1950s, from Reidsville, N.C.).

After the first frost the corn was gathered and thrown into a pile along with the pumpkins that were usually grown in the corn field.

The neighbors were then all asked in, the men to the huskin [sic—R.D.A.] and the women to quilting, so, the work and the fun began. When someone shucked a red ear which could be found now and then among the white corn, he would hollow for an extra drink of spirits which was allways [sic—R.D.A.] present at these huskins. By mid evening everyone was garenteed [sic—R.D.A.] to be in no pain. This kept up until the corn was shucked and the shucks stowed away by the younger fellows who made a game of this to see who could carry the most shucks in a single turn.

The colord [sic—R.D.A.] men were there too and they all sat at one end of the pile with their song leader on top of the pile. Many old spirituals were sung and enjoyed during the day that followed. The white men at the other end joked and discussed local events.

Supper was a real meal. Tables heaped with dishes of cabbage and bacon, turnip salad covered with boiled eggs, roast and stew beef, boiled ham and baked hen, fried chicken and all kinds of cakes, pies and preserves. There was plenty of butter and honey to go with all the rest. The men with sharpened appetites, whetted by the work and drinks of the day, marched to the tables and they attacked the layers and rows of food with the impact of an army and it fell away before them.

Celia M. Benton, "Corn Shuckings in Sampson County," *North Carolina Folklore,* 22 (1974), 131–39 (white practices, with mention of black participation, including a song with music).

At corn shuckings in general, whites and blacks shared alike in the work, though this equality would not be carried over into the social sphere. Certainly this aspect of race relations is supported by the behavior of the men. While they worked, everyone did his share, and the seating was without regard to race. When the mealtime came, if it was served outdoors, they sat anywhere they chose. If the weather was rainy or too cold, the meal was eaten indoors where two tables were served: all the white men ate first, then the plates were replaced and the black men took their places. Inviting a person into one's house to share a table implied a social equality which was not then recognized. This practice was conditioned by both races, in the black people to the extent that the oldest ones will not, even today, go to a white person's house to eat a meal.

Socializing at corn shuckings and the core work done there were chiefly the province of the men. Usually twenty to forty gathered after lunch, either about one o'clock or late afternoon, depending on the weather and the amount of work to be done. If the night was moonlit and not cold, they could plan on evening work, with the supper being served around eleven. Otherwise, they ate at the regular hour and dispersed during the evening. In either case, the meal was served only after the work was finished.

The process began as the already picked corn was brought into the area of the crib (the building or room in which the corn was stored) using what was known as a "dump cart" in recognition of its principle of operation. . . . It had two wheels and was carefully balanced. Corn was tied securely in with a piece of rope or a strip of leather. To dump the contents, the men untied the rope and manually lifted the body, which was not too difficult. Then . . . "here the corn would go, rolly out the back." The cart was drawn by a mule or an ox, and on its way to the crib, the resident children, . . . , would ride on top of the corn and be dumped gleefully out at the end.

The corn was placed around the door of the crib as it came in load by load from the field. Then the men took their places in a semicircle around it, sitting just far enough apart to have elbow room, probably about a long yard. They worked their way toward the door of the crib, and as an ear was shucked, it was thrown into—or at least toward—the door and its shuck went back over the man's shoulder. . . .

If a man could not sit on the ground or did not want to, he could sit on a basket or on one of the boxes and old chairs commonly found around a farmer's barn. In later years, rather than being always thrown at the door, shucked corn was often placed in baskets which were passed to the crib either as they were filled or after all corn had been shucked.

"Sometimes they'd have whisky and wine," Lovitt Warren said, and it added to the festive mood. "Then some of them would—" "Get happy, wouldn't they?" Mrs. Sutton broke in. "Yes," he answered, "some of them would be getting up the next morning about sunrise in the shucks." Mrs. Marshall Warren told of a neighbor who returned from a corn shucking about eleven in the morning with his lantern still lit, and one of one man who found a dozen shuckers asleep in his shuck pile the next day!

As the shucking progressed, the host, who most often provided a few jars to supplement the bottles in back pockets, took his supply around, pouring glasses full as he went. My white informants felt that alcohol was a greater attraction for black shuckers than for themselves, but this is probably shifting a moral blame, for everyone enjoyed it.

. . . As they grew happier, they began to holler and sing. Mrs. Tart said, When they'd got happy, they would be hollering, 'The corn's falling at the door.' . . . They were singing then, you know . . . but a-shucking corn, throwing it in the crib." The song she sang describes this motion.

> *Wake up, boys, the corn is a-falling.*
> *The corn is a-falling at the door.*
> *Wake up, boys, the corn is a-falling.*
> *The corn is a-falling at the door.*

. . . Eliot Best, an older black man, had sung the verse, . . . and the group, both black and white, chanted back to him this chorus:

> *Sheep a shuckin' corn by the sound of his horn.*
> *Blow your horn.*

. . . The way of singing was very much in the black tradition, with its leader-chorus structure, and was recognized as such. Mrs. Sutton said that at corn shuckings the men sang "nigger folk songs." . . . "That sounds like niggers, you know, to go right over and over the same thing." The singing continued through the day's work. The rhythm set the pace of the work, and the corn fell at the door as the corresponding words were sung. Getting the shucks up did not mean a halt to the singing, and baskets of shucked corn were thrown about wildly to the rhythm of the song being sung.

When the main job had been done, clean-up tasks remained. The shucks, which by this time lay in a huge semicircular pile, were pushed toward the crib by a few men who began the job half squatted, gradually standing more erect. Though they must have been tired, they were still singing. Mrs. Jones described the late enthusiasm of one man who must have been a leader in singing: "And there was one feller that we particularly noticed. . . . He enjoyed it so good he'd be the first one at the corn shucking and we [the children— R.D.A.] would watch through the knot hole to see how much he'd eat, and was the last one from the table. But, man, he would help them entertain, you know, when they done that. They put the shucks, you know, back in the shuck house and they would take our daddy and would tote him around by the feet and head and sing the corn shucking songs. . . ." Presumably, they congratulated him on a job well done. After supper, the party broke up at various points depending on the prevailing level of inebriation, having accomplished efficiently . . . a major task.

Other Notices of Corn Shucking in the American South

Walter L. Fleming, *Home Life in Alabama during the Civil War*, Publications of the Southern History Association, vol. 8 (1904), 99 (mentions corn shucking).

Margaret Walker Freel, *Our Heritage: The People of Cherokee County, North Carolina, 1540–1955,* Asheville N.C.: The Miller Printing Co., 1956, p. 53 (white practices mentioned).

Paul Green, "Cornshucking," in *Words and Ways: Stories and Incidents from My Cape Fear Valley Folklore Collection,* Raleigh: North Carolina Folklore Society, 1968, p. 157 (short story of white shucking).

William Uhler Hensel, *The Christiana Riot and the Treason Trials of 1851: An Historical Sketch,* New York: Negro Universities Press, 1969, repr. of 1911 ed., p. 22 (mentions corn shucking to be held).

Linda T. Humphrey, "Small Group Festive Gatherings," *Journal of the Folklore Institute,* 16 (1979), 190–201; see esp. p. 194.

William Howard Russell, *The Civil War in America,* Boston, 1861, p. 151.

———, *Pictures of Southern Life: Social, Political, Military,* New York, 1861, p. 96.

Elizabeth Lowell Ryland, ed., *Richmond County, Virginia: A Review Commemorating the Bicentennial,* Warsaw, Va.: Richmond County Board of Supervisors, 1976, pp. 335–36 (whites, brief description).

Susan Dabney Smedes, *Memorials of a Southern Planter,* ed. and intr. Fletcher M. Green, New York: Knopf, 1965, p. 151 (not described as a celebration).

The only night-work done on the place was the semi-monthly corn-shelling, in preparation for the Saturday's grinding. The mellow songs of the corn-shellers floated on the air during the hour required for this work. When they found an ear of red or blue corn, or a double ear, it was often laid aside to be given in the morning to one of the white children.

Aunt Arie, in Laurie Brunson, et al., "Corn Shuckin's, House Raisin's, Quiltin's, Pea Thrashin's, Singin's, Log Rollin's, Candy Pullin's, and . . ." *Foxfire 5* (Spring–Summer 1971), 98.

Sometimes they'd shuck till twelve at night before they'd ever get up, and sing and holler and hoop and all th'devil. And they'd take th'shuck and hide people in'em . . . ever' kin'a fun in th'world.

Florence and Lawton Brooks, reminiscences in Brunson, pp. 97–98.

We used t'have them old shuckin's. They'd just pile up their corn in their barnyard, y'know, instead a'puttin' it in their crib. And then they'd ask all their neighbors around t'come in. . . . Ever'body'uz invited. Wasn't nobody skipped. They all come together. And you never seen such corn shucks in your life.

Then sometimes they'd have it where th'man that found th'first red ear got t'kiss th' prettiest girl, and sometimes he'd shuck like th'devil tryin' t'get t'find a red ear a'corn. Somebody'd find one generally ever'time. It was funny because back then 'at was th'worst thing a boy and girl could do would be caught kissin'. That's th'worst thing you could do! . . . they'd always bury a drink right in the middle on top a'it. Then we'd have t'shuck all night to'get t'that half-gallon a'liquor.

Marinda Brown, reminiscence in Brunson, p. 99.

I always got th'biggest thrill out a'that—just th'children and me. Just th'very smallest children would get in and shuck corn, and always look for th'red ears. Ever'body that found a red ear had t'be kissed. I didn't like that much though!

Mrs. Harriet Echols, reminiscence in Brunson, p. 98.

. . . they and all their neighbors'ud get their corn gathered in, and then they'd start'n'they'd go from place't'place—maybe twice a week they'd have a corn shuckin' at a different place. And all the men'ud get in th'barn and shuck, and if there was too many women, they'd go help shuck too. And then t'others'ud cook supper—have a big supper just like we have goin' t'a church supper'r'something like that.

Samuel Alexander Harrison, "The Civil War Journal of Dr. Samuel A. Harrison, ed. Charles L. Wagandt, *Civil War History*, 13 (May 1967), 136.

Anna Hoppe, *Negro Slavery; A Review of Conditions Preceding the Civil War*, St. Louis: R. Volkening, 1935, p. 30.

Spartanburg Unit of the Writers' Program, Work Projects Administration, State of South Carolina, *A History of Spartanburg County*, Spartanburg: American Association of University Women, 1940, pp. 117–18.

Cornshuckings were jolly occasions. They occurred in the fall. . . . The farmer issued a general invitation for such a festivity, and his neighbors came, bringing slaves and families. Often a jug of liquor was buried in the center of each pile of corn and could be passed from hand to hand only when the last ear was shucked. Usually a song-leader mounted the pile of corn and kept the shuckers busy, hand and tongue.

Carol Spratte, "Wyoming County [W. Va.] Folklore," *AFFword,* 3 (1973), 26.

Bonnie Mae Nicely, reminiscence in Maggie Holtzberg-Call, *Living at Home in the North Georgia Foothills: Remnants of a Traditional Way of Life,* White County Historical Society, 1989, pp. 15–17 (Concerns White County, Ga., corn shuckings involving blacks).

Songs from Sources Printing Corn Songs without Description
William Francis Allen, Charles Pickard Ware, Lucy McKim Garrison, *Slave Songs of the United States,* pp. 67–68 (with music).

> *Five can't can't ketch me and ten can't hold me,*
> *Ho, round the corn, Sally!*
> *Round the corn, round the corn, round the corn, Sally*
> *Ho, ho, ho, round the corn, Sally!*
> *2. Here's your iggle-quarter and here's you count-aquils.*
> *3. I can bank, 'ginny bank, ginny bank the weaver.*

[Iggle is of course "eagle"; for the rest of the enigmatical words and expressions in this corn-song, we must leave readers to guess at the interpretation]

Newman I. White, *American Negro Folk-Songs,* Cambridge, Mass.: Harvard Univ., 1928, pp. 162–63 ("Patting Juba," from Greenboro, N.C., 1915–16 ms).

> Corn shucking song, patted and sung
>
> > *Whar you goin', buzzard;*
> > *Whar you goin' crow?*
> > *Gwine down to de low groun'*
> > *To git mah grubbin' hoe.*

> Fus upon yo' heel-top,
> Den upon yo' toe,
> Ev'ry time I turn aroun'
> I jump Jim Crow.

Frank C. Brown, *The Frank C. Brown Collection of North Carolina Folklore,* vol. 3 (Folksong), pp. 233–34 (song with music).
Amy Henderson, *Frank C. Brown Collection,* p. 237.

And when they would finish shucking, sometimes they would pat this:

> Juba dis and Juba dat
> And Juba killed de yaller cat.
> Juba! Juba!

Jewell Robbins, in *Frank C. Brown Collection,* p. 238.

> Run, Sallie, my gal
>   Bu-ga-lo
> Run, Sallie, my gal
>   Bu-ga-lo
>
> The bull in the meadow
>   Bu-ga-lo
> As fat as he can wallow
>   Bu-ga-lo.
>
> Seven years a-boiling
>   Ho-ma-hala-way
> Seven years a-baking
>   Ho-ma-hala-way
>
> They blowed the horn for dinner
>   Ho-ma-hala-way
> The people could not eat her
>   Ho-ma-hala-way
>
> They carried her to the old field
>   Ho-ma-hala-way
> The buzzards could not eat her
>   Ho-ma-hala-way

S. M. Holton, Jr., in *Frank C. Brown Collection,* p. 234.

Up Roanoke and down the river,
Oho, we are 'most done.
Up Roanoke and down the river.
Oho, we are 'most done.

Two canoes, and nary paddle.
Oho, we are 'most done.
Two canoes, and nary paddle.
Oho, we are 'most done.

There is where we run the devils.
Oho, we are 'most done.
There is where we run the devils.
Oho, we are 'most done.

Away over in reedy bottom.
Oho, we are 'most done.
Away over in reedy bottom.
Oho, we are 'most done.

There is where we tricked the devils.
Oho, we are 'most done.
There is where we tricked the devils.
Oho, we are 'most done.

Jack de Gillam shot the devils.
Oho, we are 'most done.
Jack de Gillam shot the devils.
Oho, we are 'most done.

Blue ball and a pound of powder.
Oho, we are 'most done.
Blue ball and a pound of powder.
Oho, we are 'most done.

Shot him in the rim of the belly.
Oho, we are 'most done.
Shot him in the rim of the belly.
Oho, we are 'most done.

> That's the way we killed the devils.
>   Oho, we are 'most done.
> That's the way we killed the devils.
>   Oho, we are 'most done.

S. M. Holton, Jr., in *Frank C. Brown Collection*, p. 239.

> Goin' down the county,
>   Bugle, oh!
> Goin' down the county,
>   Bugle, oh!
> Red breast horses,
>   Bugle, oh!
> Red breast horses,
>   Bugle, oh!
>
> Comin' in a canter,
> Met my darlin.
>
> Took her in a buggy.
> Courtin' in the kitchen.
>
> Then got married;
> Dancin' at the weddin'.
>
> We had a little baby,
> Named him Jimmy.

Charles R. Bagley, in *Frank C. Brown Collection*, p. 240.

> Hidi, quili, lodi, quili,
> Hidi, quili, quackeo,
> If you'd uh been as I'd uh been
> You would uh been so pretty O!
>
> Quinckium quanckum made a song
> And he sang it all along,
> Heels in the path and toes in the grass,
> Don't take nothing but dollar and half.
>
> The ole fish hawk said to the crow,
> 'I hope to the Lord tonight it'll rain;
> The creeks am muddy and millpond dry;
> 'Twasn't for tadpoles minnows all die.'

Caroline Biggers, in *Frank C. Brown Collection*, p. 240.

> *Jola was a coon dog.*
> *Here, Jola, here.*
>
> *Jola was a possum dog.*
> *Here, Jola, here.*
>
> *Jola was a rabbit dog.*
> *Here, Jola, here.*
>
> *Jola was a bird dog.*
> *Here, Jola, here.*

Unnamed singer, in *Frank C. Brown Collection*, p. 240.

> *'Twas only tother Sunday night,*
> *As I lay half awake,*
> *Old Satan came to my bedside*
> *And he began to shake.*
> *And he shook me hard, he shook me long,*
> *He shook me out of bed,*
> *He caught me by my neckie,*
> *And this is what he said:*

Mrs. C. C. Thomas, in *Frank C. Brown Collection*, pp. 234–35.

> *Come to shuck dat corn tonight,*
> *Come to shuck with all you might;*
> *Come for to shuck all in sight,*
> *Come to shuck dat corn tonight.*
>
> *Come to shuck dat gold grain;*
> *Whar dar's 'nuff dar ai' no pain.*
> *Ef you shuck 'tis all yo gain;*
> *Come to shuck dat golden grain.*

C. L. Walker, in *Frank C. Brown Collection*, p. 236.

> *You gwine, ain't you gwine,*
> *Ain't you gwine to the shuckin' of the corn?*
> *Oh yes I gwine to stay to morning*
> *When Gable blows his horn,*
> *Am gwine to stay till the coming of the dawn.*

Elizabeth Janet Black, in *Frank C. Brown Collection*, p. 233.

> *Won't you git up, ole horse?*
> *I'm on de road to Bright.*
> *Won't you git up, ole horse?*
> *I'm on de road to Bright.*
>
> *Sheep shell corn by the rattle of his horn,*
> > *Blow horn, blow*
> *Send to the mill by the whippoorwill,*
> > *Blow horn, blow*

CHORUS
> > *O! blow your horn, blow horn, blow!*
> > *O! blow your horn, blow horn, blow!*
>
> *Cows in the old field, don't you hear the bell?*
> > *Blow horn, blow*
> *Gals up stairs kicking up hell;*
> > *Blow horn, blow.*
> *Shuck this corn, boys, let's go home.*
> > *Blow horn, blow*
> *Shuck this corn, boys, let's go home.*
> > *Blow horn, blow*

REFRAIN (Grand Chorus, to be sung at the end)
> *Hunt for the nubbins, bang a rang!*
> *Hunt for the nubbins, bang a rang!*
> *Sheep shell corn by the rattle of the horn,*
> *I never saw the like since I been born.*

G. S. Black, in *Frank C. Brown Collection*, p. 232.

> *The mules in the old field kickin' Jimmie Riley*
> > *Jimmy-my-Riley ho*
> *The mules in the old field kickin' Jimmie Riley*
> > *Jimmy-my-Riley ho*

Minnie Bryan Farrior, in *Frank C. Brown Collection*, p. 231.

> *Old Bob Ridley, come blow your horn,*
> *Sheep in the pasture, cow in the barn,*

Old Bob Ridley, come blow your horn,
Sheep in the pasture, hogs in the corn.

CHORUS
Boys, come along and shuck that corn,
Boys, come along to the rattle of the horn;
We shuck and sing till the coming of the morn,
Then we'll have a holiday.

Old Bob Ridley, o-oh! o-oh!
How could you fool the possum so?
I picked up a rock all on the sly
And hit him zip right in the eye.

I took him down to Polly Bell,
Because I knowed she cook him well,
She made a frye [sic—R.D.A.], she made a
stew,
A roast, a brile, and a barbecue.

Unnamed singer, in *Frank C. Brown Collection*, p. 239.

Oh, de fus new ye know de day'll be a-breakin',
        Heyho! Hi O! Up 'n down de banjo
And de fie be a-burnin' and de ash cake a bakin',
        Heyho! (etc., as above)
An' de hen'll be a-hollerin' an' de boss'll be a-wakin'
        Heyho! (etc., as above)
Better git up, nigger, an give y'self a shakin'.
Hi o? Miss Cindy Ann!
Fo de los' ell an' yard is a-huntin fer de mornin'
Hi O! git alon, go 'way
En' she'll ketch up wid us fo' we ever it dis corn in;
O go 'way, Cindy Ann.

E. C. Perrow, *Journal of American Folklore*, 28 (1913), 139 (from
E. North Carolina, Mr. Scroggs).

Shuck corn, shell corn,
Carry Corn to mill.
Grind de meal, gimme de husk;
Bake de bread, gimme de crus';
Fry de meat, gimme de skin;
And dat's de way to bring 'em in.

APPENDIX II

Accounts from Interviews with Ex-Slaves

The following are works which reprint or draw from the WPA ex-slave narrative project. Most of the material was elicited in response to a query on the questionnaire, given to all fieldworkers, asking for information concerning slave holidays, mentioning the corn shucking as one possible line of response to elicit. Reference is made to one or more of the following in the headnote to the discussion. In many cases, the ex-slaves simply responded that they did not have corn shuckings, and that the corn was shucked on rainy days during the winter.

After the name of each person interviewed, a volume and page number is given referring to George Rawick, ed. *The American Slave: A Composite Autobiography,* Westport, Conn.: Greenwood Press, 1972, 20 vols., suppl. ser. 1, 1977; suppl. ser. 2, 1979. Only the Virginia materials were not included in that work; Virginia references come from Perdue, Barden, and Phillips, referenced below.

In addition to the Rawick volumes, the works which draw heavily on the ex-slave accounts are:

B. A. Botkin, ed., *Lay My Burden Down: A Folk History of Slavery.* Chicago: Univ. of Chicago Press, 1945.

Lynne Fauley Emery, *Black Dance in the United States from 1690 to 1970.* New York: National Press Books, 1972, pp. 113–14.

Katrina Hazzard-Gordon, *Jookin': The Rise of Social Dance Formations in African-American Culture*. Philadelphia: Temple Univ., 1990, pp. 42–46.

James Mellon, ed., *Bullwhip Days: The Slaves Remember*. New York: Weidenfeld and Nicolson, 1988, p. 207.

Charles L. Perdue, Jr., Thomas E. Barden, and Robert K. Phillips, eds., *Weevils in the Wheat: Interviews with Virginia Ex-Slaves*. Charlottesville: Univ. of Virginia, 1975, pp. 278–79.

Ronnie C. Tyler and Lawrence R. Murphy, *The Slave Narratives of Texas*. Austin: Encino, 1974.

David Kenneth Wiggins, "Sport and Popular Pastimes in the Plantation Community: The Slave Experience," Diss., Univ. of Maryland, 1979, pp. 203–14.

Norman R. Yetman, *Life under the Peculiar Institution*. New York: R. E. Krieger, 1970, pp. 62, 190, 223, 258, 267–68.

Referenced Interviews

Jim Allen, vol. 7, p. 6 (Miss.); Wiggins, p. 206.

Anon., in Fisk Collection, Unwritten History, pp. 106–7 (Tenn.); Wiggins, p. 208; Hazzard-Gordon, p. 43.

In cornshucking time no padderollers would ever bother you. We would have a big time at corn shuckings. They would call up the crowd and line the men up and give them a drink. I was a corn general and would stand out high above everybody, giving out the corn songs and throwing down corn to them; there would be two sides of them each trying to out-shuck the other.

Anon., in Fisk Collection, Unwritten History, pp. 255 (Tenn.); Wiggins, p. 213.

I've been to many a corn shucking at night five miles from here. There would be a crowd from Big Harper, a crowd from Little Harper, and just about every place else; we all had the best times together singing and dancing.

Anon., quoted in Emery, p. 113.

Atter the sung went down dey wuked right on de light ob pine torches and bonfires. Dem old pine knots would burn for a long time and throw a fine bright light. Honey, it was one grand sight out dar at night wid dat old harvest moon a-shinin, fires a-burnin, and dem old torches lit up. I kin jus' see it all now and hear dem songs us sung.

Anon., quoted in Emery, p. 113.

Atter supper dey started up playin' dem fiddles and banjoes, and de dancin' begun. White folkses dance de twistification up at de big house but us had a re'lar old breakdowns in ahouse what Marster let us have to dance in. Wid all dat toddy helpin' em 'long, sometimes dey danced all night. . . .

Darcus Barnett, vol. 2, suppl. 2, p. 190 (Tex.) (mentions corn shucking).
John Bates, vol. 2, suppl. 2, p. 216 (Tex.) (mentioned).
Jasper Battle, vol. 12, pt. 1., p. 71 (Ga.).

Dat cornshuckin' wuk was easy wid evvybody singin' and havin' a good time together whilst dey made dem shucks fly. De corn-shuckin' captain led all de singin' and he set right up on top of de highes' pile of corn. De chillun was kept busy a-passin' de liquor jug 'round. Atter it started gittin' dark, Marster had big bonfires built up and plenty of torches set 'round so as dere would be plenty of light. Atter dey et all dey wanted of dem good things what had done been cooked up for de big supper, den de wrastlin' matches was all in good humor and was kept orderly. Marster wanted evvybody to be friends on our plantation and to stay dat way. . . .

Sarah Benjamin, vol. 2, suppl. 2, pt. 1, p. 257 (Tex.).
James Bolton, vol. 12, pt. 1, p. 99–100 (Ga.); Wiggins, p. 206; Emery, p. 112.

Bout the most fun we had was at corn shuckings when they put the corn in long piles and called in the folks from nearby plantations to shuck it. Sometimes four or five hundred head of niggers would be shuckin' corn at one time. When the corn all done been shucked they'd drink the liquor that master give 'em and then frolic and dance from sundown to sunup. We started shuckin' corn 'bout dinnertime and tried to finish by sundown so we could have the whole night for frolic. Some years we 'ud go to ten or twelve corn shuckins's in one year.

Harrison Boyd, vol. 4, pts. 1–2, p. 112 (Tex.).

Marse Trammel gave a big cornshucking every fall. He had two bottom fields in corn. First we'd gather peas and cushaws and pumpkins out de corn field, then get the corn and pile it front the cribs. They was two big cribs for the corn we ke' to use and five big cribs for sale corn. My uncle stayed round the sale corn cribs all spring. . . .

James Boyd, vol. 4, pt. 1, p. 118; Wiggins, p. 209 (Tex. via Ga.); repr. with minor orthographic changes in suppl. 1, vol. 2, p. 366.

Sometime us have de corn huskin' and dere a doller to de one what shuck de mos' corn in a certain time. Us'd have a big dance 'bout twice a year, on Christmus an sometime durin' de summer. W'en de white folks had dere big balls we niggers would cook an' wait on de white folks an watch 'em dance, but we had lots of fun on de side. An' sometimes de visitin' white genmans would give us clothes or money. But us didn't dare to keep the money. Now, if it was prize money at a huskin' or pickin' cotton us could keep dat money to buy medicine or something we had to have.

George Washington Browning, vol. 3, pts. 3–4, pp. 115–16 (Ga.); repr. with minor orthographic changes in suppl. 1, vol. 3, p. 115.

There were many frolics in those days and other slaves would often attend, after getting permission from their masters. Dancing and singing were the main features. Before a frolic would begin the men would go to the swamps and get long quills which would furnish music by blowing through them. This music reminded one of the music from a flute. "One song we sang went like this," Mr. Browning remarked, "Shake your leg every body, Hallelujah, Hallelujah." . . . When a frolic or corn shucking was planned down on the Browning plantation they would give them permission to attend, warning them to behave themselves. Usually there would be plenty to eat and drink. To see that everyone behaved properly the master would make several trips back and forth until the frolic ended.

Jeff Calhoun, vol. 4, pt. 1, p. 190, (Tex.); repr. with orthographic alterations in suppl. 2, vol. 3, pt. 2, p. 607.

De got de big dinners on holidays. After supper was have corn shuckings, or on rainy days, and sometimes we shucks 500 bushels.

Cato Carter, vol. 4, pt. 1, p. 206 (Tex.); Botkin, p. 86.

Corn shuckin' was fun. Them days no corn was put in the cribs with shucks on it. They shucked it in the fiel' and shocked the fodder. They did it by sides and all hands out. A beef was kilt and they'd have a reg'lar picnic feastin'. They was plenty whiskey for the niggers, jus' like Christmas.

Aunt Cicely Cawthon, suppl. 1, vol. 3 (Ga.), pp. 189–91.

"We had good times at corn shuckings, too. Honey, I've seen my grandma, Icie, the cook, when they had corn-shuckings, the chickens she'd put in that pot! The big pot, hanging on one of them hooks in the kitchen fireplace; I ain't never seen a pot that big since. I don't seen 'em in stores now. They don't have'em. She put twelve chickens in that pot, grown hens, let 'em boil, put the dumplings in, called the darkies, and give 'em a plate full. Lawdy Honey, I just wish you could a been there and seen how my grandma made that gingerbread, what you called raised gingerbread. They cooked that for corn shuckings, and used it for cake. It was better than what cake is now, and they give 'em locust beer to drink with it, not this stuff they sell in bottles now, they call beer.

"We had dances," she continued, "after the corn shuckings. After they got through, the fiddler would start to fiddling and they would ring up in an old-time square dance. Everybody danced off to themselves. Just let your foot go backward (she illustrated) and then let your foot go forward (she slipped her foot forward) and whirl around. Men, too, danced that way, by themselves, and you could hear them darkies laugh! Won't nothin' in 'em, no whiskey, My! They had a good time! . . . We'd have good things to eat, . . . at corn shuckings, Marster would give everyone of the men a dram. Marster drawed it himself, had a big tin cup, and he'd tak a cupful for two men. But didn't nobody get drunk nor bother nobody."

Henry Cheatem, suppl. 1, vol. 1, p. 92 (Ala.).
Harriet Chesley, suppl. 2, vol. 3, pt. 2, p. 693.

The only fun we ever had wuz when we would have co'n shuckins and guitar playins'.

Henry Clay, suppl. 1, vol. 12 (Okla., from N.C.).

The big thing on that plantation was the corn-shucking. One every two weeks almost, and negroes from other plantations would come over to shuck for their masters and then we would go to another shucking the same way.

Louisa Collier, vol. 2, pt. 1, p. 222 (S.C.); Wiggins, p. 210.

Yes 'um, I members when dey had plenty uv dem cornshucking to one annuther barns, . . . Dem cornshuckings wus big times, dat dey us; de peoples us'd to have big dancing dere when de shucking ovar.

Kizzie Colquitt, suppl. 1, vol. 3, pp. 216–17 (Ga.).

Dar was de corn shukin' [sic—R.D.A.] wid one house for de corn an' anudder house for de shucks. Arter all de shuckin' was done, deir was eatin' and dancin'. An it was eatin' too! Dey kilt hogs, barbecued 'em, an' roasted some wid apples in dey mouf's to give'em a good flavor, an' course, a little corn likker went wid it.

Martha Colquitt, vol. 4, pt. 1, p. 244 (Ga.); Yetman, p. 62.

Dem cornshuckin's us used have show wus a sight. Corn would be piled up high as dis house, and de folkses would dance 'round and holler and whoop. He 'lowed us chillun to watch 'em 'bout a half hours; den made us come back inside our cabin, 'cause dey always give de corn shuckin' folkses some dram, and things would git mighty lively and rough by de time all de corn was shucked.

Sara Colquitt, vol. 6, p. 89 (Ala.); Wiggins, p. 204.

Next to our dances, de most fun was corn shuckings. Marse would have de corn hauled up to de cribs and pile as a house, den he would invite de hands 'round to come and help shuck it. Us had two leaders or generals and choose up two sides. Den us see which side would win first and holler and sing. I disremembers de hollers jest now. My mind is sorter missing. Marsa would pass de jug, too. Den dey sho' could work and dat pile'd just vanish.

Rachel Cruze, suppl. 1, vol. 5, pt. 2, p. 323; Mellon, p. 207 (Tenn.).

There are heaps of pleasant things to look back on. The week before Christmas was always a lively one, what with dances and corn-huskin's in the neighborhood. I've seen many a corn-huskin' at Old Major's farm when the corn would be piled as high as the house. Two sets of men would start huskin' from opposite sides of the heap. It would keep one man busy just getting the husks out of the way, and the corn would be thrown over the huskers' heads and would fill the air like birds. The women usually had a quilting at those times, so they were pert and happy.

About midnight, the huskin' would be over and plenty of food would make its appearance—roast sheep and roast hogs and many other things—and after they had their fill, they would dance till morning. Things would continue lively in the neighborhood till New Year's Day, and then they got down to work, as it was that time of the yearly cleaning and repairing of the farm took place.

Green Cumby, vol. 4, pt. 1, p. 260 (Tex.); also in Tyler and Murphy, with orthographic changes, p. 78.

De best times was when de corn shuckin's was at hand. Den you didn't have to bother with no pass to leave de plantation, and de patter rolls didn't bother you. If de patter rolls cotch you without de pass any other time, you better wish you dead, 'cause you have yourself some trouble.

But de corn shuckin', dat was de gran' times. All de marsters and dere black boys from plantations from miles 'round would be dar. Den when we got de corn pile high as dis house, de table was spread under de shade. All de boys dat 'long to old marster would take him on de packsaddle 'round and 'round de house, allus singin' and dancin', den dey puts him at de other side de table, and dey all do same till everyboday at de table, den dey have de feast.

Katie Darling, suppl. 2, vol. 4, pt. 3, p. 1049 (Tex.) (mentions nightly corn shuckings).
Louis Davis, vol. 7, suppl. 1, p. 582 (Ala.); repr. in suppl. 1, vol. 7, p. 582.

We had corn shucking, but it wasn't in the form of a party. We done the shucking in the day time. Everybody was sent to the crib together. They would sing and have good times, but they didn't have no prizes. The song they liked best was

> *Once I was so lucky*
> *Old Master set me free*
> *Sent me to Kentucky*
> *To see, what I could see*
> *Mean old banjo Thomas*

> *Mean old banjo Joe*
> *Going away to Kentucky*
> *Won't come back no more.*

Benny Dilliard, vol. 12, pp. 293–94 (Ga.); Wiggins, p. 210.

Old corn shucking was sure the big times. When all the corn was done shucked and the big supper had been eat there was dancing.

Squire Dowd, vol. 14, I, pp. 265–66 (N.C.); Wiggins, p. 210.

If we could catch the master after the shucking was over, we put him in a chair, we darkies, and toted him around and hollered, carried him into the parlor, set him down, and combed his hair.

Anderson and Minerva Edwards, vol. 4, pt. 2, p. 7 (Tex.).

Massa Gaud give big corn shuckin's and cotton pickin's and the women cook up big dinners and massa give us some whiskey, and lots of times we shucked all night.

Robert Franklin, suppl. 2, vol. 44, pt. 3, pp. 1418–19 (Tex.).

We use to have corn-shuckins an' dances on de plantation an' have slaves foh miles 'roun' come—yes un us had good music too, dem niggers sho could draw de bows 'cross dem fiddle strings.

Rosanna Frazier, vol. 4, pt. 2, p. 64 (Tex.).

Marse Frazier, he didn't work us too hard and give Saturday and Sunday off. He's all right and give good food. . . . Sometimes he has corn shucking time and we has hawg meat and meal bread and whiskey and eggnog and chicken.

Charles Graham, vol. 9, pts. 3–4, p. 68 (Ark.).

They would have corn shuckings. They would have a lot of corn to shuck, and they would give the corn shucking and the barbecue together. They would shuck as many as three or four hundred bushels of corn in a night. Sometimes they would race one another. So you know that they must have been some shucking done.

Martin Graham, suppl. 1, vol. 1 (Ala.).

Yes'm dey sho did have some hot times at the cornshuckings, when corn got ready to shuck, Moster would have hit all hauled up near de crib and would invite other slaves over, pass de licker jug round several times and get em all happy and my, couldn't dey get dat corn shucked. Dey always had a leader or general that lead all the hollers but I dis-remembers any er dem. Sometimes would be er thousand bushels er corn; it had to be put in de crib den.

Austin Grant, suppl. 2, vol. 5, pt. 4, p. 1535 (Tex.).

They had co'n shuckin's in them days and co'n shellin's too. We would shuck so many days and so many days to shell it up.

Charlie Grant, suppl. 1, vol. 11, p. 172 (S.C.) (mentioned).
Virginia Harris, suppl. 1, vol. 3., p. 943 (Miss.).

. . . When corn shucking time came we had another big party. A prize was gived to whosoever shucked the most corn. Sometimes the prize would be a quart of whiskey, sometime two or three dollars. When shucking was over, we had cake and candy to eat.

Tom Hawkins, vol. 12, pt. 2, p. 132 (Ga.); Wiggins, p. 206.

When the men got to shucking that corn, the women started cooking and they got through about the same time.

Ida Henry, vol. 7, pt. 1, p. 134 (Okla.); Wiggins, p. 208.

During de fall months dey would have corn shucking and would give a prize to de one would shuck de largest pile of corn. De prize would usually be a suit of clothes or something to wear and which would be given at some later time.
   We could only have dances during holidays, but dances was held on other plantations.

Joseph Holmes, vol. 6, p. 193 (Ala.); repr. with minor orthographic differences in suppl. 2, vol. 1, p. 11.

Den come cornshucking time, mah goodness, I jes' wud love tuh be dere now. De corn wud be piled up high an' one man wud git on dat pile, hit usually wur kinda ob a nigger foreman who cud sing an' get de wurk out ob de odder niggers. Dis foreman wid verse sumthin' lac' dis.

> *Polk an' Clay went to War.*
> *And Polk cum back wid a broken jar.*

Den all de niggers wud sing back tuh him, an' hello' a kinda ob shoutin' soun'. Usually dis foreman made up his songs, by pickin' dem up historically. But, Miss, you know what wuz de motor power ob dat shucking? Hit was de ol' jug dat wuz brun 'roun' ebery hour, dats de only time any ob de slaves really got drunk.

Lina Hunter, vol. 4, pt. 2, pp. 266–67 (Ga.); Emery, p. 112–13.

I 'members dem old frolics us had, when harvest time was over, and all dat corn was piled up ready for de big cornshuckin'. Honey, us sho had big old times. Us would cook for three or four days gittin' ready for de feast dat was to follow de cornshuckin'. De best thing dey done was 'lect a general to lead off de singin' and keep it goin' so de faster dey sung, de faster dey shucked de corn. Evvy now and den dey passed de corn liquor 'round, an dat holped 'em to wuck faster, and evvy Nigger dat found a red ear got a extra swig of liquor. Atter de sun went down dey wuked right on by de light of pine torches and bonfires. Dem old pine knots would burn for a long time and throw a fine bright light. Honey, it was one grand sight out dar at night wid dat old harvest moon a-shinin', fires a-burnin', and dem old torches lit up. I kin jus' see it all now, and hear dem songs us sung. Dem was such happy times. Wen all de corn was shucked and dey had done et all dat big supper, dey dance for de rest of de night.

Charley Hurt, vol. 4, pt. 2, p. 175, (Tex.); repr. with minor orthographic changes in suppl. 2, vol. 5, p. 1843.

Us never have much joyments in slave time. Only when de corn ready for huskin' all de nighbors comes dere and a whole big crowd am a-huskin' and singin'. I can 'member dem songs, 'cause I'm not much for singin'. One go like this:

> *'Pull de husk, break de ear*
> *Whoa, I's got de red ear here.*

When you find de red ear, dat 'titles you to de prize, like kissin' de gal or de drink of brandy or somethin'. Dey not 'nough red ears to suit us.

Uncle Everett Ingram, vol. 6, p. 216 (Ala.).

When de corn needed shuckin', it was hauled up near de crib, an' on a purty moonlighted night Marster would pass around de likker. It would be long 'til dey was all happy an' had what dey called a general. De general led all de hollers an' songs. Dey shorely did get dat corn shucked fast, too.

Squire Irvin, suppl. 1, vol. 8, pt. 3, pp. 1085–86 (Miss.).

The corn shuckings were held at night. Everybody loved to attend them. Just so the corn got shucked, the white folks didn't care how much fun we had. Some of them niggers sure could sing and the ones of us what couldn't joined in the chorus just the same. I wish I could remember that old song we sang. It started out, "Shuck, shuck, round up your corn." The rest of the words is sure left me now.

Alexander B. Johnson, vol. 6, p. 49 (Ala.).
Prince Johnson, suppl. 1, vol. 3, p. 1173 (Miss.); Yetman, p. 190.

De most fun was de corn shuckin'. Dey was two captains and each one picked de ones he wanted on his side. Den de shuckin' begins. The last one I 'tended, the side I was on beat by three barrels. We put our captain on our shoulders and rode him up and down while everybody cheered and clapped their hands like the world was coming to an end. You can't make mention of nothing good that we didn't have to eat after the "shucking."

Estella Jones, vol. 12, pt. 2, p. 347 (Ga.); Wiggins, p. 203–4.

Dey wuz always glad when de time come for 'em to shell corn. Dey enjoyed dat better dan dey did Christmas, or at least jist as much. Dey always had to work durin' de day time and shell corn at night. De overseer wuz real good to 'em. Most times slaves from other plantations would come over and help 'em. Dey used to put on dey good clothes 'cause dey want to dey best.

Henry Gray Klugh, suppl. 1, vol. 11, p. 233 (S.C.).

They had neighborhood parties fur corn-shuckings, cotton pickings, quiltings and other things. The host and hostess always have good suppers at these parties, with whiskey. They would sometimes have square dancing or cake walks, with fiddlers.

Anna Lee, suppl. 2, vol. 6, pt. 5, p. 2282 (Tex.).

. . . Yes we had corn-shucking days in the winter time when it would get so bad that we could not have dances to get together, then too our maser he sold lots of shelled corn. We shelled and shucked all day long so'es us negroes could have some way to get together and have some fun.

Lu Lee, suppl. 2, vol. 6, pt. 5, p. 1297 (Tex.).

. . . we had cornshucking parties. At the dances they used to have men with fiddles and they hollered out, "Get your partners for the ring dance." Then they had nuther dance where they have dancing up the sides from head to foot and prancing back.

Jack Maddox, suppl. 2, vol. 7, pt. 6, pp. 2531–33 and repeated on pp. 2546–47 (Ga., Miss., La., Tex.).

Judge Maddox bought a nigger man who had a three string fiddle. I used to hear him play and sing. We had to work at night too. . . . His corn shucking song was:

> *Sheep shear corn*
> *By the rattle of his horn*
> *Never seen the like*
> *Since I been born.*

Andy Marion, vol. 3, pt. 3, p. 169 (S.C.); Yetman, p. 223.

A pass was lak dis, on it was you' name, what house you goin' to and de hour expected back. If you was cotched any other house, pateroller whip you sho'. Always give us Chris'mus Day. Dere was a number of dances dis time of de year. Got passes to different plantations. Dere would be corn shuckin' different places.

Jake McLeod, vol. 3, pt. 3, p. 160 (S.C.); vol. 3, pt. 3, p. 160 (S.C.); Emery, p. 112.

When corn haulin time come, every plantation haul corn en put it in circles in front of de barn. Have two piles en point two captains. Dey take sides en give corn shuckin like dat. Shuck corn en throw in front of door en sometimes shuck corn all night. After dey get through wid all de shuckin, give big supper en march all round old Massa's kitchen en house. Have tin pans, buckets en canes for music en dance in front of de house in de road. Go to another place en help dem shuck corn de next time en on dat way.

Frank Menefee, vol. 6, p. 280 (Ala.).

Oh, dem cornshuckings! Shuck corn, drink an' holler all night long. Sometimes dey's sing:

> Dark cloud arising like gwine to rain,
> Nothing but a black gal coming down the lane,
> Nigger stole a pumkin an' started outer town;
> Nigger heered it thunder, Lord, an' throwed dat pumkin down.

A. M. Moore, vol. 5, pt. 3, p. 119 (Tex.).

Corn shucking was a big sport for Negroes and whites, too, in slavery time. Sometimes they gave a big dance when they finished shucking, but my master's folks always had religious service.

Vina Moore, suppl. 2, vol. 7, pt. 6, p. 2759 (Miss. and Tex.).

Corn shuckin was a big time too, de marster would make us shuck corn all day and den we would all eat suppah out in de yard. We younguns would all play and dance and have a big time. You don't hear of any body here doing dat way now, but we enjoyed it in dem days. Dat playin allus made de corn shuckin easy.

John Mosley, suppl. 2, vol. 7, pt. 6, p. 2803 (Tex.).

Yeah we had corn shucking and cotton seed picking. Maser would give corn shucking to us negroes so he would have his corn shucked, and he would not have to be bothered with the shucks, except to feed the cows. But the best we had was cotton seed picking, . . .

Calvin Moye, suppl. 2, vol. 7, pt. 6, p. 2843 (Tex.) (shuckings on winter rainy days).
Sally Murphey, suppl. 1, vol. 1, p. 268 (Ala.).

My but they show had good times on moonlight nights at de cornshuckings, dey would haul corn frum de field and put in a big ring and as they shucked, would throw hit inside er ring, den into de crib, corn would stay on de ground till hit rotted.

Mr. Norris, suppl. 1, vol. 2, p. 120 (Miss.) (mentions "New Year's to Christmas" weeks off).
Jeff Nunn, suppl. 1, vol. 1, p. 284 (Ala.).

When dey had cornshuckings, dey show would have good times, dey would shout and sing and drink licker and holler, "Whoo-dee, Hey whoo dee, hey, Whoo-dee."

Amanda Oliver, vol. 7, p. 230 (Okla. from Tex.).

Sometime de men would shuck corn all night long. Whenever dey was going to shuck all night de women would piece quilts while de men shuck de corn and you could hear 'em singing and shucking corn. After de cornshucking, de cullud folks would have big dances.

Mark Oliver, suppl. 1, vol. 9, p. 1666 (Miss.).

I never liked to shuck corn, so I never got no enjoyment out of corn shuckings. Heap of them liked it, and they would try hard for the prize that was offered for the one that could shuck the most.

Will Parker, suppl. 2, vol. 8, pt. 7, p. 3021 (Tex.).

Christmas time we'd have a big dinner; a holiday the fourth of July; we'd have corn shuckin' and cane shuckin', tobacco twistin'.

Reverend Lafayette Price, suppl. 2, vol. 8, pt. 7, pp. 3173–74 (Tex.).

Dem Times befo' de war dey uster hab co'n shuckin's. Dey hab a big pile of co'n in de shuck. De cap'n of de co'n shuckin' he a-settin' up on de pile of co'n. He'd git a lock givin' out and throwin' de shuck sometime' 'cause dey'd be years of co'n and de shucks jis' a-flyin'. Dey hab lotser cullud folks come from ev'ryw'er. Marster he uster be 'round' 'til all de co'n mos' shuck den he dodge 'way and hide, 'cause iffen dey ketch 'im dey "cattle" 'im. W'at I mean by "cattle" 'im? Why dey etch 'im and pit 'im up on dey shoul'ers, and dey march 'roun' wid 'im and dey sings. De cap'n he settin' on de co'n and givin' ouit de song. Dey uster sing:

> *Shuck man can't let git away,*
> *Oh, hood a laddy oh hooey.*
> *Mule want co'n and cow want shuck,*
> *Oh, hood a laddy oh hooey.*

Jenny Proctor, vol. 5, pt. 3, p. 214 (Tex.); Botkin, p. 92.

We had some corn-shuckings sometimes, but the white folks gits the fun and the nigger gits the work.

A. C. Pruitt, vol. 5, pt. 3, p. 220, (Tex.); repr. with major changes in suppl. 2, vol. 8. pt. 7, pp. 3203–4 (Tex.).

De field hands stay up in de big barn and shuck corn on rainy days, when dey couldn' wuk in de fiel'. Dey sit 'roun' and shuck de corn and sing. Dey mek up dem songs to sing, some dem spirituals and some wasn'. But I's too young to place de words.

Us chillen was put in a row in de yard and sweep de yard. Dat was us job to keep de yard clean. My gramma she was de boss over us to see dat us do right. She help us tie weeds together to make brooms to do dat sweepin'.

Junius Quattlebaum, vol. 3, pts. 3–4, pp. 283–84 (S.C.).

. . . Marster lak to see his slaves happy and singin' 'bout de place. If he ever heard any of them quarrelin' wid each other, he would holler at them and say: 'Sing! Us ain't got no time to fuss on dis plantation.'

Marster lak he dram, 'specially in de fall of de year when it fust git cool. Us used to have big corn shuckin's on de plantation at night, 'long 'bout de fust of November of every year. All de corn was hauled from de fields and put in two or three big piles in de barnyard and de slaves would git 'round them, sing and shuck de corn. De slave women would hang buckets of raw tar afire on staves drove in de ground 'round de crowd, to give light. Then was sho' happy times.

Marster would give all de grown slaves a dram of pure apple brandy, on them corn shuckin' nights, and take several smiles (drinks) hisself. I 'members so well, one of them nights, dat marster come to de barnyard, where us was all lit up, a singin' fit to kill hisself. Us was s'prised to see marster settin' down wid niggers and shuckin' corn as fas' as us was. After a spell, him stood up and too 'nother smile, then say: "Pause and let's all take a drink." Wid dat, one of de niggers grab de jug of liquor and passed it 'round to all de shuckers. The marster say: "Everybody sing." Some of de niggers 'quire: "What you gwine to sing?" He say "Sing dis song: Pass 'round de bottle and we'll all take a drink." Some of them in de crowd 'jected to dat song, 'cause they had 'nough liquor in them to 'ject to anything. Marster kinds scratch he head and say: "Well, let me git a pole and you all is gwine to sing." And singin' dere was, as sho' as you's born. Them niggers 'round de corn piles dat night h'isted dat song right now; dere was no waitin' for de pole or nothin' else. They wanted to sing, bad.

De next mornin', after dis night I's talkin' 'bout, Miss Martha, our good missus come 'round to de slave houses and 'quire how they all felt. She say: "You all can rest today and do what you want to

do, 'cause Marster Jim ain't feelin' so well dis mornin'." She knowed
what was gwine on at de corn shuckin' de night befo' but she ain't
said nothin' 'bout it.

Fanny Randolph, vol. 12, pt. 1, pp. 293–94 (Ga.); Wiggins,
p. 212.

Us niggers on Master Bog's plantation had big times at our corn
shuckings. When all the corn was shucked every nigger would get
his gal and there would be some niggers over in the corner to play
for the dance and us would get on the floor to cut some steps.

Henry J. Richardson, suppl. 2, vol. 8, pt. 7, p. 3307 (Tex.).

Christmas and other holidays were just another day to us except we
were treated to a real feast on those days. We often had log rollings,
corn huskins, and cotton pickings, but I couldn't give a good description of them as they only meant busy days for my mother, father,
Master and Mistress. Too, I shall never forget that on those days we
really did feast.

Ferebe Rogers, vol. 4, pt. 3, p. 216 (Ga.); Yetman, p. 258.

Chris'mas warn't no diffunt from other times. We used to have
quiltin' parties, candy pullin's dances, corn shuckin's, games like
thimble and sich like.

George Rogers, vol. 11, pt. 2, p. 221 (N.C.); Yetman, p. 259.

Master had three plantations an' about one hundred slaves. . . . We
had dances or anything else we wanted to at night. We had corn
shuckings, candy pullings, an' all the whiskey an' brandy we wanted.

Joe Rollins, suppl. 1, vol. 9, pt. 4, p. 1898 (Miss.).

Who-OO! Cornshuckins! Yes, dey would go from one plantation to
anoder and shuck corn—plenty to eat and whisky to drink. Lawd,
ump!

Gill Ruffin, vol. 5, pt. 3, p. 263 (Tex.) ("on rainy days. . .").
Martin Ruffins, vol. 5, pt. 3, p. 266 (Tex.).

Corn shucking was a big occasion them days and massa give all the
hands a quart whiskey apiece. They'd drink whiskey, get happy and
make more noise than a little, but better not get drunk. We'd dance
all night when the corn shuckin' was over.

Robert Shepherd (Shepard?), vol. 13, pt. 3, pp. 195–96 (Ga.); Yetman, pp. 267–68; Wiggins, p. 212.

Dem corn shuckin's was sure 'nough big times. When us all got de corn gathered up and put in great long piles den de gettin' ready started. Why, dem womans cooked for days, and de mens would get de shoats ready to barbeque. Marster would send us out to get de slaves from de farms round about dere. De place was all lit up with light-wood knot torches and bonfires, and dere was 'citement a-plenty when all niggers get to singing and shouting 'as dey made de shucks fly.

One of dem songs went somethin' like dis: "Oh! my head, my poor head, Oh! my poor head is affected." Dere wen't nothin' wrong with our heads—dat was just our way of lettin' our overseer know us wanted some liquor. Purty soon he would come 'round with a big horn of whiskey, and dat made de poor head well, but it weren't long before it got worse again, and den us got another horn of whiskey.

Den us danced de rest of de night.

Polly Shine, suppl. 2, vol. 4, pt. 8, pp. 3521–22 (La. and Tex.).

Well Maser would let us negroes have corn-shucking there once and awhile as a get together for the slaves. He would invite all slaves for miles around as we shucked the corn, shelled and sacked it, that is the way Maser sold his corn. He would get plenty of corn shelled as we put what we shelled in a different sack, and the one that shucked and shelled the most corn he would give him some kind of present, and that would make the negro work that much harder to win that present as well as talk and have a good time laughing and taking on.

Smith Simmons, suppl. 1, vol. 10, p. 1940 (Miss.).

We never did have no sort of celebration at our place. Christmas and New Years was spent like Sundays. On a place about a mile away from us they held big corn shuckings. We would hear about the enjoyment of it, but none of us didn't never get to go.

Millie Ann Smith, suppl. 2, vol. 9, pt. 8, pp. 3654–55 (Tex.).

I's seen a hundred and fifty hands on one pile of corn at corn-shuckings. They pile it up in wind rows and call in the hands from all round. The wimmen cooked up a chicken stews, tater (potato) custard, pies, cakes and all kinds of meats and vegetables. Master come round now and then and give the men a drink. The chil'ren whooped and hollered while the men and wimmen shucked co'n.

Paul Smith, vol. 6, pp. 360–61 (Ala.); repr. with minor orthographic changes in suppl. 1, vol., 1, p. 398; vol. 13, pt. 3, p. 334; Wiggins, p. 209.

... when de wuk was done and dey was ready to go to de tables out in de yard to eat dem big barbecue suppers, dey grabbed up dey marster and tuk him to de big house on deir shoulders. . . .

Uncle John Spencer, in Perdue, Barden, and Phillips, pp. 278–79.

They always selected a bright moonlight [night] for the shucking. A week or more from the time, the news began to spread around when it was going to be; and as soon as it was dark, then neighbors began to drop in.

The one with the most powerful voice was selected to stand on top of the corn pile and lead the singing. They would all get in a working mood to the tune of the shucking song.

Tanner Spikes, vol. 15, pt. 2, p. 310 (N.C.); Emery, p. 112.

Bout the most fun we had was at corn shuckin's whar they put the corn in long piles and called the folkses from the plantations nigh round to shuck it. Sometimes four or five hunnert head of niggers 'ud be shuckin' corn at one time. Dey kisses when dey fin' a red year. We started shuckin' corn 'bout dinnertime and tried to finish by sundown so we could have the whole night for frolic. Some years we 'ud go to ten or twelve corn shuckins in one year.

George Strickland, supp. ser. 1, p. 398 (Ala.)

Cornshucking was de greatest thing er tall, master took a jug er licker 'roun' and got dem tight and when dey got full, dey would histe master up and toat him 'roun' and holler, then the fun started and dey would play de old gourd and horse-hair dance, the hand-saw and case knife, dey could run dey hand up and down de saw to change der tune, Leader was on top er de pile and sing, den all would follow.

Cordelia Thomas, vol. 13, pt. 4, p. 19 (Ga.).

Mammy said dem cornshuckin's meant jus' as much fun and jolli-
fication as wuk. Dey gathered Marster's big corn crap and 'ranged
it in long high piles, and sometimes it tuk sev'ral days for dem
cornshuckers to git it all shucked, but evvybody stayed right dar on
de job 'til it was finished. At night, dey wukked by de light of big
fires and torches, den dey had de big supper and started dancing'.
Dey stopped so often to swig dat corn liquor Marster pervided for
'em dat 'fore midnight folkses started fallin' out and drappin' down
in de middle of de dance ring. De others would git 'em by de heels
and drag 'em off to one side 'til dey come to and was ready to drink
more liquor and dance again. Dat was de way dey went on de rest
of de night.

Penny Thompson, vol. 5, pt. 4, pp. 104–5 (Tex.); Wiggins, p. 209.

De other big time am de corn huskin' bee. Once a year all de neighbors comes fust to one place den to de other. At de huskin's dey
gives de prize you finds a red ear. De prize am two fingers of dat
peach brandy. When dey gits de fus' one dey works a little harder,
de second still faster, and de third, lawd-a-massy, how dem husks
dey fly! Don't get drunk, 'cause you am lucky to find as much as
three red ears at one huskin'.

John F. Van Hook, vol. 13, pt. 4, p. 81 (Ga.); Wiggins, p. 208.

. . . men designated to act as the generals would stick a peacock tail
feather in their hats and call all the men together and give their
orders. They would stand in the center of the corn pile, start the
singing, and kept things lively for them. . . .

Callie Washington, suppl. 1, vol. 10, pt. 5, p. 2191 (Miss.).
Mollie Watson, suppl. 1, vol. 12, p. 374 (Okla.).

We'd have log-rollins' and railsplittins, house-raisin's, corn-shuckin's
an' quiltin's. The old women would cook, the young women would
burn brush an' de men would roll logs or build de house. After
supper we'd dance all night.

Eliza White, vol. 6, p. 412 (Ala.) (see also Liza White).

Ev'ey now and den we would have some good frolics, mostly on
Sattiday mights. [sic—R.D.A.] Somebody would play de fiddle and
we all danced to de music. De folks sure had some big times at

cornshuckins, too. De men would work two or three days, haulin'
de corn and pilin' it near de crib. Den dey would invite folks from
other quarters to come and help wid de shuckin'. While dey shucked
dey would holler and sing:

> You jumped and I jumped;
> Swear by God you outjumped me.
> Huh! Huh! Round de corn, Sally.

Liza White, vol. 1, p. 444 (Ala.); repr. with minor orthographic
changes in suppl. 1, vol. 1, p. 444.

The folks sure had some big times at the cornshucking, would be
two or three days hauling corn up near the crib and invite folks from
the others quarters to come and help shuck; they would holler and
sing. Would sing, You jumped and I jumped and swear by God you
out jumped me, Huh, huh, round the corn Sally.

Mingo White, vol. 6, pt. 1, p. 419 (Ala. via S.C.); Yetman p. 314;
Wiggins, p. 206.

De owners of slaves use to giv' cornshuckin' parties, an' invite slaves
from yuther plantations. Dey would have plenty of whiskey an' other
stuff to eat. De slaves would shuck corn an' eat an' drink. Dey use'
to giv' cottin pickin's de same way. All of dis went on at night. De
had jack-lights in de cotton patch for us to see by. De lights was
made on a forked stick an' moved from place to place whilst we
picked. De corn shuckin' was done at de barn, an' dey didn' have
to have de lights so dey could move from place to place.

Green Willbanks, vol. 13, pt. 4, pp. 144–45 (Ga.); Wiggins,
p. 207.

. . . they . . . had a general to head off in all the singing; that was
done to whoop up the work. My pa was one of the generals and he
toted the jug of liquor that was passed round to make his crowd
hustle.

Wayman Williams, vol. 5, pt. 4, p. 185 (Tex.); repr. with some
orthographic changes in suppl. 2, vol. 10, pt. 9, pp. 4148–49; Wiggins,
p. 213.

When we gathered de corn we piled it in piles an' had corn shuckins
at night, de niggers would gather de corn out of one field at a time
an' den when de git our work done, we cook our supper an all eat

to gedder an listen to de tales told by de ole folks 'bout de war an why dey is fightin' an sing de songs dat we sing in de corn shuckin' time. When dey git's de piles of corn ready fur de shuckin, den dey lay a rail in de middle an divides de piles an' de side dat get through first is de side dat eat dar supper first. We had a song went like dis, 'bout de corn shuckin'.

> *Hit's a mighty dry year, when de crab grass fail,*
> > *Oh, row, row, row, who laid dat rail?*
> *Hit's am mighty dark night when de nigger turn pale,*
> > *De big foot nigger dat lad dat rail!*
> *Oh, row, row, row, who laid dat rail?*
>
> > *Rinktim Ranktum, laid dat rail.*
> *Show me de nigger dat laid dat rail.*
> > *Oh, row, row, row, who laid dat rail?*
>
> *When de niggers fuss, de white folks fail,*
> > *Oh, row, row, row, who laid dat rail?*
> *We are gittin dar now, don' tell no tale,*
> > *Show me de nigger dat laid dat rail,*
> *I'll stick he head in a big tin pail.*
> > *Oh, turn me loos', Let me tech dat rail,*
> *Oh, row, row, row, who laid dat rail?*

Wash Wilson, vol. 5, pt. 4, p. 197 (La. and Tex.); repr. with a good deal of orthographic change in suppl. 2, vol. 10, pt. 9, pp. 4241–42; Wiggins, p. 207.

Den dar wuz de co'n huskins er shuckin'. Dey wuz pile up 'bout a hundred or two or maybe three hundred bushels corn outside de shed. Us have corn shuckin' at night and have de big time. De fellow what owned de corn, he invite de niggers from all around, give a big supper and have de whiskey us want. Nobody got drunk 'cause meet everybody carry dey liquor purty well. After shuckin' us have ring plays. For music dey scratch on de skillet lids or beat bones or pick de banjo. Dere be thirty to fifty folks, all cullud, and sometimes dey stay all night, and build de big fire and dance outdoors or in de barn. [Wind de ball Suzy wuz one ob de ring plays.]

Dere wasn't no music instruments. Us take pieces a sheep's rib or cow's jaw or a piece iron, with a old kettle, or a hollow gourd and some horsehairs to make de drum. Sometimes dey'd git a piece of tree trunk and hollow it out and stretch a goat's or sheep's skin over it for de drum. [Dese 'ud be from one to four feet high an' six to er leetle more dan er foot ercross. Dar wuz in general two togedder ter play wid dar fingers er two sticks on dis drum.] Never see so many in Texas, [Dey had 'em in Louisiana an' on our place in Texas.] but dey made some. Dey'd take de buffalo horn and scrape it out to make de flute. Dat sho' be heard a long ways off. Den dey'd take a mules' jawbone and rattle de stick 'cross its teeth. Dey'd take a barrel and stretch a ox's hide 'cross one end and a man set 'stride de barrel and beat on dat hide with he hands, and he feet, and iffen he git to feelin' de music in de bones, he'd beat on dat barrel with he head. 'Nother man beat one wooden side with sticks.

Willis Winn, vol. 5, pt. 4, p. 204 (La. and Tex.); repr. in suppl. 2, vol. 10, pt. 9, p. 4254, with minor orthographic changes; Yetman, p. 332.

Corn shuckins was the things them days. I like to see'em come. They cooked up guineas and ducks and chickens and sometimes roast a pig. Massa kept twenty, thirty, barrels whiskey round over the place all the time, with tin cups hangin' on the barrels. You could drink when you wanted to, but sure better not get drunk. Massa have to watch he corners when corn shuckin' am over, or us niggers grab him and walk him around in air on their hands.

George Woods, vol. 3, pt. 4, p. 249 (S.C.); Wiggins, p. 210.

He said that when the corn-shucking time came, both whites and blacks would gather at a certain plantation. Everybody shucked corn and they all had a good time. When the last ear of corn was shucked, the owner of the plantation would begin to run from the place and all would run after him. When they caught him, he was placed on the shoulders of two men and carried around the house, all singing and laughing and having a good time. Then they would carry the planter into his house, pull off his hat and throw it into the fire; place him in the chair; comb his head; cross his knees for him and leave him alone. They would not let him raise a second crop under his old hat—he had to have a new hat for a new crop. The owner of the farm would furnish plenty to eat; sometimes he would have some whiskey to drink, but not often, "as that was a dangerous thing."

INDEX

FOR THE BEST IN PAPERBACKS, LOOK FOR THE

In every corner of the world, on every subject under the sun, Penguin represents quality and variety—the very best in publishing today.

For complete information about books available from Penguin—including Pelicans, Puffins, Peregrines, and Penguin Classics—and how to order them, write to us at the appropriate address below. Please note that for copyright reasons the selection of books varies from country to country.

In the United Kingdom: For a complete list of books available from Penguin in the U.K., please write to *Dept E.P., Penguin Books Ltd, Harmondsworth, Middlesex, UB7 0DA.*

In the United States: For a complete list of books available from Penguin in the U.S., please write to *Consumer Sales, Penguin USA, P.O. Box 999— Dept. 17109, Bergenfield, New Jersey 07621-0120.* VISA and MasterCard holders call 1-800-253-6476 to order all Penguin titles.

In Canada: For a complete list of books available from Penguin in Canada, please write to *Penguin Books Canada Ltd, 10 Alcorn Avenue, Suite 300, Toronto, Ontario, Canada M4V 3B2.*

In Australia: For a complete list of books available from Penguin in Australia, please write to the *Marketing Department, Penguin Books Ltd, P.O Box 257, Ringwood, Victoria 3134.*

In New Zealand: For a complete list of books available from Penguin in New Zealand, please write to the *Marketing Department, Penguin Books (NZ) Ltd, Private Bag, Takapuna, Auckland 9.*

In India: For a complete list of books available from Penguin, please write to *Penguin Overseas Ltd, 706 Eros Apartments, 56 Nehru Place, New Delhi, 110019.*

In Holland: For a complete list of books available from Penguin in Holland, please write to *Penguin Books Nederland B.V., Postbus 195, NL-1380AD Weesp, Netherlands.*

In Germany: For a complete list of books available from Penguin, please write to *Penguin Books Ltd, Friedrichstrasse 10-12, D-6000 Frankfurt Main I, Federal Republic of Germany.*

In Spain: For a complete list of books available from Penguin in Spain, please write to *Longman, Penguin España, Calle San Nicolas 15, E-28013 Madrid, Spain.*

In Japan: For a complete list of books available from Penguin in Japan, please write to *Longman Penguin Japan Co Ltd, Yamaguchi Building, 2-12-9 Kanda Jimbocho, Chiyoda-Ku, Tokyo 101, Japan.*